CIRCULAR ECOLOGIES

Circular Ecologies

Environmentalism and Waste Politics in Urban China

AMY ZHANG

STANFORD UNIVERSITY PRESS
Stanford, California

Stanford University Press
Stanford, California

Printed in the United States of America on acid-free, archival-quality paper

ISBN 9781503637962 (cloth)
ISBN 9781503639294 (paper)
ISBN 9781503639300 (ebook)

Library of Congress Control Number: 2023045393

Library of Congress Cataloging-in-Publication Data available upon request.

Cover design: Daniel Benneworth-Gray
Cover art: Courtesy of the author, taken during fieldwork in Guangzhou.

For my parents

Contents

Maps and Illustrations

Acknowledgments

The idea that I might pursue a project like this one started during three years of working and living in Beijing and Taiyuan from 2006 to 2009. I traveled widely in China while working as a project intern for the United Nations International Development Organization (UNIDO) in Taiyuan, and as an assistant producer for CBS News, and a campaigner for Greenpeace China in Beijing. This period led me to carry out a project that enabled me to deepen my connections to China. I'm first and foremost indebted to the Guangzhou residents that I met during fieldwork: sanitation workers, scrap collectors, anti-incineration activists, local activists, entrepreneurs, scientists, journalists, and homeowner activists who included me in their work, lives, and shared endeavors. Without their openness, humor, generosity, and acceptance, this project would not have been possible.

I had the great fortune of working with scholars at graduate school who instilled a sense of joy and responsibility in scholarship. Helen Siu nurtured every aspect of this project with her sharp analytical mind, encouragement, and wit. Helen, thank you for opening up your homes in New Haven and Hong Kong, and for being a window into Guangzhou. Michael Dove modeled equity and fairness in every aspect of his research and teaching and never once failed to give me exactly the right advice. Kalyanakrishnan (Shivi) Sivaramakrishnan's rigor, commitment, and dedication to his students and scholarship is unparalleled. Karen Hébert introduced me to many of the key ideas that shaped this book and made time to talk over ideas in very rough drafts. Marian Chertow and Reid Lifset welcomed me into the world of waste. Peter Perdue, Deborah Davis, Karen Seto, and Valerie Hansen broadened my approach to China.

During fieldwork, researchers in Guangzhou, Beijing, Hong Kong, and Taiwan welcomed me and shared resources and connections. I want to especially thank Michael Hsiao, Li Zhigang, and He Shenjing who connected me with fellow scholars, researchers, and resources. In China, I was fortunate to meet many fellow travelers in waste that I now call friends. I will always treasure time spent working with and learning from Chen Liwen, Zhang Boju, Gao Shiyang, Mao Da in Beijing, and Yuan Fei, Fengmei, Mountai, and Yuxian (pseudonyms to protect their identity) in Guangzhou. Thanks to Jun Zhang for opening up her home in the summer of 2012. Wang Jiuliang made time out of his schedule for an interview during my first summer in Beijing in 2010. He also generously gave permission to use his stunning photographs. Meals with Valerie Nichols, John Kennedy, Ellen Friedman, Sungmin Rho, and Dan Mattingly enriched my time during fieldwork.

To the members of the Dove Lab and EAC collective at Yale: thank you for providing round after round of feedback from grant applications to chapters: especially Luisa Cortesi, Alder Keleman, Annie Claus, Sarah Osterhoudt, Jessica Barnes, Myles Lennon, Lauren Baker, Sayd Randle, Deepti Chatti, Amy Johnson, Matthew Archer, Jeff Stoike, David Kneas, and Shaila Seshia Galvin. This book was also shaped by conversations in New Haven both in class and over pizza with Yu Luo, Minhua Ling, Jun Zhang, Aniket Aga, Maria Sidorkina, Adrienne Cohen, Rose Keimig, Atreyee Majumder, Aina Begim, Hosna Sheikholeslami, Andrew Carruthers, Kristina Douglass, Radhika Govindrajan, Ana-Maurine Lara, Lucia Cantero, Mike Degani, Sahana Ghosh, Chandana Anusha, Alyssa Paredes, Tri Phuong, and George Bayuga and many others. I thank the Wenner-Gren Foundation, the Social Science Research Council, the National Science Foundation, the Social Science and Humanities Research Council (of Canada), and the East Asian Studies Prize Fellowship (at Yale) for providing generous funding throughout fieldwork and the writing of this book. Other scholars whose ideas shaped this project during graduate school and after include: Anne Rademacher, Carol Carpenter, Erik Harms, Doug Rogers, Paul Kockelman, Marcia Inhorn, Bill Kelly, Sean Brotherton, Karen Nakamura, Ralph Litzinger, Nikhil Anand, Ajantha Subramanian, Susan Greenhalgh, and Joshua Barker.

I spent an idyllic year as a postdoctoral fellow at the Fairbank Center for Chinese Studies at Harvard University from 2016 to 2017. Special thanks to Karen Thornber, Michael Szonyi, Zhang Ling, Laura Martin, Corey Byrnes, Arunabh Ghosh, and Brian Lander who quickly welcomed me into the Cambridge community.

At NYU, I am fortunate to be surrounded by wonderful colleagues. The Department of Anthropology was especially supportive in the early years of my career when I both struggled to find my footing as a teacher and to make progress on the revisions to this book. I'm lucky to have landed in a place full of people whose scholarship and political commitments are a source of inspiration, and who took the care to welcome me into the academic community over lunches, coffees, and dinners. I'm grateful to work with and to have worked alongside Bruce Grant, Faye Ginsburg, Fred Myers, Angela Zito, Elayne Oliphant, Jane Anderson, Aisha Khan, Arlene D'Ávila, Tejaswini Ganti, Sonia Das, Anne Rademacher, Helena Hansen, Rayna Rapp, Bambi Schieffelin, Emily Martin, Sean Brotherton, Aimee Cox, Gabriel Dattatreyan, Susan Antón, Shara Bailey, Pam Crabtree, James Higham, Terry Harrison, Radu Iovita, Scott Williams, Justin Pargeter, Todd Disotell, and the late Tom Abercrombie and Sally Merry. Faye Ginsburg, Fred Myers, and Bruce Grant read drafts of proposals and chapters no matter what their schedule.

At NYU, this project was also nurtured by the Discard Studies Collective, the China Scholars Working Group, and the Science and Ethnography Workshop. I'm grateful to Rosalind Fredericks, Robin Nagle, and Mohammed Rafi Arefin for sustaining the rich world of discard studies and for creating opportunities to be in dialogue with fellow Discardians, especially Elana Resnick, Marisa Solomon, Josh Reno, Brenda Chalfin, Robyn D'Avignon, and Carl Zimring. Josh Reno has given me generous advice over the course of this project. Thanks to Lily Chumley and Angela Wu for gathering China scholars together during my initial years at NYU. Thanks to the members of RAIR, especially Billy Dufala and Lucia Thomé for generously inviting me to join in their junkyard experiments in Philadelphia between 2017 and 2019, and to Christine Hegel-Cantarella for introducing me to the New York scraps world.

Catherine Fennell, Julie Livingston, Sophia Stamatopoulou-Robbins, Antina von Schnitzler, and Michael Hathaway helped me refine an earlier draft of this book at a workshop in New York in June 2022. Their insights gave new energy and coherence to this project. I learned more about book writing with them than I did at any other point in the writing process. Special thanks to Julie Livingston for the straightforward insights and support since I began teaching at NYU.

Jessica Barnes, Camille Frazier, and Adrienne Cohen read numerous pieces and kept me going with kind words through phone calls and Zooms during the most difficult parts of writing. Thanks to Maria Sidorkina, Minhua Ling, Sarah Osterhoudt, and Jerome Whitington for taking time to read and talk through chapters.

This project has in one way or another been shaped by the thoughts and ideas of colleagues that I greatly admire. It's a privilege to share panels, workshops, and conversations with: Jerry Zee, Timothy Choy, Sarah Besky, Alex Nading, Vinay Gidwani, Heather Paxson, Bettina Stoetzer, Andrew Mathews, Paige West, Alex Blanchette, Sophie Chao, Jacob Doherty, Jonathan Bach, Waqas Butt, Zhang Ling, Mary Ebeling, John Hartigan, Ashley Carse, Alex Nading, Caterina Scaramelli, Kregg Hetherington, David Bond, Max Liboiron, Gökçe Günel, Valerie Olson, Laura Ogden, Zhang Li, Sigrid Schmalzer, Shigehisa Kuriyama, Kathleen Millar, Mark Moritz, Adam Liebman, Li Yao, Christina Schwenkel, Aman Luthra, Anthony Acciavatti, Chloe Ahmann, Stefanie Graeter, Kali Rubaii, Simi Kang, Ashanté Reese, Anna Lora-Wainwright, Raul Pacheco-Vega, Jason Weidemann, Kate Marshall, Yifei Li, Robert Weller, Angela Leung, Shubhra Gururani, Wu Kaming, Joshua Goldstein, and Stevan Harrell.

I want to especially thank Michael Dove, Shivi Sivaramakrishnan, Anne Rademacher, Tim Oakes, Corey Byrnes, Daniel Münster, Ursula Münster, Mann Barua, Thomas White, Mei Zhan, Asher Ghertner, Zhang Ling, Minhua Ling, Alex Nading, Noah Theriault, and Andrea Muehlebach, Li Yao, Darwin Tsen, and Eli Friedman for inviting me to present chapters. An earlier version of chapter 5 appeared as "From Immunity to Collaboration: Microbes, Waste, and Antitoxic Politics," in *Current Anthropology* 62, no. S24 (2021): S298–310. Thanks to Matthäus Rest and the editors and workshop organizers of the special issue *Cultures of Fermentation* for the opportunity to share this work. Thanks also to the workshop participants and reviewers for their feedback.

At Stanford University Press, Dylan Kyung-lim White was a fantastic editor and a joy to work with. Thanks for throwing your editorial expertise and energy behind this project. Thanks to the anonymous reviewers for the focused insights, deep engagement, and generous spirit toward this text and its ideas. Molly Mullin's and Catherine Mallon's edits gave the manuscript polish, and Catherine oversaw the final stages of this project with patient guidance. Liang Jiayong provided advice on graphics and Lily Demet Crandall-Oral created the maps.

To my parents, thank you for inspiring in me a sense of curiosity. Needless to say, I'm indebted to you in countless ways. Thank you especially for giving me the space to pursue unusual and uncertain things. This project was nourished by my extended family in China, through shared conversations, meals, and laughter with aunts, uncles, and cousins in Chengdu, Xian, and Wuxi. This project was also shaped by stories of my late paternal grandparents and time spent with my late maternal grandparents who raised me in my earliest years. This book was, in many ways, propelled by a desire to make sense of the formative years I spent with them growing up in Chengdu in the 1980s.

In New York, I'm especially grateful to Lornette Lewis, Lama, and Myen at Happy Feet who provided extraordinary and much needed childcare particularly during the pandemic. D'Arcy Saum read every word of this project from my graduate school application to the final draft. Thanks for being my sharpest critic and my first and last reader. To Eleanor and Lou, thank you for sustaining me with joyful interruptions.

CIRCULAR ECOLOGIES

FIGURE I.1. Tour-goers in the central control room during a tour to a waste-to-energy (WTE) incinerator in Guangzhou, 2013. Photo by author.

INTRODUCTION

AT THE START OF MY fieldwork in 2012, I attended a public tour of a waste treatment facility on the outskirts of Guangzhou. A bus drove us from the city center to a village and dropped us off in front of the Phoenix incinerator.[1] A tour guide greeted us in front of a building with a dome and a long chimney and ushered us into a lobby, then into a room where LCD screens displayed a close-up image of a flame and a garbage truck. Stopping in front of a diorama of the incinerator, the tour guide narrated the technical processes employed by the plant to treat emissions. Before leading the group upstairs, the guide directed our attention to another prominent digital display, a real-time account of pollutant emissions data—hydrogen chloride (HCI), sulfur dioxide (SO2), carbon monoxide (CO), nitric oxide (NOx), and dust. When we arrived at the central control room on the fourth floor, we could see rows of engineers positioned in front of digital panels and a large screen. Our only glimpse of garbage in the thirty-minute tour came at the tail end of the walk-through. On one side of the central control room was a deep holding tank behind a glass screen, where a metal crawl moved clumps of dark matter from one side to the other.

As a strategy to educate or move citizens to take action, tours of end-of-life waste treatment facilities typically bring citizens closer to their refuse.[2] On this tour, however, waste was notable mostly for its absence. Neither smelled nor seen, waste was stripped of its capacity to elicit disgust. Instead, the audience was treated to a choreographed display of technology that deliberately foregrounded the accomplishment of waste-to-energy (WTE) incineration, in particular, its capacity to seamlessly transform waste into energy *without* generating pollution. This tour invited urban residents to witness firsthand the efficacy of this state-sponsored technology.[3] By demonstrating the technological sophistication of WTE incineration to the city's residents, organized tours were intended to garner public support for not only WTE incinerators but for a broader approach to waste that imagined techno-scientific solutions could eliminate waste altogether.

The carefully choreographed tour was particularly significant in a moment when Chinese cities had set out to actualize a modern and sustainable system of waste management. In the first decades of the twenty-first century, Chinese cities were confronting a waste crisis. From 1984 to 2012, the year that I arrived for long-term fieldwork, municipal waste in Guangzhou increased eightfold from fifty thousand tons per year to four million tons per year.[4] A World Bank (2005) report estimates that by 2030 China will surpass the United States as the world's largest waste-generating nation. China was already the world's largest trash generating nation when, in 2018, the World Economic Forum projected that the volume of household waste in China would be double that of the United States by 2030 (Chen 2018). Like the smog that grounded flights and the rivers filled with industrial effluence, the municipal waste problem signaled China's increasingly degraded ecology.

In recent decades, journalists and academics have tended to attribute the problem of waste in China to the offshoring of waste produced by Western nations. Such accounts have focused on how the transnational flows of capital that redefined global production and consumption also created new geographies of disposal. In the process, China became *the* destination for the offshoring of electronic and plastic waste from the US and Europe.[5] This book, however, shows that both China's contemporary waste crisis and the techno-scientific approach to the governance of waste that emerged in response to it are tied to an ongoing project that leverages urbanization as a strategy for growth and development. The domestic waste crisis in China in the early 2000s was, in one respect, an index of the economic successes of the previous decades. Over the last forty years, China's embrace of a mode of state-led capitalism, an export-led model of industrialization, and the growth of an urban consumer economy have, at the same time, generated a domestic waste problem. The nation's transition beginning in 1978 from a

FIGURE I.2   In 2006, Greenpeace China released a report on the labor conditions and contamination related to the disassembly of electronic waste sent from the US and Europe to the village of Guiyu. © Greenpeace/Natalie Behring

command economy (during the Maoist period 1949–1976) to the pursuit of export-led industrialization and rapid urbanization meant that the widespread material scarcity of the socialist era was supplanted by an ostensibly modern economy of consumption and disposal. The presence of waste in cities was the material vestige of China's growth and development, the scale of its production and accumulation effectively an index of the degree to which a particular region or city had modernized its economy.

By the late 1990s, however, Chinese officials no longer regarded waste as exclusively a problem of public health and sanitation.[6] The growing amount of waste that overwhelmed municipal infrastructures was increasingly seen as a part of China's growing environmental crisis. Beginning in the late 1990s, Chinese policymakers targeted waste as an object that necessitated new environmental interventions and placed waste at the center of experiments with urban development and the creation of modern, sustainable cities. In Guangzhou, officials and planners, following in the footsteps of Beijing, Shanghai, and other cities across Asia, initiated a shift away from industrial manufacturing to create a "world city." The megacity in the Pearl River Delta, with over eighteen million people in 2022, once famous for its

FIGURE I.3   In the 2010 series "Beijing Besieged by Waste" (laji weicheng), pho-
tographer Wang Jiuliang tracked over 450 illegal waste dumps in the outskirts of
Beijing to visualize how waste produced another ring road to encircle the city. ©
Wang Jiuliang.

ports and manufacturing zones, would come to assume a place of promi-
nence in the global network of financial capital. Sustainability was a critical
part of a twenty-first-century Chinese imaginary of world cities. As a part
of the goal of creating an ecological city and realizing a model of "green
modernity," new technologies, environmental governance strategies, and
urban design would be incorporated in the city's modern office towers, central business districts, and new housing developments.[7]

The Guangzhou municipal government set out in the early 2000s to
enact a techno-scientific waste management program known as the circular
economy (xunhuan jingji). In the 1980s and 1990s, industrial ecologists in
Denmark and Germany interested in energy conservation devised a model
of enclosed industrial production. To improve the efficiency of industrial
manufacturing, waste from one industrial process, such as scrap metal or
water, was captured and redirected as an input for another (Frosch and Gallopoulos 1989). Modeled after nature, the system balances production and
consumption to create a closed loop of outputs and inputs. At the heart of
the circular economy was a vision for creating a continuous circulation of
things made possible by technical systems that would facilitate the transformation of waste into productive matter. Through better technology and
social innovation (Goldstein 2018), the approach emphasized that "the ma-

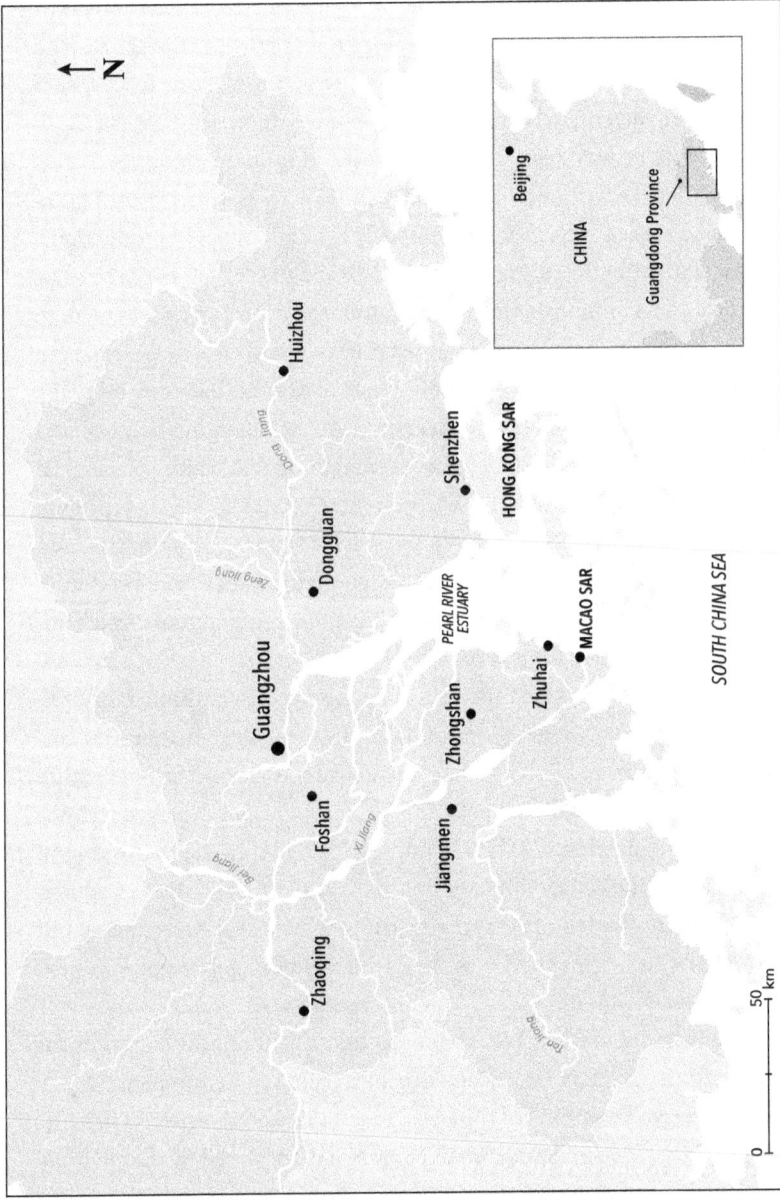

MAP 1.1 The Pearl River Delta. Map by Lily Demet Crandall-Oral.

terial loop can be closed, products ... recycled indefinitely" and the creation of "an economy that perpetually gyrates without any input of depletable resource" (Cullen 2017, 483). Modern waste management has been predominantly focused on displacement (the relegation of waste to the geographic and social margins) and containment (the segregation of waste from spaces of living).[8] At the core of the circular economy's approach to waste is an understanding of waste not as a category of thing to be discarded but as diverse matter that, through advanced technologies and governance practices, can be made to circulate continuously through cycles of production.

This book traces the social, political, and ecological effects of the circular economy as it reconfigured waste matter and waste infrastructures to align with Guangzhou's efforts to build a sustainable world city. In Guangzhou, the transformation of a diverse array of waste matter has been central to the production of urban natures and environments, to emerging political and social contestation, and to the project of imagining and making ecological cities.[9] Throughout the book, I use the circular economy as a lens through which to examine the concrete policies, infrastructures, imaginaries, and on-the-ground practices that efforts to reconfigure waste have produced. On one level, the circular economy is emblematic of the Chinese state's approach to environmental governance and engineering that encompasses policy prescriptions and technocratic projects to achieve sustainability. On another, the circular economy illuminates the ecological imaginaries embedded in its efforts to conceptualize waste matter as a novel form of nature and resource. Since the early 2000s, the Chinese state has deployed technoscience and engineering in efforts to improve the environment across broad domains including conservation, water management, agriculture, and meteorology.[10] Scholars have traced the extent to which such experiments and interventions have generated new modes of political governance and extended the reach of state power.[11] Seen in this light, the circular economy is one more instance of the application of techno-science to the environment and specifically, in this case, the making of the urban environment.[12]

The concrete enactment of the circular economy on the ground demonstrates that ecology and nature in cities are not determined by the environmental agendas of planners, engineers, or state actors. The state's efforts to foster a techno-scientific approach to waste and environmental management generated political processes, contestations, and entanglements that drew diverse urban dwellers together. When subjected to the technologies, techniques, and practices that together make up the system of waste management, the particular affordances of waste matter manifest heterogeneous and interrelated disputes, contestations, labor practices, and experiments among the city's residents. Across diverse manifestations—such as scrap commodities, toxic aerosols, and decomposing matter[13]—waste elicits ecological, social, and political imaginaries and actions.

Against the backdrop of China's experiments in the creation of ecological cities and waste management, heterogeneous waste matter has forged circulations and collectives. I use the notion of circulation to capture the diverse and emergent chains through which waste has mediated the creation and destruction of value (Graeber 2001). Waste's circulation illuminates that the creation of ecological cities depends on the eviction and displacement of rural bodies, the conversion of rural land for urban development, labor exploitation, and real estate growth. Waste's circulation in multiple forms and manifestations also prompted diverse urban communities (homeowners, peri-urban villagers, waste workers, and activists) to devise novel strategies of value-making and to articulate their own claims to the city.[14]

The collectives that have formed around waste in Guangzhou, meanwhile, suggest that science, labor, and experimentation are potent sites for an engagement with the state's techno-scientific project of green development and urbanization, formed against China's authoritarian environmental governance. In the early 2010s, waste's transformation emerged as a focus of dispute and experimental practice at three sites in Guangzhou: WTE incinerators that burn mixed waste to produce energy; formal and informal recycling practices to remove scrap commodities from the waste stream; and local experiments with novel more-than-human infrastructures[15] to use microbes to transform organic waste. The forms of political action that I witnessed during my fieldwork were a reminder that efforts at ecological improvement are not politically neutral and at times have amplified existing inequalities. On the other hand, the constitution of these ecological collectives through waste—made up of middle-class homeowners, peri-urban villagers, informal scrap collectors, and sanitation workers—points to the possibility of collaboration, mutual recognition, and parallel concern forged in response to the increasingly degraded ecologies and unequal social conditions of urban life.

Climate change and ecological degradation have brought environmental politics to the mainstream. Beyond conservation and the preservation of nature, contemporary environmentalism is increasingly oriented around racial justice, decolonization, ecological reparations, and grassroots participation (Bosworth 2022; Kirksey and Chao 2022; Parreñas 2018; Stoetzer 2022; Táíwò 2022; Vaughn 2022). China's state-led environmentalism has often been portrayed as an alternative to political stasis in the West and perhaps even as a model for mitigating the global ecological crisis, albeit one led by an authoritarian regime with little room for citizen participation, political dissent, or contestation.[16] The enactment of the circular economy in Guangzhou illustrates that techno-scientific innovation and the creation of livable cities are a crucial part of how the state devises solutions to ecological problems. In practice, however, China's approach to ecological urbanism is neither "purely" technocratic nor does it fulfill the authoritarian visions of the state. The emerging politics around waste in Guangzhou raises questions about how everyday citizens might participate in the remaking of forms of nature in cities even amid the increasingly uneven dynamics of urban growth. The transformation of waste matter both mediates and is mediated by the social and ecological dynamics of rapid urbanization: the transformation of land, daily labor practices, and the uneven distribution of pollution.

In this book, waste and its nascent urban ecological politics are ways to explore the actual political practices and possibilities of collective action that question China's state-led environmental governance. Political movements that have emerged in response to waste since the 1970s—zero waste, freeganism, opposition to incineration, and the offshoring of waste—share the assumption that environmental solutions depend on ridding nature and society of waste.[17] This book suggests that waste illuminates the material conditions and consequences of China's techno-scientific approach to urban ecological governance. Waste generates a set of grassroots engagements that suggest that the effects of techno-science are intimately connected with the nature of work and labor. Guangzhou's waste politics speak to waste's endurance and capacity to generate contestation, everyday practice, and local experimentations that prove critical to the forging of ecological cities. Waste enables a collective exploration into what counts as an appropriate technology, what kinds of relations to waste and nature we seek, and who gets to work and live in cities. Temporary, flexible, and horizontal collectives around science, labor, and everyday experimentation are key sites for thinking about emergent political practices and ecological formations in contemporary China.

URBAN EXPERIMENTS: CONSUMPTION-LED
GROWTH AND THE ECOLOGICAL CITY

The challenge of managing municipal waste in the early 2010s was the result of three decades of social and economic transformations. In 1978, only 20 percent of China's population was urban as the nation embarked on a project of economic liberalization that dismantled Maoist central planning and initiated a series of land reforms to break up the system of collective production in both cities and countryside. The household responsibility system and rural land reforms replaced collective agricultural production.[18] At the same time, China established its first special economic zones (SEZs) to attract foreign investment and to jumpstart a transition to industrial production.[19] Land reforms improved agricultural output and freed up rural labor to shift into industrial production. Guangzhou and the surrounding area were models of the labor-intensive, export-oriented industrial manufacturing that would come to define China's growth in the 1980s and 1990s. Village workshops and factories manufactured textiles, electronics, and consumer goods for the Western market and transformed the region into the "world's factory floor." The rapid pace of industrialization that followed accelerated the transformation of rural land for industrial use that caused widespread pollution and contaminated the region's riverways with industrial pollution. At the same time, the factories that attracted rural workers from China's inland provinces to coastal regions rapidly increased the region's population.

Rapid urbanization was further made possible by policy changes that facilitated the commodification of urban land and housing and the real estate boom that followed. The establishment of the country's land lease market in 1988 set the stage for a dramatic expansion of real estate development as local and municipal governments pursued land-centered accumulation to generate revenue (Hsing 2010). The liberalization of the housing market converted agricultural land to urban sprawl to meet demand for housing and industrial and commercial space. The confluence of a state policy that promoted real estate investment with a desire for homeownership resulted in a decades-long housing boom across China's cities. A nascent middle class would assume the acquisition of housing would make possible the pursuit of the good life (Li Zhang 2010). Further, agricultural land was systematically annexed and converted for use in industrial processing zones, high-tech "parks," and high-density housing (Lin 2016). By the late 1990s, China was entering a new phase of urbanization where land and real estate construction became important drivers of growth.[20] In most cities across China and especially in large coastal cities like Guangzhou, urban land has more than doubled since 1978. From 1979 to 2013, Guangzhou's urban area increased by 1,500 square kilometers at an average annual rate increase of over 11 percent (Wu et al. 2016).

By the early 2000s, stagnating employment growth, environmental degradation, and overinvestment in industry prompted another shift in policy. Throughout the 1990s, household consumption did not grow at the same pace as industrial development. Despite sustained increases in real terms, household consumption as a share of GDP fell to 38 percent in 2005, the lowest share of any major economy in the world (Lardy 2016). In 2004 Wen Jiabao (premier from 2003 to 2013) announced that the state planned

FIGURE I.4   Demolition of an urban village, 2012. Photo by author.

to abandon a long-standing and exclusive focus on industrialization and would strengthen domestic consumption as an economic growth strategy. In 2006, the State Council's "Eleventh Five-Year Plan" positioned urbanization as a way for China to transition out of a labor-intensive industrial mode of development and to serve as an engine of economic growth by boosting domestic spending and consumption.

Where China's cities were once organized around production, the dramatic economic growth of the post-reform period meant that cities were now increasingly centers of consumption. As household incomes rose, urbanization stimulated growth in a range of sectors including construction and services.[21] Guided by the goal of becoming a "moderately prosperous society" (*xiaokang shehui*), the state aimed to place a television, washing machine, and refrigerator in every household (D. Davis 2000). Cell phones, restaurants, and other consumer goods followed. China built luxury shopping malls, widened freeways to accommodate millions of automobiles, and stimulated tourism by increasing national holidays. China's megacities were now home both to a rising middle class who defined themselves through consumption, and a large rural migrant population working in a range of services to support the urban economy.

The consequences of rigid and official distinctions between urban and rural citizenship, first instituted in the Maoist era, were amplified by the process of rapid urbanization. The Maoist state adopted the *hukou* system to demarcate between rural and urban status. The *hukou* was a household registration system that assigned people and households one of two statuses: agriculture and nonagriculture for rural and urban populations respectively. Intended as a policy to prevent rural-to-urban migration, the *hukou* linked access to social services, health care, education, social insurance, welfare, and retirement benefits to local administrations (Chan 2007). In the post-reform era, even as rural migrants temporarily relocated to cities to fill the labor ranks necessary for urban growth, they were systematically denied access to urban services. As a "floating population," migrant workers depended on being able to return to their rural villages to access services such as education and health care (Ling 2019; Friedman 2022).

In the early 2000s, urban planners and policymakers set out to use comprehensive planning to transform Guangzhou into a "modern global city." In contrast to market-oriented urban growth, planners aimed by 2010 to create a modern production system, backed by a strong tertiary economy.[22]

FIGURE I.5   Guangzhou's new central business district with LEED-certified buildings, 2012. Photo by author.

Guangzhou hoped to emerge as an international financial and services center, replacing factories and ports with a knowledge and service economy. This project reflected the ambitions of the city's political elite to claim a spot in a global urban hierarchy and to become a node in a global network of finance and capital. As in other cities across Asia, Guangzhou's "worlding" experiments aimed to establish the city as a global hub through place promotion, rebranding, and the introduction of signature architecture to attract foreign capital (Roy and Ong 2011; Wu and Zhang 2007; Xu and Yeh 2003). Private developers enlisted famous architects to distinguish themselves in a crowded property market while the state planned and built a slate of mega-projects. Skyscrapers, modern infrastructure, and the arrival of international firms and businesses that followed signified the country's arrival as a geopolitical power (Ren 2011).

Across China, two decades of industrialization and urbanization had generated increasing amounts of pollution, which undermined the livability of cities. In Guangzhou, the remediation and remaking of the environment and ecology were also central to efforts to become a world city. Municipalities became increasingly concerned with improving air quality, building green space, remediating waterways, and reducing waste. Technology and green design became central to China's project of establishing a form of green modernity as a way to mitigate the effects of climate change, resource shortages, and environmental disasters. The state's pursuit of ecological urbanism relied on a series of technical adjustments (Günel 2019); the idea was that better technology and more modern, green infrastructure would move cities away from a dependence on fossil fuels and toward a green future.

Urban political ecologists have long resisted the distinction between nature and society and instead regard the production of ecologies and urban space as a sociopolitical process. The material artifacts of our built environment—for instance, water meters, electrical grids, and housing—ground political contestation and disputes and shape ethical reflection and sentiments (Anand 2017; Larkin 2008; von Schnitzler 2017). Attempts to reconfigure waste management in cities offer a unique lens on how the

FIGURE I.6   Skyscrapers in the Tianhe downtown core, 2013. Photo by author.

state's project to remake nature has amplified the existing social land-scape of growing urban-rural inequality. The mobilization of ecological features and sustainability is pivotal to the project of reinventing cities as sites of investment, spectacle, and consumption for the urban elite. At the same time, the production of urban natures has elicited contestations that reveal how the politics of labor, distribution, and access to environmental resources undergird the production of green cities (Checker 2020; Goh 2021).

THE CIRCULAR ECONOMY

On the evening of December 8, 2012, I attended a talk hosted by the Guang-zhou Municipal Urban Management Committee (Guangzhou shi chengshi guanli weiyuanhui) titled "Waste Is Besieging the City: Guangzhou Says No!" In a packed lecture hall in the bustling commercial center of Tianhe District, citizens and journalists listened as Bao Wu,[23] head of the city's recycling campaign, described rapid urbanization and an emerging waste crisis. Bao described protests in Panyu and Huadu districts (in 2009 and 2012), where homeowners and villagers living near the proposed facilities were concerned that the emissions from the burning of mixed waste would endanger the environment and their health. Bao spent the remainder of the talk encouraging citizens to "do their part" to alleviate the waste crisis by participating in the city's citizen recycling campaign and by separating their garbage into one of four categories: organics, recyclables, toxic waste, and other waste. Bao's focus on the promotion of recycling was an oblique response to a critique by protesters that, in practice, Guangzhou's WTE in-cinerators generated pollution in part because the city lacked a system of waste separation. Activists argued that WTE incinerators in Guangzhou were more likely to burn plastics and toxics because residents did not recy-cle and were more likely to burn organics because residents generated over 7,000 tons of organic waste each day, over 50 percent of the total municipal waste stream.

Critiques by waste activists illuminated the fact that the emergence and growth of a post-industrial consumer economy in post-reform China gen-erated not only an increasing quantity of waste but a dramatic change in the *quality* of the municipal waste stream. In the 1980s, ash from indoor coal heating made up a large portion of Guangzhou's waste. Today, the municipal waste stream, the stuff that flows from waste bins of households and office buildings, is becoming ever more heterogeneous, diverse, and difficult to manage. The waste stream increasingly carries the material remnants of a regime of convenience and disposability and is made up of plastic, composite matter, and paper—matter that is difficult to break apart and that often imprints its toxic marks on bodies and environments for hundreds of years over the duration of its decomposition (H. Davis 2022). Concerns about the feasibility of WTE incineration indexed the extent to which the diverse and heterogeneous streams of waste presented challenges to the state's technological solution. At the same time, these concerns led to people making connections between different aspects of the waste stream, from its collection to its treatment, and between different types of waste: organics, recyclables, and those designated for burning.

The packed lecture also revealed the degree to which waste—once the exclusive domain of engineers, planners, and municipal officials—was now an issue of widespread public debate and concern. In the 1970s, the introduction of curbside recycling and the slogan "reduce, reuse, and recycle" became a hallmark of the modern American environmental movement. That movement aligned waste management with mobilizing everyday citizens to environmental action through recycling. Environmental campaigns tend to focus on citizen behavior and to promote recycling so that a subset of the waste stream (typically recyclables) can be recovered. Bao's promotion of municipal recycling as a strategy to facilitate the success of WTE incineration in 2012, however, was not only in service of an effort to promote environmental participation. Together, WTE incinerators and recycling were critical parts of a broader state agenda to create a circular mode of waste management.

Chinese policymakers and engineers first began experimenting with the circular economy in the 1990s as a materials management strategy for promoting cleaner production in industrial sectors.[24] Engineers established pilot projects to create a closed-loop materials management system in industrial zones and eco-parks. Within a decade, however, the circular economy had become the cornerstone of a broad vision that shaped national-level approaches to green development.[25] Efforts to realize the circular economy prompted an increasingly comprehensive set of policies across diverse sectors ranging from resource extraction, industrial production, and waste management. In 2005 and 2007, the State Council launched the first pilot

FIGURE I.7 A poster inside a WTE incinerator reads "Science sets the direction of development, environmental protection gives Guangzhou its wings (of growth)," 2013. Photo by author.

projects in cities under the guise of the circular economy to reform industries like steel, nonferrous metals, coal, and textiles and to promote the use of renewable resources. In addition, the law regulated the disposal of electronic waste, batteries, tires, and packaging. The adoption of China's Circular Economy Promotion Law in 2008 elevated the circular economy to a national-level framework for sustainability, and in 2013, Guangdong Province issued its own Circular Economy Law.[26]

The 2012–2020 Guangzhou Municipality Circular Economy Development Plan offered a blueprint for how circular economy projects would be adapted to municipal planning and development. The plan stipulated that circular economy practices be central to the city's economic and urban development as a vehicle for instituting a model of scientific development, a transition to a green economy, and a shift toward a "New Urbanization" characterized by "low energy consumption, low emission, low pollution, and high efficiency" (*dixiaohao, diwuran, dipaifang, gao xiaolü*).[27] The efficient and circular use of resources would be achieved through "reduction, resourcification, and detoxification" (*jianliang hua, ziyuan hua, wuhai hua*).[28] If the aim of the circular economy in the Twelfth Year Plan (2010–2015) was to resolve a growing contradiction between ecological degradation and economic development, the pursuit of "circularity, low-carbon, and greenness" (*xunhuan, ditan, lüse*) would guide Guangzhou's transformation into an "ecological city" (*shengtai chengshi*).[29]

Under the circular economy, municipal waste management, long understood as a biopolitical imperative by the Chinese state critical for the governance of populations, was reconceptualized as a project of producing a green future. In the Republican Era, waste management was primarily concerned with sanitation and the management of germs and disease (Rogaski 2004), while in the Maoist period, the management of scrap commodities was part of a socialist project of national development. In the late 1990s, however, the introduction of the circular economy was part of a broader shift in the Chinese state's approach to environmental governance. In response to decades of environmental pollution, grassroots protests, and the influx of international NGOs, by the end of the decade, the Chinese state abandoned its previous policy of growth at all costs and began strengthening its capacity for environmental governance. As the environmental dimension of the so-called harmonious society (*hexie shehui*), the circular economy was tasked with reconciling economic and environmental goals with a social and political project to address pollution, resource scarcity, and social unrest (Naustdalslid 2014), a shift that exemplified the extent to which environmental and political ambitions were intertwined.

Scholars have observed that China's environmental governance is not only an extension or hardening of authoritarian ideological rule,[30] but a set of experiments in the production of nature. As Jerry Zee points out, the practice of "politics"—the necessity of making, containing, and securing China's political geography—is realized through ecological experimentation, or what he calls the "becoming-with a changing nature" (Zee 2022, 25). The state is an "experimental system—open and adaptive, continuously tinkered for unexpected circumstances" (25). The environmental state reiterates a tendency in Chinese governance to privilege scientific reasoning and technicist thinking and to prioritize large-scale ecological engineering (Rodenbiker 2023). China's approach to conservation "necessitates large-scale human intervention" (Zhu 2022, 190) and prioritizes engineered environments over the preservation of natural ecosystems. China's ecological governance is both flexible and adaptive, one open to being shaped by global currents and local social formations (Hathaway 2013).

The circular economy makes evident a tendency of China's ecological regime not only to experiment but also to deploy science and technology to reconfigure natures to further a project of capitalist growth and accumulation. Especially in a time of biodiversity loss, climate change, and resource scarcity, the circular economy perpetuates the idea that socioecological engineering can produce an infinite nature by dissociating waste from pollution to imagine it as an endless resource. The circular economy exemplifies an impulse in ecological modernization to resolve the contradictions between economic growth and environmental degradation through technology (Zhang, Mol, and Sonnenfeld 2007). It makes explicit the rationale behind China's approach to green development that deploys technologies and governance strategies to devise a new relationship to nature. Anticipating a future where all waste matter can once again be made productive,[31] the circular economy reconceptualizes production systems at various scales as enclosed "perpetual motion machines" (Cullen 2017). The implicit goal of the governance strategies and techno-fixes perpetuated by the circular economy is to uphold capitalism's promise of continuous growth while mitigating the environmental degradation that growth produces.

WASTE'S CIRCULATIONS

In 2013, slogans like "low-carbon economy, knowledge city" (*ditan jingji zhihui chengshi*) adorned the walls of One West Village, an urban gated housing complex in Guangzhou's western Liwan District. Every day after dinner, residents would carelessly toss plastic bags weighed down with vegetable trimmings, broken plates, and plastic wrappings into waste bins. Later, Lao Huang, one of the complex's sanitation workers, would go from floor to floor, picking up heavy overflowing bags from stairwells and move them into elevators and eventually to the lobby. He would then deposit the bags into a three-wheel pushcart, before pushing the load to the local transfer station. The daily routine of expelling waste in Guangzhou relied on the labor of sanitation workers like Lao Huang.

Waste management is most often understood as a set of infrastructures that facilitate the disposal of objects. Discard scholars working in a range of contexts have demonstrated that waste creates intimate relations of social redistribution and differentiation in a dialectic of development and disposability; the growth and modernization of certain lives and spaces demand that others be understood as unclean, dirty, and disposable (Butt 2023; Doherty 2021). Waste and waste infrastructures are useful sites to explore state retraction from and disinvestment in public services in the wake of the neoliberal turn, particularly in the rapidly urbanizing cities of the Global South (Fredericks 2018; Millar 2018). As Max Liboiron and Josh Lepawsky argue, wasting and discarding are "techniques of power" that facilitate the formation and maintenance of hierarchies that render some lives disposable in order to sustain others (2022, 7).

Sophia Stamatopoulou-Robbins, in a study on waste in Palestine, uses the concept of a "waste siege" to describe waste's perpetual presence. In place of disposability, she proposes that we understand waste as matter that cannot be easily sent away. She notes that "waste—like the total volume of water on earth—never truly disappears . . . [but] merely changes place and form" (Stamatopoulou-Robbins 2020, 23). For Stamatopoulou-Robbins, the waste siege is an "emission from within" that perpetually returns in a range of states and forms (7). The concept conveys both a broader relationship between consumerism and waste, as well as waste's relationship to the urban ecology in Guangzhou (and elsewhere).[32]

A materialist approach to discard studies holds that waste's discursive and ontological positions are neither singular nor stable, and urges scholars to trace waste's movement through "the circuits of production, distribution, consumption, reclamation, and 'annihilation'" (Gille 2010, 1050). Scholars argue that the leftovers of postconsumer capitalism are vital, heterogeneous, and "must be effaced, enrolled, exported, or expunged" to uphold the continual production of value (Gidwani and Maringanti 2016, 125). In contrast to a long genealogy of scholarship focused on capitalism's tendencies to efface, export, or expunge, waste's ubiquity and continuous presence invite an interrogation of *enrollment*, of how differentiated forms of matter produce a set of diverse networks and relations. Waste's capacity for enrollment generates indeterminate effects that might include the reproduction of the uneven distribution of pollution and displacement of harms but also the capacity to secure and distribute value and political effects. Waste mat-

ter's transformation is the very mechanism that draws together technologies, objects, bodies, and ecologies.[33]

The circular economy imagines that all types of waste can be continuously enrolled into a project of capitalist accumulation, even as waste's
afterlife produces diverse and indeterminate effects as it is transformed,
decomposed, and broken down (Gille 2010; Moore 2012). The matter
of waste—nature having been extracted, produced, commodified, and
discarded—across many states—toxic aerosol, discarded plastics, rotting
organics—persists and endures in bodies and ecologies. Waste's afterlives
exhibit the "gritty, messy, often intricate, inevitably intimate matters of in-
filtration and interdependence" between bodies and environments (Weston
2017, 11). Waste matter shows a propensity for persistence and endurance
and the capacity to continuously draw together diverse matters and objects.

In Guangzhou, waste's circulation both mediates and is mediated by
the creation and destruction of various forms of economic, ecological, and
social value.[34] Marxist scholars invoke circulation to emphasize the idea that
capital is *value in motion* (Harvey 2010) and that accumulation is a function of the continuous movement of capital through M-C-M′ (money capital, commodity, expanded money capital) (Marx 1976). Recent scholarship
treats circulation not only in reference to physical movement but also "the
transformation of value into different forms," an important process that
constitutes the circulation of capital (Cowen 2014, 101).[35] Vinay Gidwani
argues that waste is central to the logic of accumulation and produces what
he calls a waste-value dialectic. Tracing the transformation of waste under
capitalism, he uses W-(M-C-M′)-W′ to describe waste's role in the production of value. In Gidwani's formulation, "matter nature as untapped potential ('waste') is pressed into commodity production generating new forms of
waste at various moments: the moment of appropriation (when waste is enrolled into capital's circuit), in the moment of production (as leakage, chaff,
entropic exudation, and ingestion of the worker's 'living' labor) and finally
in the moment of consumption (as unusable and reusable matter)" (Gidwani
2013, 781). Waste, across various forms, marks both an external and internal
frontier, as matter that needs to be continuously transformed because of its
unruly capacity "to confound capitalism's attempts to discipline and contain
life within the domain of utility and accumulation" (781).

Gidwani emphasizes the need to focus on the multiple and changing
ways that capitalist circulation continuously generates new forms of waste

and, in the process, produces what he calls "matter nature." Neil Smith (2008) famously used "second nature" to distinguish raw, uncommodified, and inherited nature (first nature) from nature produced through human activity toward commodification, for the purposes of generating exchange value. The circular economy raises the question of how to understand the relationship between waste and nature when capital imagines that nature can be continuously transformed (i.e., commodified), where waste after commodification is put to use in the further production of value. The circular economy mobilizes both science and capital to subject matter to further rounds of capitalist expropriation after commodification and disposal. At the same time, waste's transformation illuminates how the different forms of "matter nature" generate particular effects as they circulate and redistribute both value and harm throughout the city's ecology. Waste's entanglement within Guangzhou's urban ecology reveals the ongoing dynamics of capitalism's appropriation of nature through both labor and technology. Capitalism continuously reconfigures not only human society but also the "web of life" that humans find themselves suspended in and supported by (J. W. Moore 2015).

WASTE'S COLLECTIVES

In the fall of 2009 homeowners in a housing development in Panyu learned about a proposed WTE incinerator near their complex. Concerned about the potential of the facility to disperse harmful toxins, homeowners began discussing the negative effects of toxic emissions from incineration in a WeChat group. On November 23, 2009, homeowners from neighboring complexes and from local villages gathered to protest the proposed facility. The protest was one of the largest environmental protests in the city's history. Through subsequent actions, such as petitioning officials and writing editorials in newspapers, local residents succeeded in temporarily halting the incinerator's construction. By 2012 the municipality had proposed a new location for the facility. The construction on the new site, however, was premised on the relocation of another village even further on the city's outskirts.

Almost four years later, in the spring of 2013, I waited for Yuan Fei in a ground-floor apartment of a middle-class gated complex in Guangzhou's Southern Panyu District. Arriving a few minutes late, Yuan Fei greeted a group of volunteers gathered to convert the empty apartment into a neighborhood community center. We spent the afternoon dusting and cleaning while we talked about ideas for workshops—waste reduction, upcycling, battery collection, composting—the volunteers planned to organize in the new space. For Yuan Fei and others, participation in the 2009 Panyu anti-incineration protest was only the beginning of waste activism. In 2010 Yuan Fei decided to leave his successful career as a construction contractor to form an environmental NGO, Eco-Canton. With Eco-Canton, Yuan Fei returned to communities that had been among the first and most vocal opponents to WTE incineration. Yuan Fei believed that the solution to Guangzhou's waste crisis would not come from WTE incinerators or even formalized recycling programs. Instead, waste created an opportunity for activists to "work from the ground up" (*jiediqi*).

In the months that followed, Yuan Fei and his neighbors shifted their attention to the organic waste that had troubled the technical functioning of WTE incinerators and had undermined the success of recycling campaigns. In the community center, homeowner activists devoted themselves to an experimental project fermenting organics to make a solution that they used to cleanse and purify their bodies, homes, and local riverways. Yuan Fei's narrative challenges a common characterization of China's emerging middle class as apolitical, acquiescent beneficiaries of the nation's economic ascent. The activity room at Garden Villa manifested how disputes over waste in this period generated ongoing, sustained, and unexpected connections that drew diverse things and people together.

In China, notions of the collective or collectives (*jiti*) carry a socialist valence. The Maoist era launched the project of collectivization (*jiti shengchan*), as agrarian reforms and production brigades brought social and political life into alignment with a socialist planned economy. Collectivization meant not only a mode of production but also a social and political project that set the terms of social belonging, ethics, and political reasoning. The post-reform period saw the dismantling of socialist collectives and, in the 1980s, the state relinquished control over institutions that regulated daily life by breaking up collectivist farming and liberalizing state-owned enterprises (SOEs). The creation of a commercial housing market accelerated urban development and uprooted communities. The post-reform project has also reoriented the self toward individualization rather than collective concerns (Yan 2009).

I use collectives to refer to the modes of gathering and political articulations across difference that emerged alongside the state's environmental projects. In disputes and practices around waste, diverse waste matter in transformation created temporary and emergent social and ecological interdependencies and gave rise to new political sentiments and actions. My use of collectives draws on two related concepts: publics and assemblages. Unlike citizenship, which denotes formal rights and obligations, publics capture communities and coalitions formed in response to a condition irrespective of identity and affinity. Publics capture the idea of "a community of the affected" to describe "those who are affected by the indirect consequences of transactions to such an extent that it is deemed necessary to have those consequences systematically cared for" (Dewey 2016, 69). Science and technology studies often take for granted the emergence of "publics" and "counterpublics" formed in response to controversies concerning risk, safety, and the appropriateness of technologies (Aga 2021; Callison 2014; Hess 2016). Fundamentally, the notion of a public assumes a democratic context for engaging with science, that citizens can gather to organize politically and to freely articulate their demands in existing forums.[36] I use collectives intentionally to think about emergent ecological and social formations in an illiberal context. Understood as nascent political communities, as used here collectives invite questions about *how* a shared object of concern can bring communities together to generate social and political effects where and when the state tightly monitors and limits public action.

Writing about the conditions of living and acting in a time of ecological ruin, Anna Tsing borrows "assemblage" from ecologists to describe life forms that transcend the fixed boundaries of ecological "communities" (2015, 22). Assemblages are "open-ended gatherings" that allow us "to ask about communal effects without assuming them" (22–23); They invite us to think about "unintentional coordination" across the histories, ecologies, and economies that make lifeways (23). Timothy Choy similarly uses "ecologies of comparison" to denote how knowledge-making practices have generated an "emergent web of relationships among constitutive and constituting parts" (2011, 12).

In Guangzhou, the circulation and transformation of waste generated a set of social and political relations among citizens through their engagement with the state's ecological projects. The diverse types of actions and claims around waste meant that there was not one single community of the affected. Instead, waste facilitated the formation of political strategies that evaded the state's control and collaborations that cut across class and rural/urban affinities. The specific material affordances of different types of waste made it possible for a set of distinct but interrelated disputes to emerge: scientific politics against WTE incinerators, labor politics from the recuperation and resale of scraps, and local experimentations with the transformation of organic waste.

Waste is a systemic irritant to techno-utopian attempts to continuously extract value from the circulation and transformation of nature. Systemic irritants derive their power from such cascading effects that amplify the flaws and shortcomings of not just the system on the ground but the conceits and biases that informed its design. To accommodate the systemic irritant or resolve the challenges it poses is to overhaul the structure of the system itself.[37] Mundane but fundamentally troublesome to the system, every attempt to resolve the contradictions that waste posed cascaded through different components of the system as glitches, mutations, and unruly objects that transmute, reappear, and evade efforts at absorption or elimination. The material specificities of waste challenged the vision of the circular economy which imagined waste as a neutral and homogenous substrate for recirculation and the extraction of value. In addition to troubling the vision of the circular economy, waste as a systemic irritant also generated new collectives.

In Guangzhou, organic waste was the systemic irritant par excellence. Wetness and susceptibility to decomposition particularly in the city's tropical heat and humidity, meant that organics caused problems in all phases of waste's management. Organic waste made burning waste at high temperature difficult and left valuable waste hard to extract. Organics not only troubled the vision of the seamless circulation of waste. Its central effect was to gather novel scientific, labor, and experimental collectives in a set of distinct but related disputes and inquiries, and in so doing, it illuminated the possibilities and necessity of considering the complex ecological, social, and political relations and interdependencies between objects, spaces, and residents of the city. The transformation of different waste streams—the burning of waste at WTE incinerators, the reclamation of recyclables, and local solutions to treat organics—generated a set of interconnected relations that drew diverse urban dwellers together. Science, labor, and experimentation are terrains of environmental struggle for urbanites to devise new modes of political articulation, a recognition of mutual interest, and opportunities for collaboration.

Waste collectives are post-socialist urban political formations that emerged in response to the ecological experiments of the Chinese state. In particular, the temporary, flexible, and horizontal nature of such collectives demonstrate the importance of attending to the interconnections between distinct modes of political articulation and practices. Authoritarian control continually spawns institutions, structures, and techniques of control to disrupt the potential for mass mobilization. Despite explicit constraints on political expression and collective action, scholars have charted the capacity for everyday citizens to mobilize through protests, institutionalized forms of appeals and legal action, or by disguising collective appeals as individual actions. Against the open-ended experimental nature of China's rising ecological state, the concept of "collectives" charts the types of associational life and modes of political articulations and practices well adapted to the authoritarian state's "flexible repression."[38] Waste has precipitated a set of allied, collaborative, and aggregated responses against the state's top-down environmental governance. Novel social and political collectives forged by waste illustrate that contestation and dissent are integral to the production of urban ecologies. They also suggest that different communities of rural and urban dwellers coming together through science, labor, and experimentation can lead to new modes of political action and practices.

ENVIRONMENTAL SANITATION

The actualization of the circular economy was carried out through the introduction of a new framework for waste governance, development, and planning. In the early 2000s, garbage (*laji*) was handled by the Guangzhou Municipal Bureau for Environment and Hygiene (Guangzhou shi shirong huanjing weisheng ju), which operated across municipalities, districts, and subdistricts. At the municipal level, the bureau oversaw municipal sewage treatment plants and fleets of sanitation and cleaning vehicles; their responsibilities also included cleaning up the lakes and bodies of water in the city and operating end-of-life waste treatment facilities. Each district operated a sanitation division in charge of collecting and maintaining public toilets, cleaning fleets and vehicles, and cleaning personnel. Each subdistrict (*jiedao banshi chu*) oversaw their own sanitation stations and street sweeping teams.

By the late 1990s, Guangzhou introduced its first comprehensive "environmental sanitation" (*huanjing weisheng*) plan.[39] The concept of environmental sanitation first emerged in municipal documents and increasingly reflected a shift in the conceptualization of environmental management from its initial biopolitical imperative concerned with sanitation (*weisheng*)—in Chinese literally the "guarding of life" (Rogaski 2004)—to a totalizing strategy focused on the reconfiguration of the environment (*huanjing*). In contrast to concerns about the management of germs and diseases, environmental sanitation was concerned with the measurement and regulation of industrial pollution and other aspects of the urban environment, such as the regulation of noise. By the mid-2000s, the expanding scope of "environmental sanitation" brought waste management into alignment with the project to create an ecological city.

The two iterations of Guangzhou's "Environmental Sanitation" Comprehensive Plan (2000 to 2010 and 2010 to 2020)[40] were a blueprint for the actualization of a set of technical systems and practices intended to reconfigure the organization, flow, and conversion of municipal waste according to a vision of circulation. The plans made clear first and foremost that sustainable waste management was predicated on the disaggregation of Guangzhou's waste stream. The totality of waste in the city was broken down into four distinct categories: organic waste or kitchen waste (*chuyu laji*, leftover kitchen scraps, yard waste, and anything compostable), recyclable waste (*kehuishou laji*, paper, plastics, metals, glass), toxic waste (*youhai laji*, batteries, paint), and other waste (*qita laji*, anything that cannot be easily sorted and recovered, e.g., dirty napkins and thin plastic bags). Engineers and planners recognized that a circular economy depended on systems, practices, and technologies tailored to the qualities of specific matter in the waste stream.

The Environmental Sanitation Plans were holistic and viewed waste management as embedded in broader urban planning and development. They also explicitly laid out the expansion, integration, and extension of state bureaucracy and infrastructures through waste management. The plan detailed strategies encompassing but not limited to the siting and selection of end-of-life infrastructures including WTE incinerators, the organization of collection and transfer stations, waste collection vehicles, and education and media campaigns. In 2009 the Guangzhou municipality established the Guangzhou Municipal Urban Management Committee (Guangzhou shi chengshi guanli weiyuanhui), in part to aid the reorganization of waste management infrastructures across the city, including the siting of proposed incineration plants.

Significantly, the municipal government hoped to rely on two strategies for realizing sustainable and green waste management in Guangzhou: WTE incinerators and citizen recycling. The state imagined WTE incineration replacing landfilling as the dominant form of end-of-life waste technology.[41] In 2012 most municipal solid waste (MSW) in Guangzhou ended up at the Xingfeng landfill, responsible for processing 91 percent of the 18,000 tons of waste generated each day.[42] At the time of its construction in 2002, Xingfeng was one of the largest landfills in Asia. By 2012 however, the facility was approaching capacity almost ten years ahead of schedule. The 2010 Guangzhou Municipal Environmental Sanitation Plan included a stated goal of treating over 70 percent of municipal waste through WTE incineration in the city by 2030. As of 2012 the Guangzhou municipal government planned to build six more facilities by 2018, a conclusive milestone after which WTE incineration would be the primary mode of waste treatment in the city measured by mass of waste treated.[43]

While municipal planning aimed to present a coordinated extension of state control, efforts to put the plan into practice on the ground revealed numerous gaps and discontinuities. The difficulties of realizing municipal mandates at the local level were especially apparent in Guangzhou's efforts to promote citizen recycling. In April 2011 Guangzhou mandated city-wide citizen recycling.[44] In contrast to large infrastructure projects, citizen recycling campaigns relied on coordination between street-level bureaucrats, building management companies (private companies in charge of providing sanitation service), residents' associations, and new civil society actors eager to engage in grassroots action. Recycling campaigns hinted at a reimagining of the "neighborhood" as an institution of urban governance, but more importantly, recycling positioned citizen practice, driven by a voluntaristic ethos, as the hallmark of a sustainable form of waste management. The official plan made no mention of how sanitary workers and informal collectors might participate in the collection and diversion of re-

FIGURE I.8 The 227-acre Xingfeng landfill cost over 100 million dollars to construct and began operating in 2003. Once the largest landfill in Asia, as of 2022, it is the tenth largest landfill in the world, 2013. Photo by author.

cyclables. Nor did the plan specify how the handling of recyclable or scrap commodities (*feipin*) would intersect with the existing scraps sector and the series of recycling depots left over from the era of state-run recycling under the Maoist period.

One particularly striking detail of Guangzhou's waste management strategy was that it neglected to devise a clear separation, storage, and end-of-life technology for the treatment of organic waste, even though organic waste made up over 50 percent of the city's total waste stream. In 2012 the Datianshan composting pilot project, an urban composting facility capable of handling more than a hundred tons of organic waste per day, was quickly losing government support as officials sparred over the economic feasibility of scaling up the process (Huang 2013). While some neighborhoods experimented with the separation of organics, in 2012 and 2013, when I was conducting my fieldwork, it remained unclear what the city planned to do with organic waste. While in subsequent years Guangzhou would introduce large bio-gas facilities to treat organics, state policy and planning that prioritized WTE incineration initially neglected the organic waste stream. This oversight reflected the fundamental discrepancy between an imagined circular economy and the actual compositions, circulations, and flows of waste matter.

REMAKING GUANGZHOU'S ECOLOGY

Waste's transformation changed the city's land, water, and air. Fed by tropical monsoons, the Pearl River Delta provided a fertile ground for rice and other forms of agriculture. Because of the city's long history as a trading port and center of maritime trade, it had both an outward orientation and a strong regional social and political identity.[45] By the early 1990s, the city was the site of some of the earliest experiments in land consolidation and real estate development in the country, as land-lease revenue became a key source of income for local governments. Panyu was home to early investment by Hong Kong real estate developers. Infused with outside capital, developers worked closely with officials and village cadres to transform land into commercial housing developments (Hsing 2010, 43).

In recent years, rapid expansion and political reforms have repeatedly redrawn the borders of Guangzhou's urban districts. Once concentrated in western districts (Liwan, Yuexiu, Haizhu), development pushed growth toward the east and north, absorbing villages on the peri-urban edge. In 2000 Guangzhou comprised ten city districts (Yuexiu, Dongshan, Haizhu, Liwan, Tianhe, Baiyun, Huangpu, Fangcun, Huadu, and Panyu) (J. Xu and Yeh 2003) and two county-level cities (Chonghua and Zengcheng). In 2012–2013, during the time of my long-term fieldwork, Guangzhou's ten city districts and two county-level cities took on a different configuration (Yuexiu, Haizhu, Liwan, Tianhe, Baiyun, Huangpu, Huadu, Panyu, Nansha, and Luogang, along with Chonghua and Zengcheng).[46] After I returned from the field, Guangzhou underwent two additional rounds of significant redistricting in 2014 and 2021.[47] In 2023, at the time of the book's completion, Guangzhou is divided into eleven districts, six in the historical city center (Yuexiu, Liwan, Tianhe, Haizhu, Panyu, Baiyun), and five larger districts on the outskirts of the city (Huangpu, Nansha, Conghua, Zengcheng, and Huadu).

This book's chapters document how waste's circulation amplified the social unevenness of urban growth across the city's peri-urban and cen-

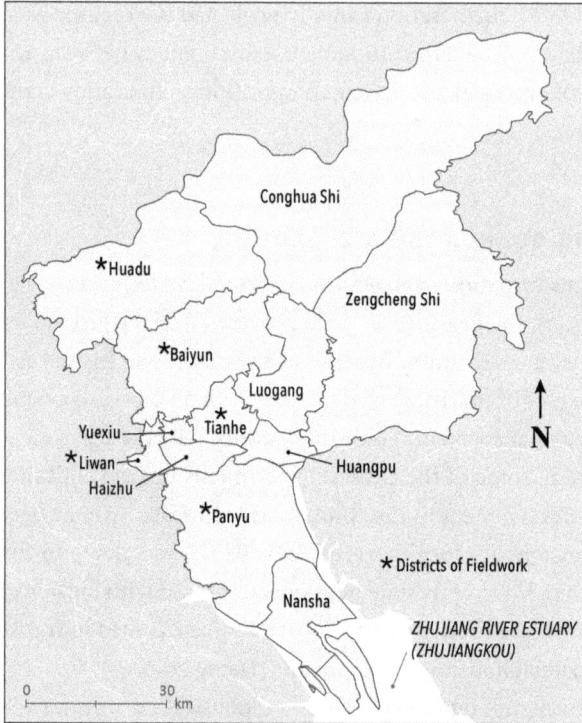

MAP I.2   Districts of Guangzhou, 2012. Map by Lily Demet Crandall-Oral.

tral districts. In chapters 2, 3, and 5, I trace the rise and aftermath of anti-incineration protests and activism among peri-urban homeowners and villagers in Panyu, Huadu, and Baiyun. In newly annexed peri-urban districts, the consolidation of rural land for urban development complicated the siting of WTE incinerators, leading to the rise of anti-incineration politics. Where waste was once relegated to distant rural sites outside the city, Guangzhou's rapid urbanization meant that rural land, particularly that in the vicinity of the urban, was now increasingly a desirable target for real estate development. As edge districts were incorporated into the city, real estate developers increasingly leveraged environmental features to market housing developments. For urban middle-class residents in Panyu and Huadu, housing developments on the city's outskirts were desirable as reprieves from the congested, polluted landscapes of the city center. A desire to defend their access to clean air and water from waste also led middle-class homeowners to devise new forms of waste politics.

The tension between rural and urban was also manifested in the process of absorbing rural villages for urban development within Guangzhou's central districts. In Guangzhou, becoming a "world city" was a function of the redesign and reproduction of urban space and of securing rural land for urban development. Chapters 1 and 4 examine how aesthetics was central to both the design and rise of governance strategies for remaking Guangzhou in the image of ecological urbanism. Once a peripheral district at the city's eastern reach dotted with sports stadiums, villages, and scrap depots, Tianhe is now the city's second-most important commercial hub. In Tianhe's central business district, the making of a modern ecological city is predicated on both the evisceration of *chengzhongcun* villages, land under rural jurisdiction surrounded by urban districts, and through signature architecture and design. Chapter 4 turns to Liwan District, in the heart of its old city. Here, too, new aesthetic and spatial principles defining environmental sustainability influenced the presence and movement of waste. In both Tianhe and Liwan, the pursuit of ecological urbanism involved the implementation of new regulations and controls regarding waste management, alongside the transformation of urban spaces. These changes constrained the mobility of rural migrants responsible for waste cleanup, maintenance, and the labor-intensive task of diverting and organizing waste.

WASTE'S INFRASTRUCTURAL EXTENSION

I take as my object of study the totality of waste in Guangzhou and treat that totality as a complex socio-technical system composed of people, technologies, objects, and practices. Research on waste in the social sciences tends to center on one type of waste matter or a singular waste site: for instance, examining the lives of collectors and sanitation workers at waste dumps (Reno 2016; Millar 2018) or militarized industrial sites (Krupar 2013; Reno 2020). My multisited ethnography is guided by and follows how different streams of municipal solid waste—organics, recyclables, and other waste—mobilized diverse groups of urban actors. I draw on actor-network theory and its insistence to not take categories such as "society," "nature," or "waste" as predefined; I follow its suggestion of tracing the interactions that assemble actors and objects in moments when they become matters of political interest or concern. My research has also been informed by Latour's argument for tracing "the connections *between* controversies" after they have unfolded (Latour 2005, 23). In particular, I focus on how waste's relations amplified and reproduced uneven structural power conditions and worlds (Fortun 2014) across Guangzhou's urban geography.

Methodologically, I keep open the possibility of change, transformation, and political agency by examining waste infrastructure through the moment of its formation, a period of what I call "infrastructural extension." Waste's circulation is usually relegated to the background of everyday urban life. Scholars have argued that infrastructure becomes visible during moments of spectacular breakdown or through mundane acts of maintenance (Star 1999). Infrastructural extension refers to the inception of infrastructural systems, in which the scale, form, and shape of infrastructure features prominently in political disputes.[48] As the Guangzhou municipality embarked upon the work of envisioning and of actualizing a green and modern waste infrastructure in the 2010s, the technologies and policies that aimed to reconfigure waste's circulation became the center of a municipal controversy.[49] The period of infrastructural extension offers a venue to witness the readjustment and recalibration of existing structures (Anand 2017), and the gap between conceptualization and implementation (Ferguson 1994; Mosse 2005). Moments of adapting existing systems toward future pathways opens up emergent modes of political action.

Ethnographers have shown that waste infrastructures are not uniform technical systems but "heterogeneous infrastructural configurations" composed of both technological infrastructures and everyday labor practices (Lawhon 2017). As complex socio-technical and political configurations, waste infrastructures enable the flow, circulation, and metabolism that govern the urbanization of nature.[50] The proliferation of social and physical conduits or networks of metabolic vehicles aimed to facilitate circulation often, at the same time, "metaboliz[ing] or provok[ing] a change in matter" (Swyngedouw 2006, 108). If the tendency of capitalist development is to generate new strategies to appropriate nature for continuous production, I trace the specific ways that waste matter's circulation generates not only changes in matter but political sentiments, alliances, and actions.

I carried out eighteen months of continuous research from 2012 to 2013, and four summers of preliminary and follow-up research from 2010 to 2018. I arrived in Guangzhou in the summer of 2010 and began to interview homeowner anti-incineration activists who had participated in the 2009 Panyu protest. Interviews with Panyu activists led me to Mei village, home to the site of the first WTE facility in the city and to homeowners from Huadu District who in 2012 also protested and lobbied state officials. A handful of activists from the Panyu protest became key informants. By the time I returned to Guangzhou to conduct long-term fieldwork in 2012, Yuan Fei, a former anti-incineration protester from Panyu, had formed Eco-Canton, an environmental NGO focused on waste. I became involved with Eco-Canton, shadowing their efforts to promote recycling in housing communities across the city.

In addition, I conducted interviews and participant observation with informal collectors and sanitation workers in Tianhe District, the commercial heart of Guangzhou's new central business district. I followed both collectors to licensed depots and guerrilla trucks in their daily routine of buying, collecting, and trading scraps. In addition, I interviewed municipal officials and bureaucrats at both large scrap sorting and processing centers. As I concluded my long-term fieldwork in 2013, Yuan Fei was returning to Garden Villa to work with participants in the 2009 anti-incineration protest to start an experimental project with organics. Accompanying Yuan Fei on his quest to find a suitable technology to process organic waste, I interviewed scientists and entrepreneurs promoting new technologies. My Chinese ethnicity and fluency in Mandarin facilitated access. My limited command of Cantonese however, marked me as an outsider and a "nonnative." With a few exceptions, I conducted almost all my fieldwork and interviews in Mandarin.[51]

CHAPTER SUMMARY

Part I, "Circulations," begins with an investigation of how rural land and livelihoods are becoming displaced in the process of creating a modern waste infrastructure and an ecological city. Chapter 1, "Alternative Circuits," traces the daily practices of informal scrap collectors in Guangzhou's Tianhe District, whose labor served to concretely and visibly manifest the goals of the circular economy, to facilitate the circulation and diversion of scrap commodities. In Tianhe District, however, the pressures of urban development and ecological urbanism increasingly encroached upon the spaces necessary for informal waste work and simultaneously displaced rural bodies by rendering them objects of disorder. Against such displacements, I trace how informal collectors mobilized strategies to stave off the forces of eviction. Informal collectors leverage their spatial and material knowledge of scraps not only to divert waste but also to stake their claims to the city.

Chapter 2, "Toxic Displacement," moves to the peri-urban edge, to the site of Guangzhou's first WTE incinerator, and its effects on surrounding villagers. By burning waste to generate electricity, WTE incinerators enact a type of circulation that relies on the techno-scientific conversion of matter, imagined to be critical in realizing the state's vision of the circular economy. The building of technological infrastructures (such as WTE incinerators) illustrates that the construction of green cities is similarly predicated on the appropriation of rural land for projects in support of urban growth. The construction of infrastructure and the continued appropriation of land in service of urban development has hastened the displacement and dispossession of rural residents.

The chapter focuses on the experience of Mei villagers as they protested the incinerator's polluting effects while simultaneously confronting the threat of their own relocation. Environmental justice scholars have shown that the geography of waste facility siting reinforces the effects of structural racism that often displace pollution to the economically marginalized, Indigenous people, and communities of color.[52] China's pervasively polluted environment, however, has created a condition of exposure that cuts across the dividing lines between the rural and the urban. The siting of WTE incinerators created an opportunity for a shared experience of pervasive exposure to cohere into political critique. Rural and urban citizens used science to contest WTE incineration by finding evidence of pollution's effects. Disputes over the operation and safety of technology and infrastructure have become a key strategy of political articulation and mobilization. Mei villagers engaged in a sustained engagement with the state through a dispute about the production of scientific data and the production of environmental knowledge. As on-site monitors, villagers uncovered key evidence that unveiled a central contradiction at the heart of China's technical policy, an attempt to rely on WTE incinerators to burn a waste stream saturated with organics. In contrast with urban homeowners protesting against WTE incineration (chapter 3), the experience of Mei villagers illustrates an important point about what makes for a successful deployment of techno-politics. What matters is not so much who can mobilize environmental knowledge in a neutral political arena, but how rural-urban relations dictate the terms of an emerging pollution politics.

Part II, "Collectives," describes how diverse waste matter generated novel ecological-political devices that allowed new collectives to form around science, labor, and experimentation. Waste's circulation and transformation generated new techno-scientific discourses, the reinvention of green laborers, and experimentations.

Chapter 3, "Technicizing Deliberation," turns to citizen disputes against WTE incineration among the city's urban middle class. Against the backdrop of Guangzhou's rapid urbanization and heated real estate market, new gated communities on the city's peri-urban edge appealed to a growing urban professional class hoping to escape pollution. In a context of political repression that explicitly limited the coordination of political action between different communities, homeowners devised strategies to scale up their battle against WTE incineration across different communities faced with the prospect of an WTE incinerator siting. In particular, they used scientific and technical discourse to generate a sustained challenge to the state. By focusing on technical detail, scientific evaluation, and rational debate, homeowners sidestepped the mechanisms of state censorship. By drawing on practices of witnessing, verification, and rational discourse, middle-class homeowners obscured the political nature of their demands and instead framed their case as a technical dispute.

As urbanites at the city's edge came to interrogate the safety of WTE incineration, a group of activists started to investigate what types of waste ended up at WTE incinerators. Chapter 4, "Mystifying Labor," describes waste activists' shift toward recycling. While official state green development discourse foregrounded and privileged technological innovation and development, the labor of workers undergirded the accumulation of value in China's transition to capitalism and urbanization. Across Chinese cities, official waste campaigns cast sustainable waste practices as a form of voluntary citizen practice, where residents, particularly the city's growing middle class, were mobilized to divert scraps. Access to recyclables and scraps, however, is also an indispensable part of strategies of livelihood for sanitation workers seeking to supplement their low wages. An ethnography of waste work—of the concrete handling of waste—reveals the forms and conditions of labor and living, of work and social reproduction that,

acknowledged or not, made possible the creation of green cities. As recycling campaigns increasingly limited the capacity of sanitation workers to
recuperate scraps, they also precipitated a politics of distribution and entitlement for sanitation workers.

Chapter 5, "Cultures of Collaboration," focuses on how the absence of a
centralized solution for managing organic waste opened a space for activists
to enlist nonhumans in the decomposition of organic waste. In 2013, four
years after the Panyu anti-incineration protest, protesters, neighbors and
friends came together to establish a community center for the management
of organic waste with a do-it-yourself method, by fermenting organic waste
to make eco-enzymes. The "magical" quality of microbes as a cleaning
solution and as agents of environmental resuscitation gripped this group
of activists. For eco-enzyme brewers, microbes and fermentation practices
anchored a novel, local solution to waste management that imagined waste
matter as an agent of ecological repair. Brewers enlisted nonhuman bodies
and life processes in a more-than-human infrastructure for the sustainable
circulation of organics. Under a new, techno-scientific approach to waste
management, enzymes that speed up the breakdown and transformation of
waste anchored local experiments to envision new ecological and political
collectives. The act of effecting a material transformation of organics drew
collectives of people and microbes into an entanglement that yielded political imaginaries and forms of action whose outcomes were neither fully
contained nor predictable.

Part I

CIRCULATIONS

FIGURE 1.1   A guerrilla waste market operating in the early evening to avoid inspections and street patrols, 2012. Photo by author.

1 | ALTERNATIVE CIRCUITS
The Spatial Politics of Informal Scraps

IT'S RUSH HOUR in Tianhe District. As the neon billboards light the evening sky, I walk beside Wang Dan, a stout man with a cigarette dangling out of his mouth, dressed in a green military top and shorts. He slowly inches his three-wheel cart into the middle of a busy intersection. The sidewalk brims with advertising songs, as men and women dressed in crisp shirts and suits pour from office buildings into restaurants and storefronts. Pedestrians sidestep and shuffle past one another and stream into the Guangzhou Metro. Stepping into traffic, Wang steadily guides his cart piled high with paper and plastic, inching forward with the crowd. We barely make it past the crosswalk before the pedestrian light changes and rapid transit buses and other vehicles speed into the intersection.

We turn left down an alley toward a truck parked along the curb. Collectors refer to unlicensed scrap traders as "guerrillas" (*dayouji*). Wang explains to me that the name captures the mobility and agility of traders who swoop in to the city for a few hours before disappearing with scraps, transporting them to processing facilities on the city's outskirts. Guerrilla trucks pull up early in the evening just as urban patrols (*chengguan*) finish their shifts.[1] Some guerrillas avoid fines by bribing local officers. Informal traders operate in a gray zone outside state regulation, but they persist by keeping track of the rhythm of urban inspectors.

Earlier that evening, I had watched Wang carefully prepare his scrap bundle for resale. As he did at the end of each day, he removed bundles of cardboard from a makeshift street corner storage space. As he squatted down to bundle scrap paper, he sorted the pile, removing and tossing flattened cardboard boxes of a sturdier quality to one side. I offered to help but Wang told me to stand aside. I watched him lay down a piece of nylon string before interspersing large pieces of cardboard with lower grade paper. From the outside, the finished bundle appeared to be composed completely of cardboard. In between the high-quality paper, however, Wang had carefully inserted paper with lower resale value, for instance, thin wrapping paper, egg cartons and old advertising. When the stack was about a half-foot high and almost too heavy to lift, he fastened the bundle with a nylon string. He then hoisted the bundle onto his cart, which was modified with two long metal rods as extensions. When the stack reached a height of about a meter and a half, he threw a rope over the top and fastened it to stabilize the load.

Wang prefers selling to the guerrilla truck collector over the licensed scrap depot. Hauling scrap is laborious, and the guerrilla buyer saves Wang from having to cart his bundles to one of the few remaining licensed depots in Tianhe's commercial center. More importantly, under time pressure to evade street patrols, the guerrilla accepts bundles that are less carefully sorted. Licensed depots require sellers to undergo a more careful inspection. Allowing mixed bundles to slip in, guerillas sacrifice quality control for speed. As an informal collector who rents a one-bedroom apartment in an urban village (*chengzhongcun*), Wang works with similar time and space constraints. With access to adequate storage space, Wang could save and more carefully categorize his bundles before resale and thus fetch a higher price. Lacking storage space, Wang has to offload his bundle at the end of each day.

By the time I met them in 2012, Wang and his wife, Lee, had worked for fifteen years as itinerant buyers (*shoumailao*), unlicensed, informal collectors who make a living collecting and reselling recyclables.[2] Informal collectors specialize in trading waste commodities such as paper, plastics, and metals with an existing market and processing chain (paper mills, steel plants) such that they can be turned into raw material for reproduction. The couple, at this time in their late forties, were based in the eastern part of Tianhe District. Their two sons remained in their home village in Hunan Province, roughly 700 kilometers northwest of Guangzhou. Every day Wang and Lee purchased, sorted, and sold recyclables collected from waste bins in households, shopping centers, and restaurants in the city center.

While the work of informal collectors like Wang and Lee takes place outside the official system of waste management, it constitutes an established channel of waste circulation that redirects scrap commodities to reprocessing centers in the city's peripheries.

Over the past thirty years, Chinese cities have witnessed growth and development that have been accompanied by state investment in infrastructure and public services. In pursuit of a mode of ecological urbanism through the reconfiguration of waste circulations and flows, the state has invested in all aspects of waste management. State strategies for achieving the circular economy backed end-of-life waste treatment facilities such as WTE incinerators that mobilize high-tech solutions to turn waste into energy, and the institution of citizen recycling. Even as the municipal government prepared to launch another recycling campaign in 2012, the work of collecting, sorting, and diverting scrap commodities away from landfills and end-of-life facilities was being carried out by informal collectors. The aggregation of commodities with resale value largely depended on an informal labor system in which rural migrants separated, sorted, and then sold scraps to middlemen (either scrap depots or guerrilla collectors).

Wang and Lee's work and the work of collectors like them constitute a "vital infrastructure of labor" (Fredericks 2018, 16), where the circulation of waste matter is achieved through and animated by human bodies and human work. Urban scholars have demonstrated that reliable access to potable water and urban services such as electricity, transportation, and sanitation have proven increasingly elusive against a backdrop of colonialism, war, occupation, and neoliberal disinvestment in the megacities of the Global South (Anand 2017; Bear 2015; Stamatopoulou-Robbins 2021; Degani 2022). Writing on *vishoka,* informal utility workers who help to connect households to Dar es Salaam's electrical grid, Michael Degani (2022) uses *parasites* to describe how informal labor came to fill the void created by a slow, dysfunctional bureaucratic system. Ad hoc strategies, daily practices, and a popular ethics of productivity enable bureaucrats, entrepreneurs, workers, and urban citizens to navigate intermittent, uncertain, and unreliable infrastructure.

Studies of waste and labor highlight the extent to which waste work has become the site for ongoing negotiations of citizenship, relations of work and exchange, and a claim to urban space (Fredericks 2018; Doherty 2021; Butt 2023). Modern waste regimes (Gille 2007) perpetuate environmental injustices and inequities by reshaping the material and infrastructural practices of waste. As Jacob Doherty points out, waste work is particularly revealing of the process of urban disposability, the "mechanisms through which people become disposable *with*, *through* and *alongside* garbage" (Doherty 2021, 13; emphasis in original). In cities of the Global South, the daily labor of informal collectors and waste pickers reveals a fundamental dynamic of neoliberal urban reform that allocates precarity through the assignment of disposability.[3] In the early 2010s, the recuperation of scraps by migrant workers constituted a de facto and effective system of waste diversion in the city, and a trade that offered a livelihood for rural migrants. At the same time, the discourses, values, and aesthetics that guided the formation of the ecological city exacerbated the unequal dynamics caused by property and real estate–driven urban development and explicitly restricted informal livelihood strategies.[4]

This chapter details how informal collectors navigated forms of spatial displacement to ensure waste's circulation in Guangzhou. The remaking of urban space in Tianhe demolished urban villages to build modern highrises and constrained the daily conditions of work and life for informal collectors. In Tianhe, the mobilization of design, ecological features, and signature projects announced the arrival of an ecological modernity and further protected the concealment of waste objects and people. Against the demolition of urban villages and sanitation campaigns that targeted bodies associated with waste work, informal collectors used an intimate knowledge of scrap matter and urban space to generate alternative circuits, to simultaneously move waste out of the city, and to stave off their own displacement.[5] Informal collectors devised a range of spatial and temporal strategies to circumvent the forces of displacement.

MANAGING SCRAPS: FROM COLLECTIVES TO DISPOSSESSION

The contemporary informal scrap collection system in Chinese cities emerged in the post-reform period following the liberalization of the Mao-era state-run recycling system. In 1957 China became the first nation in the world to introduce a large-scale, state-run scrap collection (or recycling) system. The All China Resource and Recycling Cooperative was established under the direction of the Bureau of Supply and Marketing (gongxiaoshe), the national body in charge of the distribution of food and daily provisions and supplies such as grain and oil.[6] The Bureau of Supply and Marketing was the first to set up a formal infrastructural system of state-run depots and processing centers for recyclables. Throughout cities the bureau established recycling collection depots (*huishou wangdian*) to collect household recyclables including old newspapers, toothpaste tins, pots, and textiles. The collected materials were aggregated and transported to larger sorting centers and stations (*fenjian zhongxin/zhan*) located on the city's outskirts. In sorting centers, scraps were aggregated into different categories of commodities and routed to exchange markets (*jisanjiaoyi shichang*) before finally being diverted to processing facilities and state-run factories.

The Mao era also saw the introduction of a system of materials management that encouraged everyday citizens to see scraps as a collective resource. Citizens came to associate scrap reclamation with a project of nation building. Campaigns that mobilized citizens to take their scraps to recycling depots aligned an ethic of stewardship and frugality with nationalist sentiments. Households were encouraged to adopt an ethics of frugality and to aggregate and donate scraps and metals as raw material for the nation's program of rapid industrialization and development. Insofar as the interests of the socialist state were, in theory, meant to align with those of the masses, scrap recuperation in the socialist era created and assumed a collective and egalitarian *distribution* of materials as a national and shared resource, albeit, one directed by a centralized state authority.

Post-reform, economic liberalization replaced the state-run All China Resource and Recycling Cooperative with an individual and market system to organize the reclamation of scraps.[7] State-run recycling was privatized in terms of ownership and operation; larger scrap-sorting centers were incorporated as private enterprises while smaller recycling depots ended up in individuals' hands. In 1992 a province-wide industry association, the Regenerative Resources Association of Guangdong (Guangdong sheng zaisheng ziyuan hangye xiehui) (RRAG) was formed and took on responsibility for setting industry standards and directing industry development. In the late 1990s and early 2000s, as booming urban growth and development generated growing quantities of waste in cities, the sorting and diversion of recyclables were no longer solely operated according to the state's regulation nor carried out by citizens. The scraps trade was also sustained by an informal system of migrant workers.

In the years immediately following reform, land reforms initiated a large outmigration of rural laborers from the countryside into cities. Rising manufacturing and construction drew China's agrarian population into an industrial urban work force.[8] Coastal regions like Guangzhou, which were experiencing a boom in industrial production, housing, and construction, became a destination for rural migrant workers from China's inland provinces. Those unable or unwilling to take up wage employment in manufacturing, construction, or services found work in a growing urban informal sector. Since the 1980s, an estimated 280 million migrant workers have left the countryside to live and work in China's megacities. In Guangzhou, informal collectors[9] are mostly migrants from the neighboring provinces of Hunan, Anhui, Guangxi, and Sichuan, as well as other parts of Guangdong Province.

Informality gained currency in the 1970s as a term to describe a condition of work brought about by the influx of rural migrants to cities in the aftermath of postcolonial development. In the growing cities of Ghana and across Africa in the 1960s, rural migrants took up a range of economic activities—hawking, doing maintenance work, pawnbroking—to make a living (Hart 1973). Development practitioners initially saw the informal sector as a transitional phase, a condition to be stamped out by improving labor market integration (Benanav 2019). Recent scholarship understands the informal sector as a more permanent form of surplus labor that exists alongside wage work. Informality has come to be associated with not only temporary nonwage work arrangements but increasingly a condition of labor precarity and uncertain tenure. As the genesis of the concept of informality reminds us, informality is often connected to labor precarity associated with the displacement of rural lives and land dispossession.

Migrants were not only lured by development and industrialization to move to cities. Rural land reforms in the post-reform era dispossessed rural citizens of land and accelerated the creation of an urban labor force. By breaking up collective farming, the Chinese government generated a surplus population of workers who migrated from the countryside to work in cities. David Harvey's account of capitalism's "accumulation by dispossession" describes the transformation of rural common land to private ownership and the eviction of rural landholders (Harvey 2005). In the 1980s and 1990s, however, rural migrants in China retained access to rural land and social services even as they left the countryside to work in cities. China scholars thus characterize the first decades of industrialization in China as a period of "accumulation *without* dispossession" (Chuang 2020, 13, emphasis mine). The urban sphere was a site of labor and production while ties to rural land insured workers could access social services such as education and health care. Migrants could return to the countryside through downturns in the economic cycle and gaps in irregular contracts. In the early 2000s, running deep deficits and looking for new sources of revenue,[10] local officials began selling collectively owned land, precipitating a wave of evictions that would erode networks of social security for the rural labor base (Chuang 2020). Rural modernization and redevelopment projects such as the Rural-Urban Coordination campaign (chengxiang tongchou) compelled villagers to sell their rural landholdings to support projects to modernize the countryside (N. R. Smith 2021), and by the 2010s and early 2020s, rural land was no longer a reliable social safety net for migrant workers.

As Guangzhou set out to become a world city, projects of urban development have also unleased forces of urban displacement and eviction that constrain rural migrants' access to spaces of working and living within cities. Tianhe, once a peripheral district at the city's eastern edge, is now Guangzhou's second-most important commercial hub. In the early 2000s, municipal planners proposed a new central business district (CBD) running from the Guangzhou East Train Station to the Haizhu District (Gaubatz 1999). Tianhe's urban villages would be replaced with highways, skyscrapers, upscale shopping centers, and green design. The redevelopment of Tianhe eviscerated the urban villages (*chengzhongcuns*) ("villages within cities") that once occupied the area. In 2000 Guangzhou's municipal government announced plans to eliminate 130 urban villages by 2010. Politically and legally, urban villages were rural jurisdictions where land ownership remained in the hands of village collectives and was allocated to village residents for their use.[11]

In most *chenzhongcuns* across China, residents had given up farming, built housing, and had come to rely on rent from rural migrants for their income. As an in-between space, urban villages allowed migrant workers to pursue a means of livelihood outside formal occupations recognized by the state (Chu et al. 2022). Offering cheap rent and services catering to the needs of the urban working poor, *chenzhongcuns* supported social reproduction for migrant workers. In many ways, the process of urban enclosure in the city's central districts like Tianhe parallels the spatial evictions occurring at its peri-urban edges.[12] Within Guangzhou's urban centers, the demolition of urban villages perpetuated the dispossession not only of villagers who owned land but also rural migrant workers and informal collectors who depended on *chengzhongcuns* as a source of housing.

Neil Smith argues that under the guise of revitalization, renewal, or re-development, the introduction of modern infrastructure and urban design enacts a revanchist politics in which urban space is increasingly reconfig-ured for a dominant group through the eviction and erasure of the urban poor (Smith 2005; Huang 2014). In contrast to the process of gentrifica-tion in the West,[13] "accumulation by urban dispossession" describes spa-tial evictions across cities of the Global South. As Tom Gillespie notes, for the largely informal proletariat in Accra, exclusion from both formal wage labor and housing markets precluded the development of an urban com-mons, the shared resources that undergird the reproduction of the collec-tive (Gillespie 2016). Efforts by the state to produce new spatial forms more conducive to capital accumulation (such as the pursuit of "world cities" or "global cities") enclose the urban commons that once supported an infor-mal proletariat (Caldeira 2000). The eviction of informal laborers either via physical-legal means such as the privatization of land or via expulsion from public space "mobiliz[es] . . . a revanchist discourse that frames these groups as sources of dirt and disorder" whose presence undermines the transformation of global cities (Gillespie 2016, 67).

The experience of Wen, a young woman from Hunan I met in 2012, captured how the demolition of *chengzhongcuns* perpetuated conditions of labor precarity for informal collectors. I visited Wen and her nine-month-old daughter regularly outside of Xian village where she had established a temporary collection site. Having spent years cultivating a relationship with a glass factory, Wen and her husband specialized in collecting glass. Specializing in one or two materials gave collectors a slight advantage as they were able to sell directly and at a higher price to factories without going through middlemen or brokers. However, selling directly to a fac-tory meant they needed storage space to aggregate a larger quantity of glass. For five years, Wen had searched for a reliable source of housing with an extra lot or access to additional land suitable for this purpose. When she first arrived in Guangzhou, she and her husband found a home in Yangji village, on the west side of Tianhe, which has since been reduced

FIGURE 1.2   Migrant workers returning home to a *chengzhongcun* undergoing demolition. In the background are the new high-rise developments that have replaced villages, 2013. Photo by author.

to rubble. She relocated to Xian village shortly before it was also slated for demolition and rebuilding.

She eventually found housing for her family in Yuan village, further south and east in Tianhe. In order to accommodate the family's need for storage. Wen and her husband lived in a makeshift room made of metal siding next to a row of autobody shops in a parking lot. A hot plate and rice maker in front of the house constituted a makeshift kitchen. Wen was concerned about rumors that the city would soon begin working on an extension for a subway line nearby. Anticipating another round of demolition in the name of redevelopment, Wen was already preparing for a move further east in Tianhe. Each relocation meant finding a new space to live and store her inventory. Wen explained that she would likely have to transition away from glass since finding another large space for aggregating and storing glass was a tall order. For informal collectors, housing was not only a place to live, but was connected to a capacity to forge a means of livelihood that enabled them to gain a foothold in the city. Spatial constraints for migrants and their lack of permanent, stable housing shaped which materials were recuperated and how they circulated throughout the city.[14]

A NEW GREEN ORDER: AGAINST *ZANGLUANCHA*

In the early 2000s, Guangzhou devised a plan to shift away from its focus on industrial development and manufacturing to position the city as a center of international finance. Guangzhou's efforts to become a "world city" included enlisting global architects to build skyscrapers and modern buildings. Guangzhou's pursuit of world city status, however, also foregrounded the goals of sustainability and the creation of a livable environment. Slogans like "low-carbon economy, knowledge city" (*ditan jingji, zhihui chengshi*) explicitly linked the project of elevating the city to a knowledge economy with the achievement of long-term sustainability. On the ground, however, Guangzhou's transformation into an ecological city (*shengtai chengshi*) was achieved not only through investments in green technology or LEED-certified buildings. Architecture, design, and the deployment of an ecological aesthetics were also critical aspects of Guangzhou becoming a world city.

In Tianhe, the demolition of urban villages facilitated the consolidation of land for urban real estate development and the creation of new commercial districts. In the newly constructed central business district (CBD), planners leveraged ecological features to signify Guangzhou's rise as a global, cosmopolitan urban center through the creation of ecological zones that married an environmental sensibility with commerce. Zhujiang New Town sits at the heart of the new CBD, home to a series of aboveground and underground shopping centers, hotels, and multinational offices linked together by a central walkway. At the south end of the walkway is a cluster of signature buildings, designed by global "starchitects," that include a state-of-the-art library, opera house, and stadium. The district is threaded by an urban ecological corridor[15] that features manicured landscaping, wooded waterways, and palm trees. The Tianhe CBD intersperses elements that reference nature into spaces of capital speculation and flow. A network of luxury shopping malls and seven-floor karaoke centers accompanies a new ecological zone saturated with LEED-certified buildings. The urban ecological corridor explicitly juxtaposes elements from nature with buildings designed to signify modernity. Skyscrapers tower over a blanket of greenery while a series of wooden walkways winds through high-rises with clean lines projecting upwards.

As Asher Ghertner observes, the process of creating "world cities" is often accompanied by the advent of a "rule by aesthetics" where decisions about who and what belong in a city are made through the regulation, maintenance, and orchestration of appearances (Ghertner 2015). In Guangzhou, officials interested in positioning the city as a world city rely on design and signature projects that evoke an ecologically inflected modernity in which green, orderly, aesthetic features are *synonymous* with the achievement of sustainability. Every day and night, the modern consumer city is maintained by rural laboring bodies who haul waste away, scrub city streets, and carefully tend plants and landscapes (Calvino 1997). In Tianhe, the staging of green modernity simultaneously increases the demand for sanitary labor while establishing an aesthetics of order and cleanliness that mark bodies associated with waste as targets of governance. As a state strategy, China's pursuit of ecological urbanism continues forms of land-based accumulation that perpetuate land speculation, urban displacement, and

FIGURE 1.3 The vision of Guangzhou as world city, seen here in an ecological corridor, draws on green design and nature, 2012. Photo by author.

a place-based strategy of value production through design and spectacle making (Shin 2014).

China established a series of national campaigns to rank cities according to a set of metrics, placing neighborhoods, districts, and cities into competition with one another. In Guangzhou, Sanitary City campaigns are an important part of the project to achieve an imagined green modernity and precipitate the eviction of informal collectors from urban space. During city inspection days, especially during Sanitary City campaigns held every September, each complex is evaluated against a series of targets. Sanitation inspections are an occasion for local officials (*jiedaoban*) to police the appearance of neighborhoods. Such campaigns function as a vehicle for the state to enact a rule by aesthetics, in which "a shared mode of aesthetic engagement with mutually recognizable visual markers of order or disorder" come to shape a "community of sense" and to authorize a set of governance strategies (Ghertner 2015, 7).

A new discourse characterizing qualities in need of reform in modern cities, *zangluancha* targeted informal collectors and scrap depots as objects and sites of intervention. *Zangluancha* loosely translates as dirt, chaos, and backwardness (or deficiency). *Zang* means filth or dirt and is frequently used to describe spaces or persons associated with waste work. *Luan* means chaos and disorder, but also suggests unruliness and criminality. *Cha* connotes backwardness, plotting the failure to adequately progress on a linear trajectory. In her writings on state-building projects in Israel, Emily McKee uses "trash talk" to describe the "discursive associations between purportedly dirty and disordered landscapes of a group of people and their moral and social qualities" (McKee 2015, 734). As a state discourse, zangluancha similarly casts urban space and rural bodies as targets of a project of improvement.

The discourse of zangluancha authorized a set of new urban governance strategies that increasingly marked the complex network of informal collectors who order waste as themselves a force of disorder. Like the state discourse of *suzhi* or "quality," zangluancha renders both persons and places through a set of abstract characteristics as subjects to the project of governing in an increasingly neoliberal era (Yan 2003, 494). Where *suzhi* indexed anxieties about the low quality of the population (Anagnost 2004; Kipnis 2007), zangluancha projects a desire to reconfigure persons and spaces associated with dirt, rurality, and backwardness. In urban planning discourse in China, zangluancha describes urban villages and neighborhoods, spaces of migrant life, as "cancers of the city" (Siu 2007), whose eviction would signal the arrival of modernity. Zangluancha especially attacks rural persons, bodies, and spaces who seem to threaten an abstract sense of urban order, despite the fact that rural workers carry out the work of cleanup and ordering.

At the time of my fieldwork in 2012–2013, scrap collection depots were being subjected to greater scrutiny by sanitary campaigns. During annual inspection campaigns, municipal management bureaus and public security set out to "reform" both licensed scrap depots and informal collectors. Security cameras were installed at scrap depots, ostensibly to guard against those who sell public infrastructure (pipes, wires, and street signs) off as scraps. Municipal management, however, also surveilled other aspects of operations. Licensed depots were fined for being disorderly if paper, scrap metals, and wires were not stacked neatly enough. Neighborhood safety inspection officials also dropped by for unannounced inspections in the name of maintaining safety codes. In these moments of heightened scrutiny, local security uses a presumed need for cleanliness and orderliness to assert control over a sector that has been otherwise marginalized by the state.

At the start of the Sanitary City campaign in 2012, the neighborhood security guard would alert Wang and Lee to impending inspections. The couple know that they will need to temporarily halt their business. They carefully hide their three-wheeler in an adjacent housing complex and pull a tarp over their cargo of scraps. They scrub down the sidewalk where they typically perform their trade. Wang and Lee then sit and wait, sometimes putting their business on hold for days or weeks expecting that they will be allowed to resume collection when the campaign ends. Elsewhere, scholars note that informal collectors confronting the increasing deployment of governance strategies within processes of world-class city-making use uniforms, identification cards, and codes of conduct to defend their livelihood (Luthra and Monteith 2021). Wang and Lee's voluntary compliance with their temporary eviction is an example of how collectors mobilize a range of strategies to claim their capacity to remain in cities.

CLAIMING REGULARITY

Unlike waste pickers (*shihuangzhe*) or urban gleaners who sort through waste bins to reclaim plastic bottles or newspapers, itinerant buyers such as Wang and Lee often have a permanent space with a regular clientele. From 10:00 a.m. to just after 8:00 p.m., seven days a week, Wang and Lee can be found outside a gated housing complex in the heart of Tianhe's commercial district. The complex behind Wang and Lee's collection depot was built just a decade ago, but its brick façade already appears dated next to the more recent glass high-rise and commercial complexes that were springing up in the CBD. At night, Wang and Lee close up shop by selling their collection and hiding their handwritten advertising behind the entrance. While technically outside the complex, Wang and Lee nevertheless pay a small monthly fee to the building security. Returning to the same place day after day has enabled the couple to build up a regular clientele.

Each day residents from the complex call or drop by with requests to

FIGURE 1.4   Wang and Lee's regular "street stall" in front of an urban gated housing complex, piled with sorted and organized cardboard, and bags of metal and plastics, 2012. Photo by author.

pick up newspaper, old furniture, and plastic bottles. Wang and Lee's daily work—buying, sorting, and bundling waste—is a labor of ordering, identification, and classification. In addition to the housing complex, *laoxiang* (rural migrants from the same region) working as kitchen workers, cleaners, and delivery drivers stop by to offload Styrofoam boxes, plastic bags, or large aluminum tins. At times, Wang and Lee's depot resembles a gathering space where migrant collectors meet to socialize and, at others, a market where people go to trade scrap and exchange information.[16]

"Hey boss!" (*laoban*) a collector calls out to Wang as he zips up to the depot with a stack of Styrofoam packaging on an electric three-wheeler. Xiaohui, a delivery driver with a slim build, is a regular seller. Earlier in the week, Wang and Xiaohui shared a cigarette in an air of quiet dejection. Wang was recounting the story of a collector stationed up the street whose scale was confiscated by *chengguan* (public security officers in charge of policing urban space and enforcing local regulations). The scale was worth 300 RMB, well over a collector's weekly earnings. A para-police force without the authority to perform arrests, the *chengguan* are notorious for frequent clashes with street vendors (Swider 2015). Xiaohui, listening to Wang's story, spits on the street in anger. He recounts another instance when a *jiaojing*—a member of the traffic police known to harass collectors—confiscated a modified electric three-wheeler that the collector had recently purchased to save himself from having to peddle heavy loads of scrap. Xiaohui suspects that the official immediately sold the cart—worth over 500 RMB—and kept the money for himself.[17] Wang added that he had seen street officials confiscate a whole cart full of metal only to sell it themselves. Complaints of harassment and mistreatment exchanged at the scrap depot fostered a sense of recognition among informal collectors who came to see themselves as those who share in a similar trade. The airing of grievances further solidifies collectors as political subjects who are brought together through a shared experience of exploitation by local authorities.

The work that Wang and Lee perform as informal scrap collectors was particularly vulnerable to a regime of urban surveillance and policing. Wang recalls the time that a public security officer told him, without masking the comment as a joke, that "any full-time collector is always part thief" (*yi ge shoumailao, ban ge xiaotou*). The comment invoked the stereotype of the urban poor as mired in disorder and criminality. The stereotype is hardly confined to twenty-first century China. Marx saw the *lumpen-*

proletariat as dangerous and unruly, a threat to the social stability of the bourgeoisie and to the revolutionary potential of the proletariat (Stallybrass 1990). In Guangzhou, local police derive their authority over informal collectors in part from an official stance that sees any business conducted without an official license as suspect, especially any that involves trafficking in things of uncertain origin.

To mitigate suspicion, Wang and Lee often perform daily acts of "civility from below," a type of everyday respect and horizontal relations-building that makes informal collectors and the people with whom they interact legible to one another (Forment 2018, 410). Wang and Lee are recognizable as a regular part of street life in Guangzhou. When cars pull up to the gate adjacent to their stall, Lee often runs inside to get the keys to let the residents in, always with a polite smile. When grandparents go to pick up their grandkids at the daycare center, Lee watches over their groceries. Over time Wang and Lee's performance as an informal neighborhood watch team—local security and goodwill ambassadors—worked against the view of collectors as threatening strangers. Instead, urban middle-class residents came to trust them as a familiar part of street life.

ALTERNATIVE CIRCUITS

To navigate the forces of eviction, informal collectors also leveraged an alternative geography of the city by regulating their spatiotemporal rhythms of work. Aside from their regular clientele inside the complex, Lee's outdated flip phone rang constantly with calls from cleaners working inside the 138,000-square-meter multiplex luxury shopping center across the street. In the summer of 2010, during my first visit to Guangzhou, the mall plaza was still under construction. By 2013, a familiar list of international retailers was in operation: Gucci, Louis Vuitton, and Uniqlo along with a large supermarket selling imported organic produce. The mall was part of a larger complex that, at its northern end, housed a luxurious Mandarin Oriental hotel, a rooftop garden with a German beer garden, and several Western restaurants. The shopping center is just one of many commercial complexes in Guangzhou's new CBD.[18]

Wang and Lee were not solely dependent on the collection of household goods inside the gated complex. Key members of their clientele were the cleaning staff in shopping complexes and restaurants. Each day, they traversed the private plazas of shopping malls that connected a series of commercial complexes. Even as new shopping centers proclaimed Guangzhou's status as a center of consumption and a world city, waste, its byproduct, was meant to be collected and sorted invisibly and out of sight. Wang and Lee's daily routines illuminated the infrastructural work and flows typically hidden in the city's backstage, where waste and labor move through utility rooms and less traveled corridors.

Spaces like the CBD, however, also erect invisible barriers and enact spatial exclusion. Shopping centers often employ their own private security who often interrogate collectors pulling a three-wheel cart or migrants hauling bags of cardboard, their lack of uniform distinguishing them from the cleaning staff employed by the centers. Lee is well acquainted with these encounters. To avoid attention from street police she knows how to make herself invisible. Under the watchful eyes of private security guards, she can divert the commercial center's scraps, old papers, plastics, and glass without

FIGURE 1.5 Collectors line up to sell the day's collection, 2013. Photo by author.

disturbing the orderly formal appearance of modern spaces of consumption. Wang and Lee operate in this landscape by making use of a hidden geography, a back-stage corridor of mobility and access.

One night Lee leads me into the mall complex. After a few steps, Lee rounds a corner and pushes open a door marked "utility corridor." Inside a hallway lit by fluorescent bulbs, Lee greets a cleaner interested in selling bundles of cardboard she has secured from various shops. In the middle of her exchange with the store clerk, a mall security guard catches up to Lee. Clearly aggravated, he tells her she'd been warned to stay out of the back of the mall. Lee, in a nonchalant voice, replies: "Thank you sir, I'll be gone soon." She continues her negotiations, confident that the guards will not forcefully evict her. Nevertheless, Lee works quickly to evade attention, particularly while pulling scraps from the storage room to the utility hallway. Lee shares advice on staying hidden with me: "Don't lose your scale and stay out of the way of customers."

ADULTERATION

At the end of each day, Wang and Lee move their daily collection to an informal waste market, where middlemen scrap buyers will purchase and transport scraps to a sorting center or waste market outside the city. The informal waste market is where economic value is assigned to recuperated scrap commodities. Informal collectors commonly deploy two tactics to increase the value of each bundle: arbitrage and value-added processing. Arbitrage takes advantage of small differences in price between markets. Collectors can increase the value of each bundle of scraps by purchasing scraps at one price and by selling scraps in another market with a price difference or by holding onto a commodity for a period of time until the price increases. Another strategy is value-added processing. The addition of value to a bundle of scrap can be achieved either by sorting and aggregating different types of matter into more distinguished categories, for instance by separating plastics into PET and PVC. Collectors can also disassemble or take apart different objects. For instance, collectors often strip plastic shielding from copper wiring to yield raw copper wires that can sell for a higher price.

Temporary access to space has also become increasingly difficult to obtain in the new CBD. Where guerrilla collectors set up scrap markets on sidewalks and beneath highways and overpasses, the demand for a sanitary and modern city has made it increasingly difficult to set up temporary markets. With the more limited access to space, informal collectors must pass off their bundles at the end of each day.[19] Back at the guerrilla truck, Wang is ready for the weigh-in. He had carefully mixed lower-quality paper, including egg cartons and flyers, in between higher-grade cardboard. He hoped the guerrilla buyer would purchase the entire package for the price of the higher-grade cardboard. This preparation further ensured that he could offload the small amounts of advertising and egg carton papers—he would need more of them for a distinct bundle. In this way, collectors manipulate the material quality of waste to adapt to the limits and constraints of time and space. They purposely misorder, adulterate, and misclassify scraps to maximize profit, and inadvertently, this practice also facilitates the diversion of lower-grade scraps to waste markets.

While Wang has disguised his bundle through creative layering, other collectors use a range of other strategies to increase the value of their scrap bundle: they include tricks like wetting the center of bundles or even adding sand to the perforated pieces. At the resale market, during "inspection," when scrap bundles are weighed, assessed, and assigned monetary value, scrap buyers similarly exercise their material knowledge of scraps to evaluate the bundles sold by sellers. At the weigh-in, buyers often use a scale but the assessing of value and assignment of process is a test of the eyes and the body. A seasoned and discerning buyer can guess the approximate weight of a bundle of newspapers by eyeing the height alone. Collectors who gain reputations for always selling "dirty" packages by passing a bundle of one quality off as a higher quality product are banned from returning.

On this evening, Wang pulls up at the guerrilla truck just after 8:00 p.m. Cleaners in uniform are lined up and ready to step up whenever an available scale presents itself. Pedestrians step around the spread of different bottles being counted as the sidewalk becomes a temporary waste market. When it is Wang's turn, he pulls the heavy cart as close to the scale as possible and unloads each bundle of paper. A family of three from Henan owns and operates this guerrilla truck, and Wang is a regular seller. The buyer carries a small notepad in one hand. With one eye cocked on the scale, he slips a pencil behind his left ear and begins to manipulate the weight on the top of the scale from left to right. The scale teeter-totters before reaching an equilibrium. Wang is also eyeing the scale carefully. The guerrilla buyer hands Wang a piece of paper scribbled with a few illegible numbers and then pulls out a few bills. Wang unloads his cart and hoists it to top of the waste truck where the buyer's son waits to catch each bundle before neatly stacking them toward the back of the truck.

Manipulating the composition and quality of scrap matter is common in the informal scrap trade. Informal collectors order and selectively adulterate scraps simultaneously to maximize value and to move scraps out of the city. The circulation of scraps and diversion of recyclable waste is achieved not by the ordered procession of sorting, collection, and transportation, but dictated by a set of strategies to maximize value from daily exchanges at a scrap commodity market. Strategies like the deliberate remixing of scraps illuminate the commodity chain's reliance on collectors' intimate understanding of the affordances of scrap materials, such as the weight of paper, the varieties of plastics, and the identification of adulterated bundles.

SPATIAL ADAPTATIONS

The circular economy imagines a smooth and seamless flow of different waste streams, in which scraps are sorted into distinct categories and move out of urban space. In Wang and Lee's daily spatial and labor practices we can see that the diversion of recyclables is directed by a set of adaptive strategies that collectors deploy to generate circulations of waste under conditions of spatial eviction. In Tianhe District, recent efforts to reshape the city's image according to an aesthetic of sanitized order, along with official pronouncements of building modernity and a green city, have displaced rural bodies and rendered migrants who perform scrap collection as disorderly elements. China's urban modernization schemes have generated a new contradiction in the creation of green cities: the very impulse to create a green system of scrap diversion is predicated on the displacement of existing systems.

In Tianhe's new CBD, informal collectors confront an emerging urban mode of governance that imposes a "rule by aesthetic" where aesthetic rationales authorize the reconfiguration of urban space and the eviction of people associated with waste and dirt. Greening campaigns target and evict objects and people characterized by *zangluancha* (dirt, chaos, and disorder), markers frequently associated with migrant bodies and signs of rurality, as objects of improvement or reform. In effect, aesthetic ideals that link modernity, orderliness, and ecological development exacerbate social inequality between those who produce waste and those responsible for hauling it away. State investments in the creation of an ecological and politically neutral urban development further displace the "infra-economy" responsible for fulfilling and overcoming gaps in infrastructural services in the first place.

Asef Bayat uses the concept of "quiet encroachment" to describe the "silent, protracted but pervasive advancement" of the rural poor on the propertied and powerful (Bayat 2000). Quiet encroachment describes how struggles for autonomy, distribution, and access are not only strategies of survival but also a claim to a politics of space against the state and the political elite. The circular economy is upheld by those rendered marginal to the process of building green cities, and its implementation has perpetuated alternative circulations. In Tianhe, the alternative circuits that collectors have mobilized advance a clandestine and hidden claim for the occupation of space and the right to the city. The claim is pursued through a set of horizontal alliances that collectors forge in their daily encounters with other collectors, urban citizens, and the social and material network involved in the circulation of scraps.

FIGURE 2.1 Phoenix WTE incinerator in Mei village, 2013. Phase I (building on right) has been operating since 2006; Phase II (building on left) began construction in 2012 and began operating in 2013. Photo by author.

2 | TOXIC DISPLACEMENT

Land and Pollution at the City's Edge

PHOENIX NUMBER ONE PLANT WAS Guangzhou's first waste-to-energy (WTE) incinerator. Located in Baiyun District, about 23 kilometers northwest of Guangzhou's old city center, the area immediately surrounding the plant is not an industrial zone but a village. There's no obvious dividing line between village and incinerator and, from afar, the incinerator's silver dome and tall chimney appear to rise out of a patch of farmland, with chickens roaming and feeding in its shadow. A peri-urban community of Hakka and Cantonese speakers, the village of Mei officially comprises about 6,500 registered households. Villagers in Mei have long been witnesses to the effects of pollution from the city's end-of-life waste treatment facilities. In 1991 a landfill was built in the village, and in 2006, the Phoenix incinerator was constructed there and began operations. Typical of construction in China in the early 2000s, the Phoenix facility was in violation of environmental regulations. Despite rules mandating that industrial facilities be located at least 300 meters from residences, village homes sit less than 100 meters from the incinerator.

Built and operated by the French company Veolia, at the time of its construction, the facility was touted as the future of modern waste management. The plan for Phoenix specified that the facility be built in two stages: Phase I would begin operation in 2006 while Phase II was scheduled for completion in 2010,[1] at which point Phoenix would be the largest waste incineration facility in the world. Phoenix displayed a preference for scale and centralization, key characteristics of China's environmental infrastructure. In the late 1990s and early 2000s, China looked to Western companies and relied on technology transfer to speed up development. Phase I of Phoenix was built through a build-operate-and-transfer (BOT) scheme. Onyx, Veolia's waste division, would be awarded a fixed ten-year contract to build and operate the facility before transferring ownership and operation to the Guangzhou government.[2] Phase II, however, would be built by Grantop, a Chinese state-owned enterprise that claimed to have developed their own WTE incineration technology better suited to the material makeup of local waste. The contrasting approaches to the construction and operation of Phases I and II mirrored China's changing approach to technological development, from a reliance on technology transfer in the 1990s to investments in domestic environmental technologies in more recent years. Sitting side by side, the facilities manifest Guangzhou's key strategy for creating a modern and sustainable form of waste management focused on investing and developing technological innovations.

In contrast to scrap commodities like paper, plastics, and metals that have a market value and can be easily separated from the waste stream, WTE incinerators were designed to treat a category of waste stream officially classified as "other waste" (*qita laji*) or "mixed waste" (*hunhe laji*). "Other waste" refers to matter that cannot be easily removed and diverted for reprocessing, such as diapers and thin plastics mixed with tea leaves, the stuff typically left to decompose in landfills. WTE incineration's claims as a green technology and as fulfilling the vision of the circular economy were predicated on the idea that it could transform mixed waste into clean and green energy pumped to the grid.

At the city's peri-urban edge, the construction and operation of Guangzhou's first generation of WTE incinerators had other effects. Almost as soon as Phoenix Phase I began operating, Mei villagers reported that the facility emitted black smoke and released acrid odors that burned their nostrils and left them wary of opening windows, even on hot, humid evenings. The polluting effects of WTE incinerators launched a wave of protests and petitions in Mei village resulting in arrests. But by May 2012, the relationship between the city and villagers took another turn. As the municipality was looking to build more WTE incinerators, they faced anti-incineration protests in Panyu and Huadu districts. Municipal officials were eager to shift public opinion and to build public support for this technology. After negotiating with the village council, the city authorized a team of "technical monitors" made up of representatives from Mei village who would be stationed inside the plant to oversee its daily operations. Coming after years of contentious confrontation with the state, when villager demands were ignored or met with hostility, the establishment of the monitoring team represented an important recognition of the villagers as stakeholders in Guangzhou's waste infrastructure and politics.

At the time, Mei villagers were unique in China as the first rural subjects to assume a role of technical oversight at an infrastructural or industrial facility. China's pursuit of modernization through science and technology since the post-reform period had elevated a class of technocrats, municipal officials, and engineers who steered national development (Andreas 2009). Rural citizens, both in the Republican and post-reform periods, were seen either as lacking scientific knowledge or as the target of modernization campaigns (Duara 1991; Lam 2011). Peasants and villagers have long been the target of modernization and anti-superstition campaigns and are viewed by the state as outside science (Lam 2011). The Maoist years were in many ways an exception as, at the time, the state required that experts and intellectuals learn from the masses, particularly in the realm of agriculture, through grassroots experimentations in a "*tu* science" (indigenous science) (Schmalzer 2016). The incorporation of Mei villagers into the operation of the incinerator as technical monitors marked a formal recognition of villagers as scientific subjects, capable of overseeing the operation of a new generation of environmental technology. Controversies around access to and the health, safety, and risk associated with new environmental technologies from agriculture to nuclear power expanded the realm of public participation. Across a range of democratic contexts, battles over scientific regulation, the neutrality of data, the appropriateness of technologies, and questions of distribution and access have been waged in courts, on the streets, and in the media (Aga 2021; Callison 2014; Oreskes and Conway 2010; Wylie 2018). The experience of Mei villagers suggests that peasants, farmers, and peri-urban villagers are key participants in techno-scientific controversies.

Born and raised in Mei village, Ah Wang, a steely figure in her midforties and the only woman among the monitors, was the group's supervisor. In an early meeting, she proudly recounted the long history of protests that won villagers access to the facility. For Ah Wang, years of direct confrontation forced villagers to resort to oppositional tactics that did little to curb pollution but instead provoked more repression. Ah Wang believed that access to the plant would allow villagers to help the plant operate safely and, by extension, reduce pollution. Their role as technical monitors, she believed, placed villagers on an equal footing with middle-class homeowners in Panyu and Huadu, who were using anti-incinerator protests to challenge the state's waste management and environmental governance (chapter 3).

During our first few meetings in late 2012, Ah Wang confidently told me that once inside the incinerator, villager monitors would be the "eyes, nose, and ears" of the facility. Yet over the first half of 2013, initial resolve gave way to uncertainty. Access to the incinerator did not yield clear insight into whether daily operations of the plant met safety standards. Among the thirteen monitors, none had any technical training and only one had been to university. Ah Wang feared that the state had granted them access to the facility wagering that, once inside, the daily functioning (and failures) of the plant would remain illegible.

At the end of 2013, Mei villagers eagerly awaited another announcement; the district government was about to unveil the details of a long-awaited proposal to carry out an "environmental relocation." Rumors had circulated for years that Mei village would be resettled to make way for the expansion of waste facilities in the area. Villagers were to receive compensation for selling their rural land rights to the state and would be offered apartments at a reduced rate in a newly developed complex nearby. After years of battling against waste facilities, peri-urban villagers were confronting the prospect of their own relocation.

Efforts to realize the circular economy through the introduction of WTE incineration mediated the displacement of rural lives on Guangzhou's peri-urban edge. The politics of siting waste treatment facilities illuminates the relationship between pollution and the political economy of land. Max Liboiron (2021) writes that "science always happens within land relations, and those relations are always specific to that place" (46). In the US, environmental justice scholars have shown that the siting of waste facilities— the geography of waste management—reinforces the effects of structural racism that displace pollution onto marginalized Indigenous communities and communities of color. In China, the siting of WTE incinerators amplified social divisions between rural and urban dwellers and hastened the already underway displacement of rural citizens driven by urbanization and the development of the ecological city.

The siting of WTE incinerators on the peri-urban outskirts points first and foremost to how the actualization of green environmental technology was predicated on procuring land. Mei villagers were subjected to "sustainability by dispossession" (J.-C. Chen 2013, 6), a process in which rural lives and rural communities are evicted from land consolidated for urban growth and development. Second, contestations over the process of relocation in Mei village were predicated on the transformation of not only land but of the local ecology, including air and water, by pollution that ultimately facilitated the physical eviction of residents. In her study of the effects of chemical pollution on First Nations communities, Deborah Davis Jackson uses "dysplacement" to describe the profound alienation enacted by air pollution on local residents with the arrival of heavy industry (Davis Jackson 2011). Even among communities who remain in place next to heavy industry, malodors and contamination disrupt a connection to the ecology and gradually sever ties to place. The alienation perpetuated by toxicity illustrates that one's situatedness and belonging to a place are deeply tied to the body's relation to the local ecology (Alaimo 2010; Agard-Jones 2013). Michelle Murphy views conditions of chemical exposure as generative not of alienation but of collectivities. Murphy (2017) uses the concept of *alterlife* to describe "collectivities of life recomposed by the molecular productions of capitalism" both past and future (497). Alterlife is thus both "life already altered" but also "life open to alteration" in which a shared condition of exposure gives way to new modes of action (497).

As part of efforts to implement a technocratic mode of environmental remediation for waste, the introduction of WTE incineration also pressed Mei villagers into a new mode of engagement with science. In China explicit constraints on collective action perpetuated—particularly among rural residents battling the effects of pollution—a "resigned activism" in which local agitations rarely obtained the support of scientific experts or redress from officials (Lora-Wainwright 2017). In studies of the everyday effects of living within a polluted environment, scholars argue that a central effect of toxicity is the production of uncertainty (Auyero and Swistun 2009; Nixon 2011). In Mei village, the state's techno-scientific approach to environmental remediation generated not only uncertainty, but enrolled villagers as scientific witnesses tasked specifically with documenting and monitoring pollution.

In contrast to the erasure of the experience of communities marginalized by pollution, the experience of Mei villagers demonstrates that investments in a new generation of green technology simultaneously produced a set of speculative calculations and a mode of rural scientific citizenship. In Mei village, scientific participation was thoroughly entangled with, and shaped and constrained by, land relations. The inclusion of Mei villagers as village monitors facilitated new forms of knowledge production and evaluation by rural actors of the daily operations of a so-called green technology of waste management. While Mei villagers could not marshal evidence inside the incinerator to forestall an eventual dislocation, the data they collected would contribute to a broader challenge to the city's waste policy that buttressed the techno-scientific activism of homeowners (chapter 3). The experience of Mei villagers illuminates, on the one hand, the fiction of scientific inclusion for rural citizens in China's authoritarian green governance. On the other hand, the participation of rural subjects as scientific citizens in a political performance of inclusion, even a fictional one, has the capacity to generate material effects, in this case effects that would inform and shape broader collective interrogations over the management of waste in Guangzhou.

LAND AND POLLUTION AT THE CITY'S EDGE

In the late 1980s, the municipal government announced that Mei's water reservoir had been converted into a 34.5-hectare landfill with the capacity to receive 1,000 tons of waste per day. By the early 1990s, almost immediately after it was constructed, villagers claimed that the landfill was releasing noxious smells that lingered in the village. Seasonal flooding pushed underground leachate into fields, thickening the flow of water that turned yellow, then red. Villagers dug ditches to prevent waste trucks from entering and plugged sewage drains to keep leachate from flowing into the local stream, but it seemed as though nothing could stop the waste mountain from growing. The fish in the stream slowly vanished (Wang 2011).[3]

In the late 1990s, in an effort to implement a national directive to introduce WTE incinerators as the official end-of-life waste technology for Chinese cities, Guangzhou started to look for a site for the city's first

WTE incinerator. City officials initially proposed locating it in the western reaches of Guangzhou, bordering the neighboring municipality of Foshan. The Foshan government immediately pushed back against the proposal, arguing that pollution from the site would impede local development. Officials in Guangzhou undertook another round of assessments and in 1999 identified three potential locations for the facility. According to the Environmental Impact Assessment Report for the Phoenix incinerator, Mei village was chosen for two reasons: its proximity to the city center, access to highways, and existing water infrastructure. To win over villagers, the city sponsored a trip to Macao for members of the village council, who, upon their return, hailed the technology's efficacy and safety. Villagers, however, suspected their leaders had accepted bribes in exchange for their support. In an effort to ensure that Mei villagers accepted the proposal, and to avoid further protests, the municipality promised that the Phoenix facility would be a "modern, garden facility"[4] (*xiandaihua huayuan shi gongchang*) using "German equipment, Japanese assembly, and French management."[5] In addition, the municipality promised improvements to the village water infrastructure and routine health checkups.

The Chinese state preferred WTE incineration in part because the technology required significantly less land than landfilling. Municipal officials repeatedly cited the rapid pace of urbanization and increased pressures on land use as a barrier for the construction of new end-of-life waste technology. In contrast to landfills which required the state to secure hectares of land, the process of burning at Phoenix would reduce waste mass by 97 percent, turning 1,000 tons of mixed waste into 30 tons of fly ash. WTE incineration promised to not only dematerialize waste but also to make pollution disappear. In contrast to sanitary landfills that merely contained waste, WTE incineration renders "immaterial" the mixed garbage that is fed into the facility and emerges as clean energy. As sanitation trucks enter a WTE facility, waste matter is weighed for its tonnage. The mixture of waste that arrives at the facility—napkins, plastic bags, and leftover food—is measured not in terms of its mass but in terms of its calorific (heat) value and assigned a quantity of energy expressed in kilojoules.

A key assumption behind Guangzhou's strategy for realizing the promise of a modern waste system was that advanced European technology would avoid the harmful emissions produced by conventional incineration—

noxious gases, SO2, heavy metal and dioxins, and a series of highly toxic compounds. The boiler temperature, for example, would reach 850 degrees Celsius at which point it would break down harmful dioxin. A series of scrubbers and filters would capture and sequester particles in the stream of emissions leaving the facility, rendering the exhaust "merely steam." The promised eradication of the pollution from burning makes waste inter-changeable with resource.

The state insisted that the large volume of waste designated for burning left the plant as clean and "green" electricity pumped directly to the grid. Mei villagers, however, argued from the start that the facility failed to live up to this promise. Almost immediately after Phoenix began operating in 2006, villagers noticed irregularities. Smoke emissions were white during the day, but at night Ah Wang recalled thick smoke that "makes it difficult to open windows." Noxious odors disrupted sleep, irritating villagers' throats and eyes. Villagers began to appeal to their local government, getting little response, and then began a series of protests. Ah Wang remembered 2007 as the height of the protests, and Mei entered a period of political repression and increased political surveillance.

At Mei village, WTE incineration did not eliminate pollution but en-acted a process in which a technological solution for one pollution prob-lem generated new pollution problems in different localities in other forms (Tarr 1999). Incineration released pollutants into the air, which circulates far beyond the immediate confines of the waste facility. Timothy Choy and Jerry Zee argue that understanding the modern atmosphere requires an attunement "to the moments of phase shift, where physical bodies disperse into the particulate populace of air" (Choy and Zee 2015, 213). For Mei villagers, living next to WTE incinerators provided them with a unique vantage point to observe the ways that WTE incineration effected waste's phase-shifts. In the eyes of villagers, the process of transforming waste to generate energy also generated toxic aerosols, dispersing emissions into the atmosphere, water, and land.

SPECULATION

In 2012, six years after Phoenix began operations, Mei village was expe-riencing a construction boom. Roads leading up to the village had been torn up. Inside the village, signs of construction were everywhere: bamboo poles, tied together scaffolds, workers installing new pipes. Piles of sand, bricks, and steel rods stored on the side of the road were about to turn traditional three-story village homes into ten- to twelve-story apartment buildings. Advertising plastered on walls offered dormitories for workers in the nearby cosmetics factory, construction supply shops, and family workshops.

Counterintuitively, the construction boom in Mei village was hastened by an anticipated announcement of a relocation plan. In the summer of 2012, on my first visit to Mei village, I met Ah Long, a villager in his early fifties. He told me that the beginning of the construction of Phase II of Phoenix reignited speculation about the villagers' impending relocation. "The government is offering so little money," the elderly man said. Rumors circulated that the state planned to offer each household units in a new apartment complex. The size of the unit would be equivalent to the square footage of the properties they currently owned in the village, a common land compensation scheme at the time. The rumor prompted villagers to quickly amass as much square footage as they could. Anticipating that re-

FIGURE 2.2 Mei village, 2013. These large multistory buildings without windows are being built in anticipation of a government announcement about relocation settlements. Photo by author.

location and tear-downs were imminent, the village was, at this point, in a construction frenzy. Many of the buildings have large frames, but as Ah Long explained, "No one has bothered to pay to install windows." Yuan Fei, a homeowner from Panyu, visited Mei village while organizing anti-incineration protests. He marveled at the construction boom. One of the first things that Yuan Fei noted about Mei village was that "they are building in violation of building codes" (*tamen weijian*), noting the number of buildings well above the six-story limit for villages.

Ah Yun, a skinny and pensive man, one of the oldest members of the monitoring group, always with a cigarette dangling from his mouth, spoke fondly of a "previous era of good development" (*women yiqian fazhande henhao*). He recalled his childhood in a village at the foot of a reservoir, surrounded by verdant hills, freshwater streams teeming with fish, and fertile rice patties. As he gave me a ride to the subway station one evening after his shift, he yelled to me to look at one of the remaining rice paddies as his voice dissipated in the honking traffic. As we whizzed through the village on his motorbike, he pointed to one of the unfinished buildings. "This one is mine," he said. Similar to urban homeowners caught in an overheated housing market and the real estate craze, villagers, too were willing land speculators. Walking around Mei village, you could find traces of the village of Ah Yun's childhood: ancient banyan trees with large knuckle roots sprawled in all directions, a few remaining single-story village homes untouched by construction, incense wafting from the ancestral halls (*citang*), altars of remembrance to each of the three main lineages—Wang, Qin, and Meng—and the remaining patches of green agricultural fields where the village still came together to feast on the Lunar New Year.

Yet, more often than not, the Mei village that we passed by, and that I came to know, bore little resemblance to the bucolic setting of Ah Yun's memories. Long before the arrival of the incinerator, the village had become a site of rural industry, with farmland leased to workers from interior China and collective land rented to small entrepreneurs. At the time of my fieldwork, the village contained numerous industries, including a cosmetics factory and a construction plant. At noon, workers poured into village streets and filled roadside restaurants. Migrant workers dutifully vanished at half past noon, leaving the village mostly empty during the brief nap time, silent but for the buzz of cicadas. Memories of my time in Mei village are marked by the acrid smell that greeted me each time I stepped off the bus and that lingered as I shared lunch with groups of workers on break from construction supply outlets and family workshops. I often wondered if the villagers' investment in real estate would pay off. Mei villagers, who had long lived with pollution and its effects, were faced with a difficult choice: whether to fight to continue to live in a damaged, toxic ecology or leave the place they called home. As one mother holding a baby put it bluntly to me as we stood chatting one afternoon: "Why stay around and wait for death?"

Located in a relatively wealthy region of the Pearl River Delta, Mei villagers had been beneficiaries of industrialization during the initial decades of China's reform and opening. Mei's proximity to a major urban center meant that the village avoided the abandonment common to villages across remote and interior provinces in the post-reform period. Beginning in the late 1980s, as the area surrounding Guangzhou became one of China's first designated special economic zones, small factories appeared; the area became a manufacturing hub. Villages near prosperous coastal and first-tier cities both retained the autonomy that came with land ownership and, at the same time, saw an influx of migrant workers as working-age men and women from inland areas arrived looking for work at construction sites, in restaurants and hotels, and on assembly lines.

Mei villagers became landlords and leased plots of land to migrant workers seeking housing close to the neighboring workshops or Guangzhou's service sectors. Villagers built multistory rental buildings with storefronts and opened motels, corner markets, and gaming parlors.[6] Mei villagers became land and business owners, gained wealth, and enjoyed the privilege of not having to migrate to look for work. When Ah Yun mentioned a previous era of "good development," he was, at least in part, evoking this period of wealth and prosperity. Remaining in the village granted Mei villagers the survival of their community. In contrast to villagers throughout China who left home to become migrant workers, in Mei village, cousins still finished middle school together. Relocation meant severing ties to land rights that had provided villagers a degree of continuity and autonomy.

Proximity to Guangzhou, once the source of the village's fortune, was also its curse. Guangzhou's continuous expansion and growth made peri-urban rural land valuable and increasingly consolidated for real estate development. Finite land in Guangzhou's central districts meant that peri-urban rural land was also crucial for the city's proposed waste infrastructures. While the amount of land required by incinerators was small in comparison to landfills, the construction of WTE incinerators was nevertheless predicated first and foremost on securing land.

The "environmental relocation" at Mei village was a reminder that the eviction of rural lives is frequently a necessary condition not only for China's ongoing process of urbanization but its transition to green development. In China, industrial development and the subsequent pursuit of a mode of urban speculation and growth perpetuated both the enclosure of rural lands and the eviction of rural lives (Chu 2014; Hsing 2010; Ren 2011; Yeh 2013). More recently, as China has turned toward a mode of green development that includes the development of eco-cities, the introduction of new renewable energy infrastructure and the creation of ecological services and preservation zones has unleashed a wave of "green grabs" that have enclosed rural land for environmental projects (May 2011; Chen 2013).[7] Tania Li suggests that capitalist development is usually understood as an inevitable teleological process along a path in which those whose labor is not needed on the land move seamlessly and naturally into other sectors of the economy (T. M. Li 2014). Viewing the displacement of rural lives as an inevitable process, however, obscures the specific and contingent ways that agrarian livelihoods can be perpetually displaced.[8] In this sense, "environmental relocation," as the state referred to it, was and is a euphemism for a process—not at all unique to Guangzhou or even China—in which land and resources have been expropriated in the name of green and sustainable development (Corson and MacDonald 2012, 263). However, as the experience in Mei village demonstrates, the process of evictions also created opportunities for negotiation.

Villagers rightly saw relocation settlements as a once-in-a-lifetime opportunity and sought to mitigate the loss of their land and community by securing as much compensation as they could. "If you want us to move," Ah Yun paused, "you have to be clear about how much you are willing to offer." The relocation meant the further consolidation of rural land for infrastructure construction and that the Mei village of Ah Yun's recollections would all but vanish. Yet no one had to tell Ah Yun that relocation presented perhaps one of the last opportunities for accumulation through the transfer of land. "We've lived here for generations," Ah Yun said, "if I had more land, I would build even more buildings." The fate that Ah Yun most wanted to avoid was the loss of his wealth in the process of relocation (*yue ban yue qiong*). Nothing was more important than securing a good settlement at the moment when the terms of relocation were negotiated. A good settlement meant alleviating the precarity of the work and future of his son, who, at the time, worked as a temporary water delivery driver.

The rush to build was somewhere between a rational, calculated decision and a mode of inexplicable (desperate) action in response to uncertainty. Awaiting the decision that would shape the course of their future, villagers threw money into construction and built upward despite little to no concrete information about the actual scheme the state would use to compensate them for their land. In the face of displacement, Ah Yun leveraged his most valuable possession, land, as a way to create an economic opportunity. If control over land was viewed as providing peasants autonomy and was the source of a revolutionary force during the Maoist era, under China's rush to urbanize, rural citizens were pressured into adopting another accumulation strategy. Mei villagers felt they needed to exchange their autonomy of landownership to become landlords in high-rise buildings.

FICTIONS OF POLITICAL INCLUSION: RURAL CITIZENS AND SCIENTIFIC PARTICIPATION

In 2012, in the midst of the speculative building frenzy in the village, Mei villagers were officially installed as technical monitors at the Phoenix incinerator. In 2012, ahead of plans to build more facilities and amid growing public protests, the state was eager to win public approval. The safety of Phoenix, Guangzhou's first and only WTE incinerator, was the subject of widespread scrutiny from other communities across the city also faced with proposals for new WTE incinerators. The municipal government held up Phoenix as an example of the future of waste processing for the city. Other peri-urban communities protesting incinerators, where the protesters were mainly middle-class professionals and homeowners, looked to Mei village monitors for evidence and insights as local witnesses with firsthand accounts of the daily operations of the plant. Living in a village on Guangzhou's peri-urban edge, the villagers' fate became embroiled not only in the politics of relocation at Mei village but in a broader debate over technology, pollution, and the risks associated with ostensibly green infrastructures like WTE incineration.

The everyday experience of communities living in the midst of industrial pollution, where environmental knowledge has been destabilized, has been characterized as one of uncertainty accompanied by an overwhelming sense of "doubt, disagreements, suspicions, fears, and endless waiting" (Auyero and Swistun 2009, 4). The claims that WTE incinerators were high-tech, modern, and safe occasioned a contested politics of verification and witnessing that transformed rural villagers into scientific subjects. The looming presence of WTE incineration presented villagers with a new avenue for political action.

Before villagers were formally appointed as "technical monitors," they had already formed an alliance with homeowner activists to document the impact of pollution on the village. In late 2009, homeowners from Panyu, agitating against the proposal to build a WTE incinerator in their neighborhood, collaborated with Mei villagers to produce a list of cancer victims near the Phoenix incinerator. The data suggested that the rate of cancer had increased twentyfold in the five years since the incinerator was built.[9] The collection of cancer data was an act of popular epidemiology, a strategy undertaken by communities to independently aggregate data in order to map the distribution of harm in relation to spatial proximity to pollution.[10] In the West and in Japan, communities living with toxicity often mobilize citizen science to produce material evidence of pollution in order to counter attempts at obfuscation or denial by the state or corporations (Irwin 1995; Ottinger 2013). Lay experts' authority to claim knowledge is a function of their status as local witnesses with intimate knowledge of conditions often unavailable to outside experts (Wynne 1991). The villagers' findings were discredited by the Guangzhou Center for Disease Control, which concluded that there was no statistical or scientific basis for claims of an increase in cancer rates. In Guangzhou, as elsewhere, particularly in cases of low and dispersed forms of toxic exposure, popular epidemiology has often faced difficulty in establishing a link between exposure and illness (Morimoto 2023; Shapiro 2015; Vogel 2013). Yet, what is most significant in this case is how the state's top-down control of research institutions circumscribed the practice of popular epidemiology. Journalists from independent news sources in Guangzhou claimed that researchers from the state-run Center for Disease Control never conducted a full investigation in Mei village.

If the state intended merely to stage the illusion of public participation through their invitation to villagers for scientific inclusion, villagers seized the opportunity to expand the scope of what they saw as their ongoing work of pollution monitoring in the local community. The appointment of villagers as technical monitors, on the one hand, represented a relatively naked attempt to co-opt and neutralize political opposition. Public process and participation are common features of techno-scientific regimes of environmental governance and, especially in liberal democracies, scientific governance is, at least in theory, accompanied by expansive and meaningful public participation (Rowe and Frewer 2000; Wynne 2007). Lay actors not only become a part of the process of public oversight, but citizen scientists can regularly mobilize localized knowledge to challenge the claims and expertise of outsider scientists (Wynne 1991). Communities seeking to document and communicate the impact of pollution often formalize, standardize, and routinize evidence-gathering so they will be taken more seriously by institutions and legal and state actors (Ottinger 2010). Science and technology studies (STS) scholars, however, point out that the expansion of NGOs and citizen groups to monitor risk is one way that neoliberal governances individualize the assessment of risk and harm and perpetuate the state-sponsored normalization of disasters (Kimura 2016; Petryna 2002; Polleri 2019).

Yet, even when corporations and states take advantage of legal institutions and power, scientific participation can still function as a potent mode of political action by those who take part in it. At Phoenix, even in the context of top-down, authoritarian governance, the state valorized (to a limited extent) participatory citizenship as a signal of advancement and modernity. The enfranchisement of rural subjects as scientific citizens, and the incorporation of political processes and rituals like public participation, existed, at least in theory, to fulfill some of the self-conscious aspirations of China's project of techno-scientific modernity. Even though China formally endorses public participation, there is little in the way of official procedures on the ground. With regard to the debate over WTE incineration, the terrain of public participation has thus become an important arena in which individuals and NGOs can work within existing channels to advocate for scientific inclusion.

Having pursued an oppositional politics based on a wholesale rejection of WTE incineration, Ah Wang was well aware that accepting the state's invitation and assuming the role of technical monitor entailed a change of strategy. Becoming technical monitors meant that villagers would be incorporated into the state's project and that their participation would at a minimum legitimize the construction of new environmental infrastructure. Village monitors were enlisted to complement the efforts of the plant's technical personnel and the municipality's institutions of pollution oversight. In exchange for the opportunity to participate as scientific citizens, Mei villagers ceded a more vocal tactic of localized opposition.

In Mei villagers' early encounters with waste infrastructure, the capacity to mobilize against pollution required only that villagers point to observable traces of leakage and contamination. Their authority and reliability as local witnesses relied on tracing, identifying, and documenting pollution's observable effects. As technical monitors, villagers documented evidence of the plant's malfunction with the aim of improving plant safety: "Whenever there was a bad smell, we called the village head, who would alert the factory." For some monitors, the decision to collaborate was pragmatic. Ah Wang explains: "It became clear that the incinerator wasn't going anywhere. If we can't relocate the facility, our job is to make sure that it is working better." Ah Wang seemed to affirm a technique of neoliberal governmentality in environmental governance, which expanded scientific participation and citizen science—but did so in order to regulate citizen conduct in an age of pervasive toxicity and contamination (Kimura 2016; Polleri 2019). From one perspective, the technical monitors were a performative gesture of political inclusion, which enrolled rural citizens who were previously excluded from scientific and political governance. In this particular case, scientific inclusion was meant to neutralize a challenge to a state-sponsored technology. Yet the incorporation of villagers as scientific monitors revealed that China's techno-scientific modernity also encouraged the aspirations of citizens for "politically good forms of governance" (Ezrahi 2012). Villagers agreed to their role, hoping to seize the opportunity to actualize a more inclusive model for the governance of risk. Political regimes, whether liberal democratic or authoritarian, are constituted through partial and unstable performances (Ezrahi 2012). The opportunity to be inside the facility presented an opening and opportunity for rural citizens; Mei villagers translated the state's performed inclusion to materialize evidence of toxicity and risk.

THE 850-DEGREE CONTROVERSY

Shortly after gaining access to the facility, it became evident to Mei villagers that they would be left on their own to pursue the work of monitoring. Aside from a brief introduction, villagers were offered no technical training. Waste engineers at the plant largely ignored them and excluded them from daily operations and planning meetings. After much lobbying, Mei village monitors secured an empty room on the second floor of the facility to use as an office. They furnished it with couches, desks, and two computers. The team decided that the daily work of monitoring would be based on physical presence. They agreed on a strategy of continuous occupation of the facility. Divided into teams of three, monitors worked eight-hour shifts. Monitors on the overnight shift would sleep inside the office despite the fact that all lived within walking distance of the plant and could arrive at a moment's notice. They determined that continuous presence was necessary to legitimate their position as witnesses on hand of all that would happen inside the facility.

One evening early in June 2013 I joined the monitors for their night shift. I watched as the sky darkened outside the large windows to the front of the monitoring room. Around 9:30 p.m., Ah Yun and Qiang, a younger monitor in his mid-twenties, put on helmets, picked up flash lights, and hung digital cameras around their necks, preparing to conduct the last round of evening patrols. Ah Yun and Qiang followed a designated route through the facility: moving down from the fifth floor, the smoke room (the site of a reported pipe explosion a few months earlier), to the central control room on the fourth floor, and from there down through the second, and finally, to the ash pit on the ground floor. The patrol usually took around twenty minutes. Ah Yun recorded data—mostly emission levels of air pollutants such as HCI, SO2, CO, and NOx along with dust and boiler temperature levels—in the monitors' notebook.

In the office, Qiang passed the time by watching a soap opera set in the Nationalist period with a loud soundtrack blasting from the computer. Around 11 p.m., Ah Yun prepared to turn in for the night. The monitors spread out on the two large sofas and unfolded a cot from behind the couch. Having decided that he couldn't sleep, Fan lit a cigarette and decided to go and watch the waste trucks pull in at the entrance. At 1:30 a.m., Ah Yun and Qiang once again grabbed their hard hats and set out for another round of

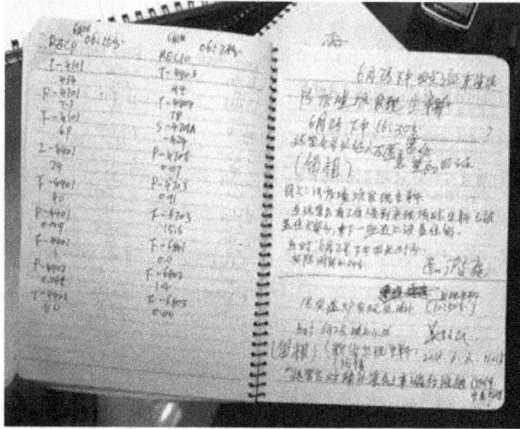

FIGURE 2.3   Village technical monitors' notebook with
daily logs from their patrols, 2013. Photo by author.

inspections. My sleep was repeatedly interrupted by the noise of the industrial facility, first by a random alarm at 2:50 a.m., and then again at 6:00 a.m., when I awoke to the sound of office cleaners arriving for work. Ah Yun was already up and headed off to brush his teeth before handing off the night shift. Around 8:15 a.m., the first Veolia engineers arrived at the plant.

Inside the facility, most shifts passed without event. Patrols were routine, repetitive, and ritualistic. Yet over the days and weeks, the second-floor village monitoring office came to resemble an extension of Mei village itself. As the villagers' daily lives and the plant's rhythms blended into one, the patrol office became an impromptu break room frequented by engineers, drivers, and shift managers who stopped by to chat, drink tea, or share a cigarette.

Villagers once noted the visible effects of pollution in the area surrounding the WTE incinerator through the harm registered as illness in their bodies. The challenge that monitors faced inside the plant was how to track technical malfunctioning in real time. Inside the facility, visible signs of pollution were difficult to track; technical instruments were responsible for measuring and calibrating pollution. WTE incineration and pollution require a regime of perceptibility reliant on technical instruments as a mode of knowing (Murphy 2006). On their daily patrol, villagers observed engineers watching digital representations of the fire in the incinerator alongside charts and statistics, which villagers lacked the capacity to interpret.

With no technical training, village monitors were forced to devise techniques to monitor the daily technical operations inside the facility. Village monitors honed in on moments of change, irregularities, and inconsistencies at the plant. Continuous access provided monitors with a unique vantage point as they could observe and see the functioning of the plant outside moments of public display or inspection.[11] Ah Wang noticed that the main panel that displayed emissions data would often stall and that emissions would remain at zero for long periods after the boiler was shut down for maintenance or repair. Ah Wang's team started to record a variety of technical mishaps and irregularities that were apparent even to those without scientific knowledge or technical training.

Routine patrols and continuous observation enabled village monitors to uncover crucial evidence to challenge the proclaimed efficacy of WTE incineration. One of the most well-publicized technical specifications of WTE incineration is that the plants rely on the boiler temperature reaching 850 degrees Celsius in order to safely break down dioxin and other pollutants. Dioxin refers to a group of harmful and persistent chemical compounds generated through the burning of mixed waste. Safety measures for capturing and removing dioxin include sustained burning at a high temperature combined with a high-tech filtration system. Lü Zhiyi, deputy secretary general of the Guangzhou Government, boasted that the pollution mitigation capacity of the Phoenix incinerator was comparable to foreign technology and that the air released from the facility met EU standards. The boiler temperature, however, was critical to ensuring that the facility was operating according to safety standards.

In August 2012, three months after they had installed themselves onsite at Phoenix, villagers brought evidence of the failure of the WTE incineration to the Municipal Urban Management Committee (J. Li 2012). During the city's monthly petition meeting, villagers reported that on three separate occasions during their patrol, unburned plastic was found at the ash pit. Villagers offered photographic evidence, and the story circulated in the local media. The photographic evidence of unburnt plastic punctured the illusion of WTE incineration techno-scientific sophistication. Photography's unique association with scientific truth and objectivity made the often opaque and technological details of WTE incineration at once legible and communicable. The photo was undeniable proof that undermined the promise of the technology to dematerialize pollution.

By bringing the evidence of unburned plastic to public attention, village monitors inadvertently revealed another technical issue with burning waste.[12] Forced to account for the presence of unburned plastic to the public, municipal engineers attributed the problem to an unusually wet rainy season that made it difficult to sustain high temperatures in the boiler. Prompted by the evidence presented by Mei villagers, the municipal engineer's technical explanation revealed a central connection between the material quality of the waste stream and its suitability to the end-of-life technology used to treat it. Through their explanation, the engineers had clearly and openly conceded that the ability of boilers at Phoenix to sustain burning at 850 degrees Celsius was related to the composition and quality of the waste stream. The quality of waste itself was not uniform and, instead, shifted and changed depending not only on the weather but fundamentally on the practices that fed the waste stream. The materiality of the waste stream in Guangzhou not only revealed a problem with the daily operations at Phoenix, but also led to fundamental questions concerning the rationale for relying on WTE incinerators to burn a waste stream that was, relative to waste streams elsewhere, notably wet.

The connection between the safety and efficacy of WTE incineration and the material quality of the waste stream attracted the attention of anti-incineration activists. Homeowner protesters, in particular, seized on the evidence provided by Mei villagers and began to elaborate this connection to build a larger argument to challenge the legitimacy of WTE incineration itself (see chapter 3). Building on the controversy, homeowners questioned whether WTE incineration was the appropriate choice of technology given that the waste stream in Guangzhou is made up of over 50 percent organics. The high percentage of organic waste in the Guangzhou waste stream threatened to undermine the state's rationale for adopting WTE incineration as the key technology for the elimination of waste. The controversy was an instance where rural citizens, despite a lack of technical training and playing a narrow role in a performance of scientific citizenship, nevertheless mobilized firsthand access to generate scientific evidence. The controversy would prove crucial for middle-class homeowners as they pushed back against the prospect of siting WTE incinerators in their own communities. The evidence generated by village monitors, however, did little to help Mei villagers to stall or to advance their goals leading up to their relocation.

URBAN DISPLACEMENT

In the summer of 2018, I returned to Mei village. The bus station in front of the subway had been rerouted, but the same row of electronics stores blasted loud music into the hot summer air as I emerged from the metro. The once bumpy road had been paved, but I could see that another segment of road, slightly ahead, was being torn up. I was on my way to meet Ah Wang, outside the plant, at a restaurant at the front of the village. I walked past Phoenix before our meeting. Phase I and Phase II of the facility now stood side by side, one round and one rectangular structure, each with a column of white steam wafting from its chimney. The entire front entryway to the plant was now blocked off. A large LED display erected at the front entrance displayed real-time emissions visible to anyone passing by, but when I stopped to snap a picture from across the street, a security guard waved me away. Mei was now a hollowed-out village. Demolition had not started in earnest, but the once clean village streets were littered with broken pieces of construction material and garbage. Empty beer bottles and laundry decorated hollow steel and concrete windowless frames. Two thirds of the village households had already moved out.

Ah Wang greeted me at the neighborhood restaurant and confirmed that the monitoring group was still active. She was more interested, however, in describing the many changes that had taken place in the village. In the final compensation scheme, each family member who met the age requirement (eighteen for women and twenty-two for men) was allotted 280 square meters of housing compensation, equivalent to three or four apartments in the proposed relocation housing. The final municipal government compensation scheme skirted the feverish building strategy of villagers. The first wave of village resettlements had been completed earlier that year. Many families had moved to the resettlement housing even as the new housing complex was still being fitted out.

Ah Wang, however, still refused to move. She would rather live in a village, even one where she did not grow up, than move into a high-rise. Using her savings, she was in the process of purchasing a house in another village. What if urban expansion would dismantle the new village too? I asked. Ah Wang shrunk back in her seat and replied, "We'll deal with that day when it comes."

In the official story of Guangzhou's drive to build its new system of waste management, the city's waste crisis was resolved through investments in an ostensibly green technology that created an enclosed form of circulation that converted trash to energy. WTE incinerators promised to simultaneously dematerialize waste, generate clean energy, and eliminate pollution, all while conserving land. The siting of WTE incineration could only be achieved through more difficult, prickly political feats: winning public approval and overcoming opposition from rural villagers and the broader public. The on-the-ground operation of the technology, however, was shaped by other forms of circulation at the peri-urban edge: the expansion and growth of urban land, the displacement of waste, the city's political ecological transformation, and the gradual removal and transformation of rural lives. Even as the state's capacity to achieve their technological feats is predicated on multiple displacements, the story of Mei village reveals the fraught engagement by rural villagers as scientific citizens. For Mei villagers, a project to transform Guangzhou into a modern green city resulted first and foremost in the alienation of communities from land as pollution transformed the local ecology. China's pursuit of green urbanism through building advanced technological infrastructure hastened the conversion of rural land and the eviction of rural bodies that had become central to its urbanization.

The story of Mei villagers also reveals how rural subjects in China negotiate and act, albeit in a conflicted manner, against and alongside displacement. Faced with outcomes they had little control over, Mei villagers sought to resist displacement through the production of speculative value *and* through the production of scientific knowledge. Mei villagers mobilized within the terms dictated by the state and by the broader project of authoritarian scientific modernity. Their long-term engagement with pollution was determined simultaneously by their private interests but also by aspirations for broader inclusion as participants and contributors to a collective and nascent antipollution waste politics in the city. Although the scientific inclusion of village monitors was part of a state strategy to co-opt political opposition through a performative expansion of scientific participation, the villagers' participation elevated them, even if briefly, as legitimate participants in a public dispute over science and technology. As technical monitors, Mei villagers gathered evidence critical for the formation of a citizen-led debate on the risks posed by a technological scientific modernity.

Villagers drew on modes of evidence-gathering that surfaced a key fact to anchor the emergence of Guangzhou's waste controversy—the mismatch between the materiality of the city's waste stream and the state's central waste technology. The 850-degree controversy and the experience of villagers ultimately laid the groundwork for a growing public interrogation not only of pollution but the efficacy and rationale of selecting WTE incinerators as the official technology to treat waste. The opportunity to act as technical monitors enabled rural citizens in Guangzhou to gather evidence to expose the latent, often invisible, and uneven distribution of pollution (Davies 2022). In Mei village, scientific participation expanded strategies of political action for rural subjects to overcome conditions of uncertainty, ignorance, and doubt against exposure and risk. The monitoring efforts of Mei villagers would prove critical for homeowner anti-incinerator activists across the city. Panyu and Huadu activists (chapter 3) built on the evidence provided by Mei villagers to expose the mismatch between the materiality of the waste stream and the choice of the end-of-life technology that anchored the city's emerging waste collectives.

Part II

COLLECTIVES

FIGURE 3.1 A gated housing complex in Panyu, 2012. The landscaping and artificial lake contributed to its marketability as a "green community." Photo by author.

3 | TECHNICIZING DELIBERATION
Toxicity and Homeowner Techno-politics

LATE ONE EVENING in November 2009 in Siyuan, a housing development in Panyu District in the southern part of Guangzhou, an internet thread in a neighborhood online discussion board caught the attention of Nianji. A post titled "Waste Incineration" reported that the local district government had just announced plans to build an incinerator with the capacity to treat 2,000 tons of waste per day. The incinerator would be built in Wangjiang village, a mere ten kilometers from Nianji's home. His curiosity piqued, Nianji searched Baidu (the Chinese version of Google) and found articles linking WTE incineration to harmful chemicals like dioxin. Nianji wasn't alone in growing alarmed. In just a few weeks, the thread "Waste Incineration" had over two hundred comments. Siyuan residents also began to mobilize in person. A group of homeowners organized a trip to Mei village, the site of Guangzhou's first WTE incinerator. Villagers in Mei, who had lived next to an operating incinerator since 2006, confirmed the Siyuan homeowners' suspicions about the polluting effects of incineration. A team of volunteers moved to organize offline by circulating fliers in the Siyuan parking lot to get the word out to neighbors.

On a Sunday morning later the same month, a homeowner with the internet handle "Mountai" donned a face mask and headed to the subway holding a sign that read "Protect Green Panyu." Mountai rode the subway to the crowded Tianhe New Town shopping center. She strolled around the busy plaza for over two hours before returning back to the underground.

As she emerged close to her home, public security officers were waiting to take her to "tea."[1] Mountai wrote up the day's events and posted them to the homeowner discussion board that evening. The post went viral and attracted the attention of local media.

Panyu homeowners' organizing efforts culminated on November 23, 2009. During a scheduled public petitioning day at the recently established Guangzhou Municipal Urban Management Committee (Guangzhou shi chengshi guanli weiyuanhui), hundreds of homeowners and villagers gathered.[2] Homeowners from Siyuan and several adjacent complexes, along with villagers from Wangjiang, staged one of the largest and most well-publicized urban protests the city had seen. After the protest, Yuan Fei, one of the key organizers at the Panyu protest, along with Mountai and Nianji, appeared on the cover of a January 2010 issue of *Nanfang People Weekly*, a prominent magazine with a national readership, alongside a headline that read "Panyu Power." Panyu homeowners and Mei villagers were invited later that year to appear as guests to debate the harms of WTE incinerators on a popular nationally syndicated CCTV television series.

In early 2010, the Municipal Urban Management Committee halted the Panyu incinerator project temporarily and in 2012 announced that the facility would be relocated to a site near a more remote village, thirty kilometers further south in the district. The Panyu protest, however, would turn out to be an early milestone in the history of anti-incineration debate and action in Guangzhou. In 2012 homeowners from the northern district of Huadu engaged in similar actions including protests, petitions, and writing editorials to contest a proposed incinerator. Huadu activists drew heavily on the playbook of Panyu homeowners and echoed many of the critiques that Panyu homeowners voiced against WTE incineration. When incinerators were announced in Zhengcheng and Longgang districts in 2013, residents organized protests and used the same arguments and strategies as Panyu and Huadu activists.

Over the last decade, anti-incineration protests have become among the most prominent forms of urban environmental action across China. The introduction of WTE incinerators has sparked protests in Hubei, Hunan, Guangdong, Shandong, Hainan, Jiangxi, and Zhejiang provinces. In Guangzhou, proposals to build new WTE incinerators, a central strategy for realizing the circular economy, motivated a succession of protests across different peri-urban communities. Middle-class peri-urban homeowners from the city's recently developed real estate complexes emerged as a key demographic participating in antipollution activism.

Homeowner protests against the siting of unwanted infrastructures such as waste facilities are often characterized as NIMBYism ("not in my backyard"). NIMBY was first applied to homeowners in California in the 1980s who used the language of environmentalism to thwart development projects and to preserve low-density neighborhoods. NIMBYism has since been used to characterize local resistance against unwanted infrastructure and development. NIMBYism is often framed in opposition to environmental movements and as a category that describes those who mobilize the discourse of public concerns in service of local interests or property (Hsu 2006; Michaud, Carlisle, and Smith 2008). NIMBYism has become the default framework for understanding the rationale and logic of a propertied class who reject proposed developments and whose opposition very rarely scales up to a broader social movement.

China scholars, however, note that NIMBYism fails to capture the complex and evolving dynamics of the nation's emerging anti-incineration protests. In the early 2000s, for example, anti-incineration action led to broader policy advocacy focused on debating public procedure around technological facilities in China (Bondes and Johnson 2017). Scholars attribute the shift to the adoption by the Chinese state of a softer stance toward anti-incineration protesters and the environmental NGOs who had emerged and mediated contention between the state and local communities (Wong 2016; Lin and Kao 2019). Very little attention, however, has been paid to the homeowners who constituted a core group of anti-incineration activists or to home ownership as key to an emplaced understanding of environmental mobilization. Just as peri-urban villagers' engagement with anti-incineration politics was shaped by the broader dynamics of urban expansion, the participation of homeowners in relation to pollution and risk was also intricately tied to urban development. In Guangzhou, the scope and ambition of homeowner anti-incineration protesters exceed NIMBY concerns. To take seriously homeowners' concerns over the toxic potential of WTE incineration means thinking with the inseparability of chemical entanglements between bodies and land. China's anti-incineration protests show that the state's efforts to achieve ecological urbanism through technoscience simultaneously invited new environmental articulations.

New gated housing developments at the peri-urban edge emerged as sites of collective action that challenged a state-sponsored technology. The tendency of gated communities to market environmental amenities— fresh air and clean land—to homeowners, amplified a recognition of the inseparability of bodies and land that gave way to a new mode of discursive critique. Homeowners' shared focus on the inadequacy of technical oversight of WTE incinerators aggregated into a collective challenge to China's reliance on technological solutions to achieve the circular economy. In a context in which political repression limited the coordination of political action between different communities, homeowners devised a set of strategies to enable anti-incineration critique to scale up to a public concern shared by a variety of communities battling WTE incineration.

Anti-incineration protesters devised a distinctive rhetorical style that foregrounded scientific neutrality and bureaucratic procedures to challenge the state's reliance on technological infrastructure. Rather than focusing on how the siting of local incineration would impact local stakeholders in terms of rights, distribution, and harm, they framed their concerns about the state's scientific policy in explicitly and exclusively technical and apolitical terms and as an issue of broader public concern. In the US and elsewhere, communities battling toxic exposure have often mobilized citizen science to collect evidence of contamination to counter and challenge the state and corporations, and they explicitly frame contamination from waste as a question of rights and justice (Irwin 1995; Checker 2005; Ottinger 2013). In the case of homeowner anti-incineration activists in China, protesters advanced their claims instead by appealing to the state to uphold established technical procedures and scientific evaluation. By focusing on the technical procedures surrounding WTE incineration, homeowners sidestepped being seen by the state as those who overtly challenged official policies or rejected a state-sponsored technology. This self-conscious strategy by homeowner activists to depoliticize and technicize their critique is a strategy to sustain dialogue between state and citizen over technical risk, a strategy that would ultimately enable them to challenge China's technoscientific approach to waste management.

TRANSFORMATION AT THE CITY'S EDGE

The popularity of newly developed gated complexes on the city's peri-urban edge was driven by the middle class's pursuit of housing. The real estate–led development that transformed Panyu is an example of the broad remaking of peri-urban zones in cities across Asia. As the population of Guangzhou grew in the 1980s and 1990s, land prices skyrocketed in the old central districts. In response to urban expansion in the early 2000s, officials annexed the neighboring counties of Panyu and Huadu, which became new districts of the city (Wu and Yeh 2007).[3] In Panyu and Huadu, land-lease revenue became an important source of income for district and local governments, and Panyu in particular was an early site for Hong Kong investment. Infused with outside capital, developers worked closely with officials and village cadres to transform land into commercial housing and enclaved housing developments (Hsing 2010, 43). In Panyu, the Huananbankuai (the South China Plate), a suburban district development that is home to over 300,000 people, was one of China's first and largest suburban housing developments (Li et al. 2020), set amid a patchwork of villages and small-scale industries.[4]

During the Maoist period, *danwei* (work unit housing) ensured that the social collectives forged in relation to a mode of production (*jiti shengchan*) extended to the realm of social life. The *danwei* dominated the socialist urban landscape where workers shared their neighborhoods and living quarters with coworkers. Post-reform, urban life shifted from the *danwei* to another type of gated enclosure. As the population of Guangzhou grew, new private gated communities like Siyuan became a site of community formation. New private gated complexes offered housing for the influx of middle-class workers moving to Guangzhou from other provinces, or local residents while older urban neighborhoods within Guangzhou were being demolished for redevelopment.

The housing boom in Guangzhou made newly developed peri-urban real estate communities particularly attractive to the middle class. A large portion of the participants in the 2009 Panyu anti-incineration protests were residents from one of the three large complexes in Huananbankuai: Siyuan, Yu Complex, and Garden Villa. For home buyers and young families battling the pressures of the overheated real estate market in the city center, new housing developments offered a range of housing options (apartments, townhouses, single-family villas) for a lower price. Peri-urban enclaves not only provided housing but typically also amenities such as markets, restaurants, schools, and even hospitals.

In the summer of 2012, I was seated in a coffee shop near the main entry gate to Garden Villa with three homeowners who were active participants in the 2009 anti-incineration protests. All three were middle-class professionals with young children: Wuxi worked in a technology start-up, Guiyang was a civil servant in the provincial government before becoming a stay-at-home mother, and Yun Tan ran a small family business. Whenever the three women came together, and in lulls in our discussions about waste, the conversation drifted to after-school activities and which markets offered the best produce. When I asked what prompted their participation in the Panyu protest, they each prefaced their answer by recounting their decision to purchase homes in the complex. "I moved here in 2009 right around the time of the incinerator announcement," Yun Tan recalled, gesturing to Wuxi and Guiyang. "We moved here earlier, in 2003, Gui Yang in 2007," said Wuxi. "I was pregnant at the time, and the housing stock was very tight in Guangzhou. In the center of the city, there was intense competition to buy, and over here [Garden Villa] there were many more options and also luxury housing," Yun Tan added.[5]

"I think that a lot of people move here for the air quality; for me the environment was a key concern," Guiyang said. "When I moved here, I instantly felt like we had left Guangzhou behind. As soon as I stepped off the *louba* (private bus service run by the complex), it felt like I was somewhere entirely different." Guiyang conveyed the feeling of leaving the dense urban center for a more spacious landscape, and her answer touched on an unanticipated selling point of peri-urban gated communities like Garden Villa, which distinguished themselves by their environmental features. Yun Tan noted that the fresh air, the lack of noise and congestion, and the manicured landscape projected a vision of an environment shielded from toxicity. Yun Tan's sensitivity to air quality reflected how pervasive exposure to pollution has generated a particular "atmospheric attunement" to air pollution in China's citizens (Choy and Zee 2015; Calvillo 2018; Nguyen 2020). Yet, many aspects of what Yun Tan described as the community's environmental features—greening and manicured landscapes, the lack of noise, architecture and design that emphasize a clean, green aesthetic—had little to do with air pollution. Instead, in Garden Villa, environmental quality was also achieved through the creation of a particular environmental aesthetic. At Garden Villa, a 400,000-square-meter artificial lake sits in the center of the development, with swans, a fleet of pedal boats, and a large fountain that shoots water into the air. With frequently swept roads and sidewalks, careful landscaping, and manicured lawns, the complex emulates an updated garden city aesthetic, a planned community with ruralist ideals which contrasts with the dense, congested city center (Sze 2015).

As peripheral districts became bedroom communities for the city's white-collar middle-class workers, Guangzhou underwent the "spatialization of class" (L. Zhang 2010). The rise of the middle class in China since the 1980s was anchored not by a relation to production but by a relation to consumption, particularly of housing. Commercial housing replaced the socialist *danwei* unit as the site for accessing services for social reproduction, once provided by the socialist state—of child-rearing, leisure, education, and health.

In Guangzhou, housing developments on the outskirts of the city grew as part of a booming, speculative real estate market. Against a backdrop of pervasive pollution, peri-urban housing developments were marketed and portrayed as protected enclaves, refuges from pollution and environmental risk. Due to their proximity to the urban center, peri-urban districts were also the preferred sites for environmental infrastructures designed to support Guangzhou. The siting of WTE incinerators at the peri-urban edge reinforced the logic of the displacement of pollution to the city's outskirts, where peri-urban space was transformed into a pollution sink (Tarr 1996). Set outside the city center but close enough for daily transport, all six of Guangzhou's proposed WTE incinerators were sited in newly incorporated peri-urban districts. Unlike in the US, where WTE incinerators and landfills have often been located in marginalized communities (McGurty 2007; Pellow 2004), the pace of urban development in China meant that an emerging middle class found themselves living next to waste facilities.

ECOLOGIES OF PERVASIVE EXPOSURE

During our interviews, when I ask about what type of pollution she feared most, Yun Tan replies without hesitation: "We're most concerned with chemical pollution." She continued:

We see no obvious improvements with air quality. The state has remedi-
ated the river ways. They used to be black. At least they no longer smell
as bad. . . . [When it comes to] industrial pollution, many industrial
plants don't abide by regulation or standards. There are no restrictions
[to the release of emissions]. Officials in charge of inspection are cor-
rupt! They won't conduct any monitoring. If they are caught polluting,
they must pay a fee and they can carry on as usual.

The popularity of housing developments like Garden Villa as environmental reprieves reflected pervasive concerns over pollution among China's middle class. Throughout the 1980s and 1990s, the de-collectivization
of rural land transformed the areas around Guangzhou into a patchwork
of production centers and workshops, a manufacturing base for industries
ranging from textiles to electronics and paper mills. Weak environmental
regulations meant industrial pollution went effectively unchecked. Even as
national policy and urban centers started to pursue a policy of environmental remediation in the early 2000s, the evidence of ubiquitous and pervasive
pollution and contamination was widespread in the form of thick smog and
pesticide run-offs, bromide-laced rice, and contaminated food. In contemporary China, toxicity was not associated with a single source or a place,
but understood as inescapable, a pervasive toxin (*du*) in contemporary
urban life (Lamoreaux 2019). New gated communities, particularly in their
planning and marketing, emphasized environmental quality in contrast to
the damaged ecologies and pollution created by industrial development.[6]
Through careful attention to green space, design, landscaping, and sanitation, gated communities emphasized their capacity to offer environmental
amenities unavailable in the crowded, disorderly, and polluted city center.

For residents, the announcement of proposals to burn waste close to
peri-urban housing complexes recalled the ubiquitous toxicity many had
sought to escape. In our conversations, Yun Tan and Guiyang reflected frequently on the legacy of industrialization in Guangzhou in the post-reform
period. The siting of WTE incinerators provoked action by threatening to
release toxic emissions into spaces marketed and understood as ecological refuges. Citizens saw the state's pursuit of green development through
technology to be a continuation of older industrial development policies
that relied on technological development for growth. Situated next to gated
communities that claimed to be secluded and private paradises, WTE incin-

erators amplified fears about toxicity, and those fears catalyzed an emerging anti-toxic politics.

Waste and incineration emerged as prominent sources of widespread, urgent concern because they touched on a sense of shared and embodied risk. Manuel Tironi's "hypo-interventions" capture the minor but life-enabling acts that sustain an ethical response to chemical harm in the absence of collective action (Tironi 2018, 439). The shared affects, sentiments (Marres 2012; Fennell 2015), and everyday awareness of the pervasive condition of toxic exposure elevated an ethical orientation and individual concern to collective action. Among urban homeowners, the introduction of WTE incinerators prompted new modes, strategies, and discourses to challenge the state's techno-scientific mode of green development.

TECHNICIZING DELIBERATION

Three years after her famous protest, Mountai was a regular contributor to *Nanfang Weekly* and *Xinkuai Bao*, two of the most popular newspapers in Guangzhou. When I interviewed Mountai in 2012 and asked her why she believed Panyu activists were so successful, she paused and said, "We engaged the government [in a dialogue] across space" (*women gen zhengfu gekongduihua*). In interviews, homeowner activists repeatedly used "dialogue across space" (*gekongduihua*) to describe the strategies they deployed to engage the state. The expression captured how homeowner anti-incineration action shifted across sites and between communities. The dialogue took place online and offline, through both institutionalized channels and direct protests. The notion of "dialogue across space" resembles a discursive public, a "large-scale political subject" or collective united by mediated modes of social interaction self-consciously formed in relation to a shared concern (Cody 2011).

"Dialogue across space" describes a rhetorical style that homeowners mobilized to generate a broader forum for the public evaluation of technical risk. In a context with explicit limits on speech and action, anti-incineration action generated a network of homeowner activists who spearheaded public debates and sustained disputes against state policy through an appeal to neutral-technical discourse. One of the central tactics of authoritarian control is to explicitly break up or splinter any anti-state factions within communities to prevent them from aggregating into a collective demand.

The tendency to "technicize deliberation" is one way that communities of homeowners protesting against WTE incineration have been able to sustain a broader critique of WTE incinerators as a state-sponsored technology. If the "ideal means of authoritarian rule is demand, not deliberation" (He and Warren 2011, 271), a focus on the technical elements of waste technology offered a means for homeowners to engage in an evaluation of waste technologies.

Sitting in a busy restaurant close to the Garden Hotel where I regularly interviewed Mountai, in Yuexiu District, I listened as she discussed a series of newspaper editorials she had recently authored. Waste management was an increasingly popular topic of discussion especially in online forums and social media, and it was the subject of widespread coverage by journalists.[7] Mountai's editorials were evidence that in-person protests translated into longer-term engagement by homeowner-activists that often entailed a shift in their strategies. In her editorials and blog posts, Mountai has explicitly broadened her critique of WTE incinerators beyond Panyu to challenge the logic and rationale of selecting WTE incinerators as *the* official technology to treat waste in Guangzhou. "I believe that it's not enough to just reject incineration. The ability for the state to control and limit dialogue far exceeds our own capacities. We must consider this question from another angle. How do we make waste a point of focus not only for those who are affected by waste but everybody. I found a venue to let all of Guangzhou know that this is a problem that we all need to consider."[8]

Mountai's soft-spoken manner faded away as she listed the editorials she had published:

> First, I challenge the idea that WTE is a nontoxic form of waste treatment. I point to secondary pollution from burning, which is even more difficult to contain. My second article raises the question of whether it's important to first recycle or to incinerate. If you recycle first and remove all the organic waste, then WTE incineration can no longer claim to be a technology that treats biomass, which jeopardizes WTE incinerators' ability to claim biofuel subsidies. My third article addresses the mayor's trip to the US and why the Chinese model differs from the US. There's ample land in the US for landfills . . . the US has not built a single new WTE incinerator since 1995.[9] It's a joke to adopt a technology that the US has abandoned. I suggest Japan and Taiwan as models forward. In

my fourth article, I pointed out that the plan to increase WTE incinerators needs to involve the public and outside experts. We need surveys
and consultations. My fifth article uses the Datang incinerator[10] as an
example to question the procedures of site selection. Siting the incinerator in agricultural land is not reasonable. Much research points to the
contamination of soil. The siting of incinerators should take place on
former waste facilities. The city's growth is too rapid. Any vacant land is
quickly converted into residential districts.

In Mountai's words, technical dialogue enabled homeowners not only
to present themselves as stakeholders in waste management but also to
frame the question of whether WTE incinerators pose risks to a broader
public.[11] Mountai's self-conscious focus on technical detail, scientific evaluation, and rational debate sidestepped state censorship concerned with
discussions of rights, distribution, and harm. Across both print and online
media, homeowner activists generated spaces for public debate and framed
WTE incineration as a question of technological risk.

Mountai's editorials critiqued the state's claims that the construction
and adoption of Western WTE incinerators in and of itself constituted the
achievement of a modern and sustainable form of waste management. She
points out that, unlike developed nations such as Japan and the US, China
adopted WTE incineration without introducing environmental regulations concerning monitoring and technical oversight. Furthermore, China
lacked channels of public involvement, including third-party monitoring
and community participation in site selection and risk evaluation. She also
criticized officials' reliance on technology transfer to "catch-up" to the West.
In national imaginations of development and modernization, technological
adaptation has served as a powerful paradigm for national elites (Prakash
1999), where non-Western nations can "catch-up" to an "ideal" West by
adopting a similar technological framework.[12] Yet, as Mountai points out,
technology transfer necessitates not only the import of technological hardware but also the establishment of structures of public oversight to mitigate
risk. Mountai's editorials frequently drew a comparison between how WTE
incineration was deployed in China and other national contexts to illustrate
how local material and political conditions shaped technological outcomes
(Jasanoff 2004). Comparison, here, is a knowledge-making practice that
draws together multiple locales and often illustrates how one object travels

across different contexts and place (Swanson 2018; Choy 2011). By noting the shortcomings of safety protocols in China, Mountai critiqued the idea that the introduction of technology alone can bring about a universal outcome.

Implicit in Mountai's editorials was another key argument: the state's choice of WTE incinerators did not fit with the city's waste stream and the recycling practices that composed the material qualities of waste. As Mei villagers revealed, waste high in organics compromised the capacity of the WTE incinerator to meet safety standards by making it difficult to reach the necessary temperature to eliminate toxins (chapter 2). Mountai's editorials highlighted an ironic contradiction in China's environmental policy: despite the inefficiencies of burning wet waste, WTE incinerators qualified for subsidies for biofuels (as a technology that generates energy from biomass) because of the high presence of organics (over 50 percent by mass).

Unlike citizen scientists, the primary strategy of Panyu homeowners was not the production of science; they did not devise their own instruments and tools to capture exposures outside of the designated time and space of official datasets (Kimura 2016; Ottinger 2010; Wynne 1991). Panyu homeowners also differed from the "enunciatory communities" which form in the *aftermath* of disasters and leverage shared experiences of harm that have already transpired (Fortun 2001, emphasis mine). Instead, Panyu homeowners were battling the *potential* for exposure and an anticipated future risk created by the ways that China imagines it can arrive at a techno-utopian green future. Panyu homeowners' critique enacted a prognostic politics, where they made a calculation of potential exposure in anticipation of future risk based on past evidence (Hébert 2016; Mathews and Barnes 2016). By technicizing deliberation and dialogue across space, homeowners constituted a "verifying public," an objecting minority formed "in situ" or close to the debate over the terms of the science itself (Stengers 2005, 160). To verify here means to mobilize technical details in order "to put what is given into question" (Mackenzie 2013, 482).

FROM PANYU TO HUADU: AN EXPANDING CONTENTION

As Guangzhou set out to build WTE incinerators in other peri-urban districts, Panyu homeowners' tactics became an unofficial model for other communities. At the time of the Panyu project's announcement in November 2009, a facility was also planned for Huadu District in nearby Fengshui

County. The suspension of the Panyu project after the protests in 2009 also halted the Huadu project. In early 2012, however, a homeowner found a posting on the Huadu District office's website announcing the project's reinstatement. The homeowner posted the announcement to a neighborhood discussion board, and in May 2012 homeowners from several gated complexes organized a street protest with villagers. From May 2012 to the end of 2013, Huadu homeowners occupied the local district office during monthly petition days.[13] In petitions, appeals, and online discussions, Huadu homeowners cited the technical arguments of Panyu homeowners and the evidence gathered by Mei villagers to challenge the rationale for siting the facility in their district.

On a cool February morning in early 2013, I arrived outside the municipal management bureau, close to the Sun Yat-sen Memorial Hall. A reporter from *Nanfang Daily* stood with a small crowd of homeowners from Huadu district waiting for the office to open. I walked up to meet Tina, a homeowner from Ying Yuan housing complex, whom I had interviewed a week prior. In our interview, she recounted that she had accidentally learned about the proposal to build an incinerator from a neighbor. "Nobody told us about this project," she told me, her shaky voice betraying her anger. "We feel cheated by the state." Tina's anger was directed not only at the lack of adequate community consultation but at the prospect that the apartment she so carefully selected away from the city center because of its promise of better air quality would soon be contaminated. She had followed the Panyu protest closely and was wary of the dangers of toxic emissions from WTE incineration. From her perspective, news of the facility was muted because, she suspected, if the authorities told Huadu residents about the project the news would surely invite backlash.

Tina thought of herself as a *laobaixing*, a commoner who normally kept out of politics. For the last three months, however, she had become a regular fixture at municipal petitioning sessions. Petitioning (*xinfang* or *shangfang*) is an institutionalized form of appealing and managing grievances in China. Citizens write letters or visit officials to communicate their grievances. Petitions are useful as a valve that releases pressure by allowing citizens to air their grievances and, in some cases, to challenge central policy by appealing to local officials (Chen 2012). For Huadu anti-incineration protesters, the municipal management bureau's monthly in-person petitioning day represented an opportunity to directly engage city officials and bureaucrats.

On this February morning, a group of five homeowners sat across from state officials. The first homeowner, a middle-aged woman, addressed the bureaucrat: "There are rumors circulating online that a potential location for the incinerator is Fengshui County. We would like more information. Our district is densely populated, with villages, a water reservoir, and numerous new housing developments. Polluting the local reservoir will impact hundreds of thousands of people. We'd like to know when this decision will be made."

Another homeowner added: "We are still worried. There are rumors on the internet that the Development and Reform Commission will select Fengshui. We want to inquire whether this is the case. Fengshui is densely populated, close to villages, farms, and most importantly a water reservoir. There are also housing developments. There are upwards of 300,000 to 400,000 residents. If you pollute the reservoir, the impact will be huge."

The state official paused before asking the group of homeowners a simple question: "Are you opposed to incineration or opposed to the site?" The question was intended as a Catch-22. If homeowners admitted to being against incineration, they would be taking a public stance against national policy. Since local governments were in no position to alter national directives, such a position would be easily dismissed by municipal officials. However, if homeowners admitted that they were only concerned with *siting*, their demands were also not worth engaging because local officials could

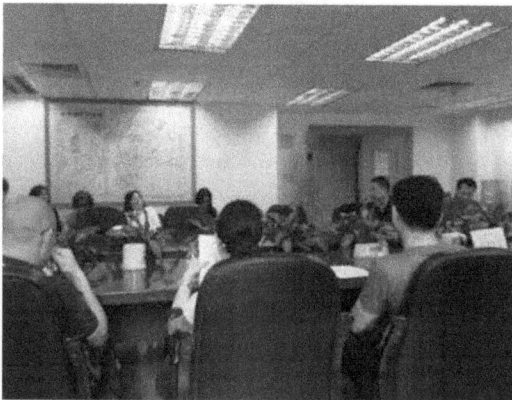

FIGURE 3.2   Huadu residents petitioning the local
district government, 2013. Photo by author.

easily dismiss them as NIMBYs, defending narrow and private interests, whereas the local government was accountable to a public need and obligated to introduce technologies that would achieve a more efficient waste treatment system for the city. Local communities were often charged with NIMBYism, accused of placing a narrow set of interests above the public good. In the eyes of state officials neither position constituted a legitimate challenge to municipal policy.

Xu, a district official, clearly laid out the state's position:

> Concerning WTE incineration, the government (*zhengfu*) must weigh and measure different scenarios. We have to take into account costs. Siting is dependent on the cost of waste transportation. We have to think about the overall impact on the environment ... on the local air quality, on the local water source, and population density. We can't just oppose WTE incineration because it's in front of us, if you build it in front of other people's homes, they will also oppose it on the same principle ... This is how the state has to think about this situation. We [the state] are fair and reasonable (*gongzhen heli*). We can't only consider just one side, we have to weigh many interests. This is my position.[14]

The state, according to Xu, was the vanguard of the people and charged with administering the technocratic processes and calculations that assured delivery of a public good. Xu ventriloquized a discourse of state legitimation established early in China's socialist era of mass-line politics in which legitimacy was derived from a capacity to rule on behalf of the people. In Mao's classic formulation of mass-line thinking "all correct leadership is necessarily 'from the masses, to the masses'" (Mao 1965). As the vanguard of the people, the party's role is to concentrate the interests of the people into meaningful shape and then to propagate the resulting ideas back to the masses (Chen 2012). Xu's reiteration of this logic rang familiar but hollow to petitioners. In the post-reform era, the state ceded the authority to govern to a class of technocratic experts (Andreas 2009). Yet, increasingly, as those technocratic experts aligned with the political interests of an elite—developers, party bureaucrats—they were alienated from the new "masses," the rising urban middle class.

Through their appeals, Huadu homeowners transformed an officially sanctioned forum, where the state once dictated the terms of speech, into a site of technical deliberation, where official procedures and governance were scrutinized and challenged. In appeals to the state, homeowner activists carefully framed their own position within what the state considered as permissible forms of critique. A homeowner responded to the official's charges by making the case for a middle ground that abided the limits of dissent:

> I'm not opposed to incineration, this is national policy, a decision that is out of my hands. I am personally against incineration, but since the country has no other solution but to pursue incineration as a policy, it also doesn't matter even if I'm opposed to it. I can only say that you can't build it [WTE incineration] in densely populated neighborhoods. Build it somewhere more remote. This is the least that the state can do.

In officially sanctioned arenas of political appeal under state authoritarianism, scholars have noted that the supplicant usually adopts the authorities' language to frame their argument in anticipation of how they might be received (Fitzpatrick 2005, 156). In exchanges with state officials, however, what becomes immediately clear is that homeowners can engage the state on such grounds because of their capacity to debate according to terms that are dictated by the state. The state official aimed to delegitimize homeowners as those driven by a narrow desire to defend one's own property. In response, homeowners reflexively broadened their case to matters of technical consideration based on urban density. Homeowners quickly adapted their rationale from advocating for a local issue to a broader public concern.

Anti-WTE incineration activists in the US have similarly deployed a form of "flexible alliance" to frame incineration as sometimes "everyone's problem" and other times as a local problem to avoid being considered a narrow interest group (Ahmann 2020). In Guangzhou, a focus on technical conditions of siting helped homeowners to depoliticize their demands in order to speak on behalf of a broader public interest. By focusing on the technical elements of the siting and operation of WTE incineration, homeowners are engaging "boundary-expanding contentions" that move beyond the state's allowable framework of actions (O'Brien 2003). In this case, homeowners broadened their appeal by presenting themselves as the "masses," who came to speak against the technical policies of a governing elite.

FIGURE 3.3   Huadu protesters oppose the siting of a proposed WTE incinerator near their housing developments, 2013. Photo by author.

A PUBLIC CONTROVERSY

From 2009 to 2012, what began as a localized homeowner protest against the siting of WTE incineration in Panyu evolved into a citywide debate over the rationale for and implementation of Guangzhou's vision to create a modern and sustainable form of waste management. From 2012 to 2013, newspapers and magazines in Guangzhou—ranging from more liberal publications like the *Nanfang Daily* and *Xinkuai Bao* to the state-leaning *Yangcheng Evening News*—provided daily coverage of issues related to municipal waste management. In May 2012, the city established an official group of citizen monitors tasked with overseeing the roll-out of waste policies in the city.[15] The group—including engineers, representatives from related businesses and associations, homeowner anti-incineration activists, journalists from the *Nanfang Daily,* and academics from local universities—initiated a series of urban forums to encourage public debate and participation.

Through their anti-incineration activism, homeowner activists from Panyu and Huadu were connected to a translocal network of antipollution activism. Yuan Fei and Fang Fang attended workshops on pollution and chemical safety with activists and civil society groups from across the country; the workshops were run by the Beijing NGO Green Beagle along with international partners such as the International POPs Elimination Network (IPEN), Arnika (an international NGO from the Czech Republic), and other NGOS in China. In 2012, a Beijing environmental activist launched a lawsuit against Guangzhou's Environmental Bureau after the bureau failed to respond to a series of requests for the release of pollution emissions reports at the Phoenix incinerator mandated by the new Open Access Information Law (OAI). The increasingly national and international networks of anti-incineration action also helped shape the perspective of homeowner activists, who came to see themselves as emerging environmental subjects engaged in anti-toxic politics.

Through the course of their anti-incineration action, a core group of homeowners in Guangzhou, who started out by protesting a set of localized concerns about pollution, emerged as visible, prominent, and public environmental actors who also critiqued other aspects of the city's waste management policy. In the course of the controversy, the urban middle class focused on the technological rationale informing the state's approach to waste. Oscillating between online discussions and debates and offline political acts, homeowners self-consciously shifted the terms of debate on WTE incineration into a public evaluation and debate of the safety of WTE incineration technology. If the state sought to legitimize WTE incineration by appealing to advanced science and technology, the strategy of "technicizing deliberation" represents an "authoritarian dilemma of modernization" in which the very institutions and logics producing modernity generate a parallel mode of engaging the state (Lei 2018, 6). Homeowners seized on technical detail as a means of enlarging and sustaining the terms of debate. Their strategy compared the workings of WTE incinerators across local and international contexts, evaluated evidence gathered by communities across the city, and established a connection between end-of-life technology and the daily practice of waste collection that composed the city's waste stream. Anti-incineration action enabled homeowners to forge new ties with their neighbors through a shared attunement to pollution and suspicion of the state's institutions of pollution oversight. Their way of mobilizing was to transform their affective experiences into new strategies of not only protest, but also ongoing deliberation, discourse, and critique.

Homeowners devised a strategy to sustain a public evaluation of technological risk in a context of authoritarian control. By foregrounding techno-political discourse to address the shortfalls of WTE incineration, homeowners made it possible for challenges of state-sponsored infrastructure to coalesce across communities in a context where the state worked to break up and splinter collective action. Homeowners learned to self-consciously privilege the neutrality and rationality of technical procedures to cultivate and sustain a terrain of deliberation. They produced coalitions between different communities of anti-incineration protests to generate a bottom-up critique of pollution control and safety procedures. Technicizing deliberation allowed them to forge an alliance between distinct communities while obscuring the political nature of their demands, allowing the debate to linger, build, and endure. For activists like Yuan Fei, the Panyu protest and its interrogation of WTE incinerators prompted him to focus on the composition of the waste stream and the importance of recycling.

If one prominent feature of "technicizing deliberation" was, in Mountai's words, a capacity to engage in a "dialogue across space," homeowner deliberation in Guangzhou also raised the question of who can be seen as a valid participant in spaces of deliberation. In Guangzhou, the knowledge politics of technical deliberation remains primarily a strategy wielded by an urban middle class, comprised of educated professionals. In anti-incineration debates we can see how China's urbanization drove middle-class homeowners, among the most well-resourced urbanites, to not only succeed in stalling and relocating WTE facilities but to amplify the rise of a nascent waste politics. Technicizing deliberation as a strategy assumes that a condition of participation is the knowledge of how to speak in the forums and spaces where the technical features of WTE incineration are evaluated: newspaper editorials, petition meetings, and protests. Groups of homeowners came to see themselves as anti-incineration activists who collectively mobilized a "rational" discourse to establish a neutral terrain in which different communities of protesters could convene in a collective challenge to the state.[16] As a strategy of scientific knowledge and discourse, technicizing deliberation precluded villagers and waste workers from participating in public forums.

FIGURE 4.1 The four-bin recycling system and poster in front of Liwan Court, 2013. Photo by author.

4 | MYSTIFYING LABOR

The Political Economy of Recycling

IN MAY 2012, THREE YEARS after the Panyu protest, I went to meet Yuan Fei, a homeowner anti-incineration activist whom I first interviewed in 2010, in the office of the recently formed NGO called Eco-Canton. While I waited for Yuan Fei, I greeted and met the organization's core members for the first time: Da Dun, a village protester from Panyu; Fengmei, an environmental activist; and Yuxian, a researcher and volunteer from Hong Kong. Yuan Fei, in characteristic fashion, burst into the room a few minutes behind schedule. Excited and slightly out of breath, he wiped his forehead with a handkerchief before pulling a folder from his backpack. He proudly passed around a document that certified Eco-Canton as a registered NGO. For Yuan Fei, the formation of Eco-Canton signified a turning point; he was leaving behind a successful career as a building contractor to become a professional activist.

The core members of Eco-Canton had all come to waste activism through anti-incineration action. At the organization's first meeting, they were unanimous that Eco-Canton should focus on recycling. In 2011 Guangzhou had become the first city in China to enact laws mandating recycling. By 2012 bus stops, walls, and other public spaces were adorned with advertisements and public announcements. Eco-Canton hoped to seize on the momentum as districts across the city started to experiment with different models of waste separation. Members of Eco-Canton believed that a focus on recycling would allow them to work at the neighborhood level to address how everyday citizens dealt with their trash. Aligning with an official state campaign also offered a degree of security and protection as they established themselves as an NGO.

For Yuan Fei, an interrogation of the technical aspects of WTE incineration during the Panyu protest led him to redirect his attention to recycling. Panyu activists had determined that the efficacy of WTE incineration as end-of-life waste technology was, at least in part, a function of the practices of waste collection and sorting *before* waste reached landfills or incinerators. They concluded that the safety of WTE incineration was compromised by the "mixed" waste stream fed to the facility. The mixed waste that arrived at end-of-life facilities was officially classified as "other waste" (*qita laji*) and was comprised of over 50 percent organics in addition to thin plastics and different types of toxics (such as batteries). Activists stressed that the "inadequate" quality of mixed waste was due to the city's failure to introduce a formal citizen recycling campaign, thus allowing waste unsuitable for burning (e.g., batteries) to end up in incinerators. As waste activists shifted their focus to the city's recycling program, they quickly discovered that the high organic composition of the waste stream in Guangzhou was not due to the absence of a formal recycling system but also *because* of the city's widespread and effective *informal* recycling system (chapter 1). Even as official recycling campaigns failed to motivate citizens to voluntarily sort their trash, informal collectors, sanitation workers, and even the occasional middle-class homeowner were already effectively diverting high calorific materials like paper and high-quality plastics away from the waste stream. By the time garbage reached the incinerator, organics, low-quality plastics, and other hazardous materials made up the bulk of the mass left to burn.

In Chinese megacities, ongoing and substantial state investment in techno-scientific infrastructure did not diminish the importance of the everyday labor practices that diverted and ordered waste. Since 2012, the implementation of the city's official recycling campaign has reshaped the livelihood practices of the city's sanitation workers. China's efforts to build green cities are realized not only through the introduction of end-of-life facilities like WTE incinerators but by remaking the labor practices that constitute an infrastructure of circulation that is responsible for organizing, collecting, and moving recyclable waste (*huishou laji*). Citizen recycling campaigns rearranged the process and spaces of waste disposal and exchange and thus raised questions about who had and has the right to claim ownership of scraps. The practices of diverting, sorting, and recuperating scraps anchored negotiations and contestations among middle-class residents, the state, and sanitation workers over the types of labor that counted as "sustainable" and "green."

In voluntary citizen recycling programs, municipal governments positioned citizens as stewards responsible for shepherding recyclable material including paper, plastics, and organics away from end-of-life processing facilities. These programs continue to be a key component of how the Chinese state imagines a modern and sustainable waste management system. The push for voluntary citizen recycling programs in China in many ways echoes the introduction of curbside recycling programs in the US, when in the 1970s, recycling and cleanup became the hallmarks of the modern American environmental movement. In post-reform China, state recycling campaigns fundamentally encroached on the capacity of a growing migrant population to buy, sell, and recuperate scraps for their livelihood, and in doing so, diverted those scraps from neighborhoods, alleyways, and waste bins.

In Guangzhou, citizen recycling campaigns erased the political economy and labor practices behind scrap reclamation; the voluntary diversion of recyclables (whose primary value is sustainability) was privileged over sanitation work (the labor of cleanup and informal diversion of recyclables). When it came to waste work, the association of formalized recycling campaigns with the rise of a green middle-class environmental consciousness perpetuated a green mystification, which obscured existing systems of scrap diversion.

Mystification was central to how Marx understood how "the social and economic character impressed on things in the process of social production" comes to stand in for value (Marx 1987, 225). Scholars have demonstrated that the production of green economies increasingly facilitated both the securing and obscuring of undervalued forms of precarious labor in the name of sustainability (Castellini 2019).[1] The creation of green communities remained reliant on scrap labor and the largely informal scrap trade, even as voluntary citizen recycling campaigns cast sanitary work (the people who perform it, the value of scraps, and the existence of commodity markets) as invisible, inefficient, dirty, backward, and necessarily ready to be subsumed by greener and more modern forms of waste recuperation.

The debate over who has access to recyclables in urban communities, however, also yielded an opportunity for sanitation workers to articulate a politics of distribution and moral economy. The practices of waste reclamation in Liwan Court recounted in this chapter reflect a moral economy of claims-making, echoing what Amiel Bize calls "the right to the remainder." Bize argues that categories like "leftover" and "remainder" enable the economically marginal to articulate an entitlement to a particular kind of share (Bize 2020, 476). Sanitation workers claim scraps as an in-kind supplement to wages, their entitlement anchored to their proximity to waste and dirt. Waste work's association with dirt, therefore, not only facilitated the process by which certain bodies were deemed to be disposable, but the association also grounded waste workers' articulation of a moral economy of entitlement. The exchange and reclamation practices in Liwan point to how the *free disposing* commonly found in regimes of consumption makes possible practices of *free taking*. The disputes at Liwan Court that I recount in this chapter, meanwhile, make clear that the channels, flows, and practices of waste's diversion are not only sites of governance and control but sites for negotiations over who has the right to "take" and claim the remainders of consumption—scraps.

LIBERALIZING SANITATION WORK

The campaign to formalize citizen recycling that kicked off in 2012 was not the first attempt by the Chinese state to motivate citizens to recycle. As recounted in chapter 1, following the demise of the socialist state-instituted recycling system in the early years of the post-reform era, recycling became the domain of informal collectors, rural migrants who came to depend on the selling and recuperation of scraps for their livelihood. Urban citizens, once motivated by a nationalist ethos to bring scraps to depots to encourage national development, now sold their scraps to informal collectors, typically migrant workers (Wu and Zhang 2019). Yet, scraps and resale depots across Chinese cities were not only the domain of informal collectors. Construction workers, kitchen staff, and grandmothers also came to sell recyclables. Aside from informal collectors, sanitation workers (identifiable by their uniforms) were one of the most common presences at scrap depots.

In the post-reform era, shifts in the structures of sanitation work made sanitation workers depend on scrap sales to subsidize their wages. During the socialist era, sanitation workers were employed by municipal sanitation bureaus. Despite low wages, as state employees, sanitation workers had access to a range of welfare benefits including subsidized housing, sick leave, and holiday pay. In addition, workers enjoyed redistribution and compensation in the form of rationing and payments in-kind, including meal tickets, grains, oils, and other household items. Sanitation workers were part of the revolutionary proletariat workforce lionized by the state as socialist heroes and entitled to an "iron rice bowl."

The dismantling of the socialist work regime meant that sanitation services would increasingly be provided by private firms competing in a market. Guangzhou was one of the first cities in China to experiment with privatizing its sanitation services, beginning with the privatization of road and river cleaning services in 1995 (Chi 2008). In 2002 and 2004, the Ministry of Construction issued official policies that authorized the contracting out of public services, including sanitation work, to private companies.[2] Since then, Guangzhou has become a leader in the marketization of sanitation with about seven hundred sanitation companies operating by 2008 (Renmin Web 2013). The municipal government turned previously permanent public sector jobs into limited time contracts (typically three years) and issued wage contracts to the lowest bidder (Xu and Dou 2021). Reforms in 2008 divided public sector sanitation workers into two groups: those managed directly by the city and those managed by district- or street-level governments. District governments further privatized their cleaning services and independently procured contracts from private sanitation companies. Officials at the Guangzhou All-China Federation of Trade Unions reported that, as of 2013, about 60 percent of the 40,000 sanitation workers in Guangzhou were employed by private contractors, while the remaining 40 percent (those in charge of transporting municipal waste and those working in landfills) still enjoyed state benefits.[3] Predictably, contract work drove down wages as contractors competed with one another on price. Liberalization left sanitation workers among the lowest compensated of wage workers.

Scholarly studies of strikes, unionization, and worker petitions in China have been based, to a large extent, on the experience of industrial workers typically in factory settings. The rise of collective labor action in China in the early 2000s was composed of both veteran state workers responding to the dismantling of the socialist welfare system (pensions, severance, job tenure) in state-owned factories, as well as a rising young proletariat class laboring in private industry demanding higher wages (Lee 2007). Labor action involved worker petitions, appeals through the legal system, and spontaneous protests and strikes (Lee 2007).[4] An analysis of the modes of political agency and forms of actions carried out by workers in the tertiary sector, particularly in China's megacities, however, is still emerging. From late 2012 through 2013, as Guangzhou's municipal government launched another round of citizen recycling campaigns, the media reported thirteen mass strikes by sanitation workers in Panyu, Tianhe, Yuexiu, and Liwan districts. Where factory work and the growing services sector favored younger workers, sanitation and cleaning services typically relied on older workers and those with limited opportunities to compete in higher paying sectors. The wave of sanitation strikes in Guangzhou represented unusual pushback from a labor sector often perceived to have little organizational structure or to hold little power.

Growing municipal sanitation worker strikes of 2012 and 2013 were the result of marketization and outsourcing that reflected a broader process of the informalization and the degradation of work across and within sectors (Sanyal and Bhattacharyya 2009). Sanitation workers commonly reported labor abuses, including unpaid holidays and no compensation for work-related health problems and injuries. Yet the declining working conditions experienced by sanitation workers was due not only to shifts within the structure of labor, but also to the conditions of living. In China's megacities, there is a growing discrepancy between wage compensation and the cost of living. In 2012–2013, sanitation workers frequently complained of rising rents fueled by real estate speculation and of long commutes between home and work. Wulong, a sanitation worker for a private contractor whom I interviewed in 2013, told me that he had to rely on a second job as a delivery driver to pay his rent.

Sanitation workers hired by private companies in gated communities like Liwan Court answered to private building management companies and had even less power to organize strikes or other forms of political action. In addition, as internal migrants without urban registration (*hukou*), sanitation workers under private contract, like other migrants throughout China, lacked access to state services including health care, education, and other benefits that supplemented wages for those in possession of Guangzhou urban registration.[5] In these conditions, the ability to collect and sell scraps, discarded and ready for the taking, emerged as a critical form of wage subsidy. Hao Zhang and Eli Friedman use the concept of "ancillary informal work" to describe informal work that occurs alongside and subsidizes and stabilizes conditions of formal employment (Zhang and Friedman 2019). As a form of "ancillary informal work," the selling of scraps complicates the clear division between wage and nonwage work. By proposing to shift the practices and the organization of the waste stream, recycling campaigns also encroached on an existing terrain of value production that has been a lifeline for sanitation workers.

BUILDING GREEN COMMUNITIES

The formalization of recycling campaigns positioned urban citizens as the vanguard of sustainability. In 2011 the city kicked off another round of recycling campaigns focused on educating urban citizens to undertake a "participatory" role in waste sorting. The slogans and campaigns made explicit that recycling initiatives were part of a larger urban governance strategy that linked concerns with health and well-being to a scientifically inflected mode of green urbanism. In Guangzhou, the city became saturated with slogans like: "Promote recycling, create healthy living" and "To build a smart Guangzhou, low-carbon Guangzhou, and a happy Guangzhou"(*jianshe zhihu Guangzhou, ditan Guangzhou, xingfu Guangzhou*).[6] The allusion to "smart Guangzhou" evoked the pursuit of "smart" or "knowledge" cities where digital technology, interwoven into the physical space of the city, promised to facilitate not only financial flows but the attainment of sustainability and well-being. If the state was primarily responsible for the production of the physical infrastructures associated with modernity, recycling campaigns suggested that citizen participation was also critical to the state's attempt to transform Guangzhou into a world city.[7]

Recycling campaigns not only fit seamlessly into a particular state vision of sustainability, they also enabled the state to enact pilot projects to bring about green urban development at the neighborhood level. Civil society groups were critical to such experiments and to the state's capacity to create green communities through waste. In 1997 the grassroots environmental organization Global Village started China's first efforts to promote citizen recycling in Beijing (Boland and Zhu 2012). Pilot projects were quickly absorbed by the state, and by 2001 the State Environmental Protection Administration (SEPA) (guojia huanjing baohuju) launched a pilot and then a national-level initiative to promote green communities. Campaigns promoting community recycling were launched in China's eight largest cities, including Guangzhou.[8] Green communities represented the first wave of state efforts to chart a comprehensive city-level environmental management strategy. Green community campaigns were launched in tandem with local urban governance reforms that sought to shift governance responsibilities away from the work unit (*danwei*) (Bray 2005) and to invest in a new system of community and neighborhood governance (*shequ jianshe*). Green community programs also encouraged citizen participation in local sustainability projects that promised to improve residential space, environmental infrastructure, and to encourage more ecologically minded behavior (Boland and Zhu 2012, 149).[9] Despite the emphasis on public participation and community self-governance, *shequ* committees largely operated under the direction of "street-level" offices (*jiedao banshichu*) charged with implementing local-level campaigns such as recycling. The *shequ* model reinforced a top-down mode of state-governance charged with delivering a set of state-mandated goals (Boland and Zhu 2012).

During the Maoist period, state-led mass campaigns were critical in mobilizing the collective labor needed in national reconstruction (Perry 2011). In cities, improvements in public health, beautification, and sanitation were often achieved through the mobilization of citizen labor (Rogaski 2004). The failure of previous recycling campaigns signaled, for Yuan Fei, a citizenry who had grown tired of the slogans, public launches, and fanfare of post-socialist state campaigns. Yet, urban citizens had invested little in the formation of committed grassroots communities, whose autonomy and self-governance, he believes, were critical to the success of such efforts. While neighborhood-level officials speculated that the failure of recycling campaigns was due to a lack of state investment at the local level, residents like Yuan Fei attributed its failure to apathy and to a lack of trust in state campaigns. For many activists, conversely, recycling campaigns were a vehicle for cultivating a different type of subject, one who not only abided by the state's vision of sustainability but who could be moved toward broader political participation, including the governing and maintenance of their own community.

Yuan Fei's interest and involvement in neighborhood recycling began long before the formation of Eco-Canton. In the summer of 2010, less than a year after the Panyu protest, I first visited Yuan Fei and Da Dun when they became volunteers at "Green Family," where they went door to door collecting paper, plastics, and other recyclables in Siyuan complex. The group of volunteers, made up of mostly middle-class residents, would separate the bags of mixed recyclables—grouping papers, plastics, and metals—in front of their neighborhood community center. The public performance— middle-class residents squatting and sorting through waste, picking through bags of soda cans or organizing cardboard (labor commonly performed by migrant collectors and sanitation workers)—attracted attention. Green Family members pooled their money and purchased a three-wheeled cart to haul sorted recyclables to an informal collection depot just outside the complex. Each week the proceeds from the sale of recyclables were put toward community events to raise environmental awareness. As a former anti-incineration activist, Yuan Fei believed that as a grassroots organization, Eco-Canton could mobilize the support of citizens who were not only interested in the diversion of scraps but in investing in their community. He claimed that through recycling he could "teach people how to be citizens." Yet, as Eco-Canton would come to discover, the successful diversion of scraps involved the participation of not only residents but sanitation workers, who performed the daily labor of recovering scraps.

AN EXPERIMENT: *LAJIBULUODI*, "NO WASTE TOUCHES THE GROUND"

In July 2012, the Guangzhou Municipal Urban Management Committee's Recycling Division announced that all 131 street-level governments would begin promoting pilot recycling projects. The various street-level districts were divided into four categories (A through D). The sixteen A-level districts were given the most aggressive targets and tasked with diverting 80 percent of recyclables from the waste stream. Built in 2003, and classified as an A-level district, Liwan Court had already been the site of several pilot campaigns. Plaques on its front gate proclaimed it as a "green community" where, as early as January 2010, residents participated in an experimental project that encouraged citizens to separate wet waste from dry. The community was once again selected as a pilot site in 2013 in part because, as home to mostly white-collar workers, including many city bureaucrats and local street-level government officials, the building manager believed that the high "moral quality" (*suzhi*) of the residents would make the campaign more likely to succeed.

In the spring of 2013, four brightly colored waste bins were placed prominently at the entrance gate to Liwan Court and announced the start of a new round of recycling campaigns. The four bins corresponded to the city's four-stream waste recycling system introduced in 2012. Blue bins were for recyclables, green bins for organics, pink bins for toxic waste, and grey bins for other waste. The four bins represented not only a place to aggregate waste but an attempt at establishing a method to regulate the practice of "placing" to prompt a shift in the habits and behaviors that governed how residents disposed of their trash (Gregson, Metcalfe, and Crewe 2007). As early steps toward what waste officials and planners hoped would be a broad restructuring, reordering, and redirection of waste flows, the bins were critical nodes in a planned infrastructural network that would condition how waste was collected, aggregated, and moved. Unlike the water pipes, train tracks, or cables through which matter or information flowed mostly seamlessly, the movement of matter through waste infrastructure was made possible only through the labor of collection that placed discarded waste objects on a designated path of circulation.

Throughout my research in Guangzhou, municipal planners and officials repeatedly described a desire to create an enclosed (*fengbishi*) system of waste management. The term "enclosed system" (*fengbishi*) describes a spatial and aesthetic characteristic that typifies modern waste systems. In the concrete and sanitized halls of apartment complexes, making waste management modern meant making trash imperceptible. Trash would be stored in receptacles, hidden in stairwells, separated from the spaces of daily life. New *fengbishi* waste trucks (introduced by the Municipal Urban Management Committee) enclosed waste to conceal odor and the unsightly process of decomposition. Waste labor was similarly required to remain hidden. In windowless basement rooms or utility closets, sanitary workers manually sorted recyclables, their labor ensuring the sustainable processing of waste even in the face of failed citizen recycling campaigns. The enclosure is a standardized apparatus aligned to the aesthetic order of modern living in contemporary China. In these new, ostensibly environmentally minded communities, waste, a harbinger of disorder and disease, needed to be kept at bay.

Recycling campaigns not only regulated disposal practices but reconfigured ownership of scraps, which had been, in effect, a "free" resource for the urban poor.[10] In her study of waste collectors on a landfill in Rio de Janeiro, Kathleen Millar notes that waste work offers the types of flexibility and autonomy that provide a refuge from both conditions of precarity and wage labor. Patrick O'Hare similarly observes that for waste pickers in Uruguay, landfills offered a strange form of security (O'Hare 2019).[11] Waste's transgressive potential lies in the fact that it is not only capital's excess but also a speculative object with the capacity to sustain and to create wealth for those outside formalized channels and categories visible to and recognized by the state. Formalizing waste work enacts a process of enclosure that limits access to collective resources that sustain communities (Gidwani and Baviskar 2011). In the wake of the liberalization of scraps, the capacity to buy, sell, and recuperate scraps in neighborhoods, back alleyways, and from waste bins, served as a resource commons for the urban poor and the growing migrant population who labored in cities. In gated housing complexes, where informal collectors are prevented from freely entering, sanitation workers, hired by private sanitation companies, helped to broker the recovery of scraps to the private market.

State-sponsored recycling campaigns, however, proposed that the voluntary diversion of scrap commodities by citizens was a fundamental component of a sustainable system for diverting waste. In June 2013 the Liwan District government asked Eco-Canton to facilitate the roll out of a citizen recycling program in an urban housing development. In the year since they formed, Eco-Canton had already designed and conducted a citywide survey on why citizens were hesitant to recycle, and they had attempted to devise a recycling scheme in an office building. An opportunity to facilitate the recycling campaign at Liwan Court, however, represented a unique opportunity. Eco-Canton believed that if their pilot experiment in this typical middle-class community proved successful, they could use the model to encourage recycling in similar complexes across the city.

Eco-Canton soon discovered the challenges of motivating citizens to recycle. Residents at Liwan Court exhibited patterns of waste disposal typical of high-rise apartment complexes across Guangzhou. The presence of pests like cockroaches and rats along with the hot, humid tropical climate meant residents took out their garbage at least once if not twice a day. Food scraps are especially susceptible to generating odors as they decompose. Families were eager to expel trash from the household, but most were unaccustomed to paying for trash bags. As a result, most families reused grocery bags from wet markets to hold their trash—thin, flimsy, and small plastic bags handed out for free. The bags tore easily and spills were common, another reason families typically tossed out waste frequently. At the stairwell landing on each floor, where households deposited their trash, most families paid little attention to which bin they tossed their waste in and very few noticed the posters recently placed by the recycling campaign, instructing them to sort their waste into the appropriate receptacles. Several weeks into the recycling campaign, very little had changed. Two generic black bins sat on the stairwell of each floor, one labeled "recyclable" and one "other waste." Most communities, even those selected as pilot sites, had too few of the colored bins to service all their buildings. As Eco-Canton began their project, the specialized bins that had been installed at Liwan remained stubbornly full of mixed garbage.

Volunteers from Eco-Canton speculated that campaign fatigue had set in.[12] Eco-Canton proposed an experiment using an approach from Taiwan called "No Waste Touches the Ground" (*lajibuluodi*) that had achieved success in a comparably dense Asian city and that would distinguish their efforts from the state's top-down environmental campaigns. Faced with its own waste crisis in the early 2000s, Taipei initiated reforms that succeeded in producing one of the highest recycling rates in the nation. *Lajibuluodi* eliminated shared waste bins from housing complexes and, instead, each evening at designated times, waste and recycling trucks traversed city streets. Residents would collect the day's waste and wait to dispose of it at waste trucks under the watchful supervision of municipal sanitation workers. Citizens who came with unsorted garbage would be turned away.[13]

Hoping to experiment with a modified version of the *lajibuluodi* system in Liwan Court, Yuan Fei proposed that each building remove waste bins from stairwells. Each day, at a designated time, sanitation workers with volunteers from Eco-Canton would supervise citizen recycling and waste disposal until, he hoped, recycling had become part of residents' daily habits. After months of negotiation, the building management company finally agreed to a one-week experiment.[14] As Yuan Fei recounted, on the day the program started, residents were quickly outraged at the inconvenience. Building management had to mediate between angry residents who lashed out at NGO members. Within a few hours, the building's garbage bins were restored to their original positions in the stairwells.

Lajibuluodi was a failure, but the pilot project opened the once hidden practices of waste disposal to public scrutiny. Where once waste bins were where anyone could come to retrieve recyclables, the formalization of recycling established new norms around who could and should direct the quality, quantity, and direction of waste flow. To Eco-Canton's surprise, resistance to the program not only came from urban residents but also from the building's sanitation workers. Members of Eco-Canton had anticipated that sanitation workers would support the change because placing waste bins downstairs was, on the face of it, a labor-saving strategy. Resistance among workers revealed that, in addition to being a temporary holding place, waste bins demarcated ownership. Mediating, on the one hand, disposal and, on the other, recuperation, bins were a liminal space, a temporary commons, where the relinquishing of ownership at the moment of disposal legitimized retaking in "free" space, effectively concealed, out of sight, and thus outside regimes of surveillance. The pilot project showed that citizen recycling threatened to disrupt an existing set of livelihood practices formed around waste bins.

THE LABOR OF DIVERSION AND CLEANING

Sanitation services at Liwan Court were contracted out to a private company called Everclean. Staffed primarily by rural migrants, Everclean had about twenty employees at Liwan who took care of all of the sanitation needs of the twenty-one high-rise buildings within the complex, along with the recreational facilities, which included a community center, a swimming pool, and a basketball court. Each worker was paid a monthly wage of 1,600 RMB (around $266 USD) and given four days off per month. If they chose to work on these days, as most did, they received overtime, which brought their wages for the month up to 1,810 RMB (around $300 USD). During the summer months, workers were offered a 30 RMB/month subsidy to work in temperatures that typically hovered in the high 30s to low 40s Celsius.

Each cleaner was charged with maintaining one building and, on an evening in the fall of 2013, I accompanied Wang, a thin man in his late fifties, on his collection route. At 6:00 p.m. Wang and I took the service elevator to the top floor and we worked our way back down, one floor at a time, collecting the building's trash. Wang dumped the trash from the stairwells into one bin, collapsing two floors into one. He then made a second trip from the top to the bottom, stopping every other floor to pull two or three buckets into the elevator downstairs.

Working alone, he used the waste buckets to stop the elevator door from closing while he wheeled the bags to the front entrance of the building, where they were piled up along the sidewalk. Before long, another cleaner arrived on a bicycle attached to a three-wheel cart to lift the trash bags and wrestle them onto the cart, one at a time. Unsorted waste is weighed down by a significant percentage of organics. I tried to lift one onto the cart and the bag ripped easily, bones spilling onto the sidewalk. "You can't grab onto the corners, it will tear," Wang instructed me, and he demonstrated that the way to ensure that the bag didn't spill was by holding it close to the body, the juices of the rotting food waste dripping out of the bag. While government recycling campaigns teach residents to use waste bins to organize their waste, Wang's collection route revealed that waste is made to move literally through the physical labor of sanitation workers. Liwan Court's achievement of a sanitary and waste-free condition of living depended on some bodies willingly engaging in forms of "waste intimacy" involving a proximity to and embodied exchange with objects and filth so that others could preserve their own cleanliness and distance from waste (Butt 2023).

Earlier in the collection route, as we crammed into the elevator with a large wheeled bin used to haul out the bags of trash, Wang pointed to tiny black spots on the ground that he had been "docked points" for. These "docked points" would translate into deductions from his wage. He told me that building management had complained that the marks were from leakages from waste bags but he attributed them to residents who threw cigarette butts and gum on the floor. Each month building management would deduct 3,000 RMB from the contract with Everclean if they discovered spots or filth in the complex. In June 2013 the deduction was increased to 10,000 RMB. Under pressure from building management, Everclean had recently instituted the point system to help ensure that workers delivered

FIGURE 4.2   Wang wrestles a bag of waste onto a cart before hauling it to a compacting station, 2013. Photo by author.

quality service. The company passed city penalties down to workers, and Wang's already low wages were further diminished.

Sanitation workers bore the responsibility of upholding cleanliness standards, essential for transitioning Guangzhou into an ecological city. However, by virtue of their proximity to dirt, workers also came to be associated with dirt or filth, and their presence was perceived as a threat to cleanliness and order. Wang, a quiet, shy man, was careful not to leave any traces behind as he headed off on his bicycle to transport the piles of trash out of the complex to the local compacting station. Hua, another cleaner who had been sweeping the courtyard, had already hauled buckets of water to clean the concrete where the bags of trash had momentarily rested.[15]

Another sanitation worker, Chuang, however, told me that to be clean and remain free of filth was impossible: "There's no way that this can be clean" (*zhe ge ganjing bu liao*). For Chuang, the physical filth of her body is attributable to the moral filth of the residents that sanitation workers clean up after. She remarked to me, "We're not dirty, they're dirty" *(women bu zang, tamen cai zang)*, referring to residents who litter and spit. Sanitation workers are acutely aware of not only how dirt marks class, caste, and labor hierarchies, but of how waste labor also redistributes the burdens and costs of filth. Yet, as Chuang's comment suggested, workers are not only keenly aware of how they are perceived but also devise their own critiques of the urban middle class based on the uneven distribution of the burdens of cleanup. For Chuang, the distinction between dirty and clean bodies isn't always clear: those deemed clean due to their separation from dirt are often those responsible for filth.

Studies of the relationship between waste and labor show that capitalism has produced a labor force that is not only subjected to exploitation but made ever more expendable and disposable (Doherty 2021; Yates 2011). The logic of disposability that applies to objects is similarly applied to people and space, rendering humans as waste (Bauman 2004; Doherty 2021). Sanitation workers have habituated themselves to working under stigma and duress. Their proximity to dirt has made them become "so accustomed to their bodily presence inciting disgust that they come to expect and preempt it" (Resnick 2021, 225). For sanitation workers in China, the stigma amplifies the ways that the demands of neoliberal urbanization have eroded their capacity for work and living. In such a climate of super-exploitation, the capacity to recuperate scraps is not only a wage supplement or a form of "ancillary work." By 2013, the right to reclaim scraps undergirded an emergent collective effort by sanitation workers to claim resources central to their capacity to remain in the city.

THE INTERNAL WASTE MARKET

In early 2013 sanitation workers at Liwan Court requested a pay raise. Everclean's management rejected the request but countered with an alternative proposal: instead of increasing their pay, the sanitation company would buy scraps directly from workers. For the workers, the proposal meant they could sell recyclables they gleaned directly to management instead of hauling the scraps to another market. In this arrangement, Everclean would assume responsibility for sorting and selling the aggregated scraps, and workers would receive a portion of the income from the sale of recyclables that they recovered in the building. The new arrangement was presented by Everclean's management as the equivalent of a raise to the workers. Sanitation workers, in turn, saw scrap recuperation as a form of payment in kind. While this new arrangement promised to secure a buyer for the scraps that sanitation workers collected throughout the day, the requirement that all workers opt in precluded them from freely selecting a buyer for their scraps. Although Everclean presented this arrangement as a compromise that provided workers a wage subsidy, the arrangement would also yield a marginal gain for Everclean. Everclean, for their part, pocketed the difference between what they paid the workers for scraps and what they earned from selling the aggregated scraps to resale markets.

The proposal by building management exploited existing patterns of scrap recuperation in the building. Each morning at 5:00 a.m. and then again before lunch, cleaners visited each bin in the building to pick out recyclables before carrying out daily trash collection. One day I sat on the curb outside the Everclean office with Hua during her break. Hua, a cleaner in her forties, told me about a grandmother who liked to get up even earlier than the cleaners to sift through the trash bin. "The grandma is going through trash bins on the thirteenth and fourteenth floor again! She goes through them at 4:00 a.m.! What are we going to do about her? She leaves a mess too!" Hua exclaimed to another group of workers sitting across from us. Hua's outrage illustrated that the cleaners saw the recyclables as their entitlement, a view reinforced by Everclean's proposal to formally incorporate scrap recuperation into their payment arrangement. In the view of sanitation workers, in exchange for their closeness to waste and their willingness to endure the burdens and risks associated with dirt and disease, they were "granted" the privilege to recuperate things from the bins. Often the first to shuffle through the bins, they recovered bottles, cans, wires, used electronics, and other objects. Hua interpreted the grandmother's reclamation practice as not only an economic infringement but as a violation of the moral economy of distribution, of who could rightfully claim scraps.

Hua's story yielded an insight into the moral economy of sanitation workers, of how they understood who possessed the right in the housing community to take and to reclaim scraps. In her study of the diversion of fuel in East Africa's roadside exchange markets, Amiel Bize describes the moral logic of gleaning as the "marginal's right to remainders" (Bize 2020, 474). Drawing on European texts from the seventeenth and eighteenth centuries, Bize shows that prior to the enclosure movement, these texts defended the right to glean as reserved for "the poor and alien" (Bize 2020, 474). In particular, as Bize writes, "villagers . . . the indigent, the young, the old and women . . . were allowed to enter fields after a harvest to pick up what had been left behind" (Bize 2020, 474). The picking up of crops, often intentionally left by landowners, yielded a meaningful subsistence and constituted a cultural system of redistribution. Moreover, those who gleaned came to recognize and claim their entitlement to the remainder itself.

It is useful to think about the practice of waste recuperation in Guangzhou, too, as a form of urban gleaning. In Liwan Court, concessions made between a privatized sanitation company and its workers invited sanitation workers to understand and see their own entitlement to recyclables as a form of wage subsidy. Bize argues that the moral economy of gleaning illustrates how "redistributive obligations become re-routed through work relations" (Bize 2020, 476). In Liwan Court, sanitation workers' understanding of their entitlement to, and their active collective participation in, upholding this system of scrap recuperation also demonstrates how everyday practices of labor enable those with little recourse to collectively mobilize to articulate a morality of redistribution.

Everclean's management used to their advantage the fact that sanitation workers at private companies had very little power to collectively organize. They attempted to subsume existing scrap recuperation practices into an "in-kind" supplement that could be converted into cash. Around 5:00 p.m., the small cleaners' office became a scrap market. Xian, a cleaner from Hunan, had recovered a large red metal tin used for the burning of incense; the hefty, durable piece of metal was a valuable recovery. Huang, a skinny worker in his fifties, had less luck. He spread a mundane array of bottles and papers across the floor. Xu, the sanitation manager, weighed each bundle and recorded the type and prices in a notebook. For example, Huang: "31 catty (jin) of paper, 11 catty (jin) of plastic, 1.7 RMB, 5 RMB = 27 RMB." The collected scraps are stored in two sectioned-off spaces at the back of the building. Two or three times a week, Xu and another cleaner, Zhu, bag up each type of scrap to take it to a local resale market.

FIGURE 4.3 The manager of Everclean, the private sanitation company for Liwan Court, shows me how the office of the sanitation company has been converted into a scrap holding space, 2013. Photo by author.

Zhu, from Sichuan, who had worked for the company for over ten years, was in charge of hauling scraps to a waste market for resale. He told me about the discrepancy between the prices that the company offers to cleaners and the price that scraps fetched from informal collectors, stationed immediately outside the housing district. In September 2013 while the sanitation company offered 30 cents RMB per catty of paper, scrap buyers just outside the complex a few blocks away were offering 40 cents RMB/catty for the same bundle.[16] Everclean's command of storage space further gave them the capacity to undertake several iterations of sorting—dividing the bundles of scraps into finer categories that were more attractive to scrap markets and, in some cases, holding inventory until they could get a better price. For the sanitation workers of Liwan Court, however, Everclean's scheme was perceived as preferable to formalized recycling, because at a minimum, it recognized and preserved the capacity to recover scraps for sanitation workers.

For sanitation workers, daily proximity to trash and dirt had placed them in a position to reap the value from recuperating scraps. Kathleen Millar notes that waste matter has a dual characteristic, as "both toxic and life-giving" (2018, 32). Recyclables, for example, encompass both things that can be predictably transformed into value and things associated with dirt and disease. Recyclable waste's dual characteristic as hidden value and its association with dirt makes scrap matter a latent form of resource for gleaners, sanitation workers, and the urban poor. For sanitation workers in Guangzhou in 2013, however, the question of who could reclaim scraps also animated a terrain to articulate a moral claim to resources.

MYSTIFYING LABOR:
A MORAL ENTITLEMENT FOR TAKING

Waste labor provides a critical site for examining how contemporary environmental governance strategies are transforming what was once thought of as dirty work into green labor. The labor practices of sanitation and recycling in Liwan District are examples of how sustainability initiatives mystify and obscure existing political economic claims to waste. Urban recycling campaigns promote the rise of a middle-class environmental identity to foster a green city, while simultaneously obscuring, and foreclosing on, the right of the urban poor to reclaim resources. By reassigning who and what types of environmental work are recognized as "green," and who can access waste scraps as a material resource, recycling campaigns facilitate the flow of resources, wages, and profits away from workers.

While NGOs like Eco-Canton would discover that environmental campaigns shifted who had access to waste, their push for citizen recycling continued to focus on middle-class residents. The rise of citizen recycling campaigns, however, enacted a subtle shift in how sanitation workers understood their own role, not only as those responsible for cleanup but as those possessing an entitlement to waste as resource. In 2013, the concrete labor of waste work fostered a growing realization by sanitation workers of their collective entitlement to scraps. Sanitation workers articulated a right to scraps as "leftover," by resisting proposals that assumed recycling to be a voluntary green activity devoid of economic value and unrelated to questions of distribution. The shift in the allocation of the right to reclaim recyclables allowed sanitation workers, who had lost their ability to organize collectively amid liberalization, to perceive themselves as workers with a common stake in and right to determine the conditions of their own labor.

FIGURE 5.1 Panyu anti-waste activists brewing eco-enzyme solutions in Garden Villa, 2013. Photo by author.

5 | CULTURES OF COLLABORATION
Eco-enzyme and More-Than-

Human Collectives

IN MAY OF 2013, I met Yuan Fei and other anti-incineration activists to turn an apartment into a new community center in Garden Villa. We passed the day mopping the floor and dusting old shelves. Yun Tan and Guiyang, who I had met through their participation in the Panyu anti-incineration protest, introduced me to their neighbors Fang Fang and Ling who also participated in the 2009 protest. Around lunch time, Yuan Fei took a small seed envelope from his backpack and pointed to the bottom of the envelope, where "09/10/20" (the date October 20, 2009) was stamped in small print, marking the date of purchase. Yuan Fei asked the group if we knew what this meant and we shook our heads. Yuan Fei smiled as he began to recount the story.

On October 20, 2009, Yuan Fei was returning to his housing complex after a trip to pick up gardening supplies. As he approached Siyuan's front gate, he found his neighbors circulating fliers, and he learned that the Panyu District government had proposed building a WTE incinerator nearby. For Yuan Fei, October 20, 2009, was a turning point. It marked the day he became involved in Guangzhou's waste crisis. After learning of the proposal, Yuan Fei devoted himself to organizing, and following the success of the Panyu protest, he went on to form the NGO Eco-Canton in 2012. Today, as he was gathering gardening tools to help set up the community center, he came across the bag of seeds he had purchased nearly four years prior. "I didn't get to garden that afternoon, as I had planned to," he said with a wry smile. The group of us made our way outside the apartment to a small patio. Guiyang and Yun Tan turned the soil in the small garden. Yuan Fei opened the envelope and sprinkled the seeds into the dirt.

While Eco-Canton turned its attention to promoting recycling in housing districts across the city, Yuan Fei began to feel increasingly detached from the community of anti-incineration activists he had grown close to while organizing. After the announcement of the relocation of the Panyu incinerator, many activists went back to their daily lives. Over occasional get-togethers and holiday celebrations, he sensed that many remained deeply invested in the waste crisis. Yuan Fei believed that the communities where Guangzhou's anti-incineration activists first emerged and mobilized were uniquely positioned to forge a grassroots anti-waste movement. The establishment of the community center in Garden Villa brought anti-incineration citizen activists together to experiment with new forms of waste action.

The space of the community center was donated by a neighbor in Garden Villa, and others contributed money to a small fund to support the group. That afternoon, the organizers reflected on the fact that while protests had stopped the construction of a waste facility, they had so far failed to address the root of the waste crisis. The newly formed Green Family Center, its name a reference to the neighborhood recycling initiative that Yuan Fei first spearheaded back in 2010, would not only complement the state's promotion of citizen recycling but, they hoped, host activities that would fundamentally reduce the amount of waste being produced. The assembled group all believed that the solution to the city's waste crisis would emerge from within the local community (*xiaoqu*).

In the months after the establishment of the community center, Green Family experimented with a range of activities from hosting a flea market and DIY craft workshops to the exchange of secondhand goods and the collection of batteries and recyclables. A volunteer suggested that they try offering a workshop on how to make eco-enzyme (*huanbao jiaosu*), something that no participants were familiar with at the time. Eco-enzyme, also known as garbage enzyme, is a solution made from the fermentation of organic waste—typically kitchen scraps or produce. Kitchen scraps are cut up and mixed with a solution made of one-part brown sugar, three parts kitchen scraps, and ten parts water. Left to ferment for three months, the resulting cloudy brew was used as a household cleaning product, an alternative to chemical cleaners, shampoos, and detergents.

The brewing of eco-enzyme was already a popular household activity among middle-class urbanites in Malaysia, Taiwan, and other parts of East Asia. Its popularity stemmed from a growing environmental awareness and the emergence of a conscious consumer who endorsed or preferred so-called natural products over the use of chemicals or synthetics.[1] Yun Tan and other Green Family organizers were initially enthusiastic about eco-enzyme as a method to reduce and divert organic waste. However, not long after the initial workshops, they began to claim that the brew itself could be useful in many ways. They encouraged workshop participants to experiment with how to use the solution—applied to the skin as a serum and bug repellent, added to plant soil as an organic fertilizer, and poured into rivers to cleanse them of chemical pollutants. In the months that followed, however, participants began to ferment the brew for ingestion. Participants devised new recipes that replaced food scraps with fresh, edible ingredients: brews made from pomelo peels and honey fermented to cure stomach discomfort and indigestion, for example, or rosehip buds to fortify the skin against aging.

Remarkably, within a few months of its introduction, eco-enzyme brewing eclipsed all other activities at the Green Family community center. Both the Green Family organizers and the DIYers who attended the workshop espoused the myriad capacities of the solution. Brewers insisted on the observable material effects of enzymes, including sleeker hair and revived plants. Over the following months, brewers scaled up their production of eco-enzyme and, instead of using empty two-liter water bottles for brewing, Green Family members purchased forty to sixty-liter containers. Boxes of brown sugar piled up in the former living room like bricks, and participants often jokingly complained that their hands were sore from chopping up fruit peels and vegetables. By the fall of 2013, eco-enzyme solutions were the dominant, if not the sole, focus of Green Family and the community center at Garden Villa.

The brewing of eco-enzymes illuminates the material and political effects of the transformation of organic waste in a local, do-it-yourself experiment. Microbes and their material effects on organic waste were at the center of a collective inquiry into how to transform waste into an agent of

FIGURE 5.2   Large jugs used to store eco-enzyme in the backyard in Garden Villa, 2014. Photo by author.

ecological restoration. These experiments, carried out by a group of former anti-incineration activists and their neighbors, sustained an ecological relation to waste in the aftermath of a more direct engagement with the state and the political sphere. In workshops and in conversations with one another, eco-enzyme brewers focused their discussions on techniques of fermentation and sidestepped politics. Participants' enthusiasm for and financial investment in developing a home remedy would nevertheless sustain a broad experiment into the form that urban environmental politics might assume in the wake of a novel, public, and visible clash over incinerators and the state's environmental governance. For homeowner activists in Garden Villa, microbes and their material effects on organic waste opened up an experimental space for the production of new social and political infrastructures of collaboration. Microbes decomposed waste and in doing so, enabled the recomposition of social, political, and ecological collectives.

For the waste activists of Garden Villa, the eco-enzyme brewing they took up in the wake of their participation in the anti-incineration movement catalyzed a microbiopolitics. They became invested in the proliferation of microorganisms as a mode of inquiry into how humans ought to live with one another (Paxson 2008). The enthusiasm for eco-enzyme brewing is reminiscent of a recent "microbial turn" in scientific research and in the broader culture that challenges a once dominant association between microbes and disease. Scientists, health researchers, and environmentalists have become increasingly interested in the role of microbes in facilitating the development of healthy bodies and ecosystems (Benezra 2023, Benezra, DeStefano, and Gordon 2012; Paxson and Helmreich 2014). In the realm of politics, art, and food, microbes feature prominently in experimental projects to create alternative social and political movements. A probiotic turn in environmental conservation in late-modern Western scientific contexts similarly "us[es] life to manage life," by "working with biological and geomorphic processes to deliver forms of human, environmental and even planetary health" (Lorimer 2020, 1–2). The "probiotic turn" shows a preference for diverse and uncertain outcomes (Lorimer 2020). In the Garden Villa eco-enzyme project, micro-agencies of change in organic matter through the process of fermentation incited a "form of vital responsiveness of all living organisms that can be neither predicted nor controlled for" (Jasarevic 2015, 58).

The official plan for environmental remediation in China imagined complex socioeconomic problems as solvable through investments in large-scale centralized technology. The eco-enzyme, on the other hand, captured a do-it-yourself (DIY) ethos, the sense that everyone can participate in making (Lindtner 2020, 2).[2] In their scientific experimentation, participants became saturated with an "affect of intervention," a feeling of "agency and control, a sense that alternatives to dominant structures at various spatial and temporal scales were possible" (2). Yet, as the brewers demonstrated, the power of eco-enzymes to bind participants is inseparable from the unpredictable nature of the material effects of transformation.

Science and technology studies scholars point out that ecological survival depends on forging novel assemblages, practices, and strategies to reconstitute heterogeneous collectives of human and nonhumans.[3] Feminist theorists have advocated experiments that, in a departure from individualism, emphasize co-laboring, reproduction, and survival (Fournier 2020; Tsing 2015). The eco-enzyme project represented a form of microbial advocacy that mobilized agency at a microbial scale where the speeding up of decomposition and material transformation is tied to the production of new infrastructures of ecological repair. The collective local experiment offered a counterpoint to China's top-down centralized techno-scientific solution to waste.

In Garden Villa, the fermentation of waste incited an ecological experiment that, rather than expelling waste, transformed it into an agent of environmental resuscitation. Eco-enzyme experimentation led to a grassroots response to pollution, and a more-than-human anti-toxic politics. Brewers became invested in the proliferation of microbes to neutralize the waste that had previously been the target of a sanitary regime of containment and expulsion. Through fermentation, waste could be reincorporated into bodies and ecologies. Eco-enzyme transforms waste into a material medium to combat a pervasive environmental toxicity and to forge new connections to the health of bodies, ecologies, and communities. An investment in the cultivation of microbes to speed up the transformation of waste also contributed to the scaling up of social and political investments. Like the brewers, I am less interested in scientific explanations of how microbes work to achieve the cleansing or resuscitation of bodies or the local ecology. Instead, I am concerned with examining how the material effects of microbes catalyzed the political and ecological project of the brewers. For brewers, fermentation and the materiality of microbes revived an enthusiasm for collective action under a repressive authoritarian regime. In China's authoritarian context, eco-enzyme brewing enabled citizens to collectively act to address pollution in ways that transcended state-sanctioned petitions, overt protests, or quiet resignation (Lora-Wainwright et al. 2012; Van Rooij 2010).

SYSTEMIC IRRITANT: THE PROBLEM WITH ORGANICS

As anti-incineration activists point out, the state's emphasis on investing in WTE incineration and in recycling downplayed the extent to which organics in Guangzhou's waste stream posed a challenge to the city's waste management strategy. In 2012 organic waste made up over 50 percent of the total municipal waste stream; residents in the city generated over 7,000 tons of organic waste each day. Local composting projects were nearly impossible to carry out; Guangzhou's dense urban high-rises offered little to no access to community green space. During the latest wave of the city's push to formalize recycling, housing communities experimented with requiring residents to first separate organic and nonorganic waste. Few citizens obliged and sanitation workers were often left with the work of separating organics.

Left unsorted, organic matter creates problems during all phases of collection. In Guangzhou's intense tropical heat and humidity, vegetable peels and other kitchen scraps were susceptible to rapid decomposition. Garbage quickly rotted in stairwells between household disposal and collection. While informal collectors were motivated to separate plastics and paper, as of 2012, residents in the city lacked an incentive to separate their organics. Left in the waste stream, organic waste rendered other types of matter more difficult to recover. During transportation, decomposed organics leaked and emitted smells that clung to the bodies of sanitation workers, and they left a trail of liquid behind waste trucks.

As anti-waste activists discovered, in 2012 the city lacked a centralized technological solution for the processing of organic waste. That year, the Datianshan composting pilot project, an urban composting facility capable of handling more than 100 tons of organic waste per day, was quickly losing government support as officials sparred over the economic feasibility of scaling up the process. 2012 also saw a nationwide food safety scandal over the reuse of gutter oil. Cooking oil collected from sewage drains was being reprocessed on a large scale and distributed to restaurants and grocery chains, stoking citizens' suspicions about the safety of any reuse of organic waste. Without a centralized solution, Guangzhou's organic waste typically became part of its stream of mixed waste, transported to the city's end-of-life facility where it posed another challenge for waste treatment. As noted by Mei village incinerator monitors (chapter 2), at WTE incinerators, wet waste, with a lower calorific value or heat value, poses a challenge for burning, decreasing the efficiency and compromising the safety of WTE incinerators. Anti-incineration activists have argued that China's high organic waste content posed a clear challenge to the efficacy and rationale of the state's decision to invest in WTE incinerators.

The lack of a centralized technology for treating organics in Guangzhou stood in contrast to China's long history of organic waste reuse. In premodern China, fermentation was the dominant method of treating humanure and for converting organic waste into an agricultural resource. Manuals dating back to 1149 AD describe a range of techniques to turn manure and waste products into oil cakes, hemp waste, and bean-curd liquor, and were designed to accomodate different soil conditions and crops (King 1927). In the early twentieth century, Beijing's sewage system was designed exclusively for the drainage of wastewater (Gamble 1921). Human waste primarily moved out of the city through a network of night soil collectors who gathered humanure to be processed and used as agricultural fertilizer in the countryside.

Bio-gas treatment, otherwise known as anaerobic digestion, was another common technology of organic waste treatment. Anaerobic digestion uses microorganisms to break down organic compounds in the absence of oxygen. Compared with composting, which releases carbon dioxide with little value, anaerobic digestion produces energy. In the 1960s and 1970s, the government subsidized the installation of both household digesters and centralized plants across the Chinese countryside.[4] Gas produced from the digester is used primarily for cooking and to supplement electricity and to run generators. The digested slurry and sludge are used to cultivate earthworms as feed for poultry and fish, and to grow mushrooms and lotus roots. While small-scale bio-gas facilities were once popular with rural households, the idea of using bio-gas for organic waste in Guangzhou in 2013 was just getting off the ground. Commonly used to treat and reduce the volume of wastewater and sewage sludge, bio-gas technology has seen only limited use as a treatment for other forms of organic municipal waste.[5]

CATALYSTS OF TRANSFORMATION

Yuan Fei and other waste activists saw the large proportion of organics in the city's waste stream and the city's lack of a centralized solution to treat organic waste as an opportunity for Eco-Canton. Yuan Fei set out to discover a sustainable solution for the city's waste and began to meet with local entrepreneurs trying to push a range of localized solutions to treat organics, ranging from in-sink garburators, food pulverizers, and biological decomposition technologies, including vermicomposting and the breeding of black soldier fly larvae (Zhang 2020a, 2020b).[6] In the words of waste activists, organic waste catalyzed a period of *baihuaqifang*[7] of experimentation and opening. A lack of state-sponsored technology for organic waste in 2013 created a unique opportunity for local communities to experiment with their own strategies outside state initiatives.

The popularity of eco-enzyme among the members of Green Family, however, took Yuan Fei somewhat by surprise. About four months after our first interview, I visited Yun Tan—an accountant, mother of two, and once an active participant in petition meetings and protests against the proposed Panyu WTE incinerator—while she was co-hosting a workshop on the brewing of eco-enzyme solution. Seated on a couch, holding a small 50 milliliter clear spray bottle filled with a liquid solution the color of cantaloupe, Ling urged two women sitting across from her who had come to the workshop to stick out their hands. She sprayed the contents of the bottle on one woman's wrist. "This is great as a mosquito repellant, and I've been using this [eco-enzyme] shampoo for my hair for the past few months," Yun Tan exclaims while running her fingers through her own ponytail, "and it's now shinier, sleeker, and darker."[8] Halfway through the demonstration, Yun Tan stood up from the couch and handed each of us a pamphlet. The title, Chinese characters in a comic book font, read "eco-enzymes save the world." Beneath it, a four-line slogan across the front announced, "With the simplest action, the most economic method, we can alter our living environment."

Yun Tan told me that in her initial use of eco-enzyme, she didn't have many expectations until she used it on her hair and noticed its effect. Fang told me a similar story about using the formula to rejuvenate a dying plant. Most of the workshop participants agreed that what convinced them of the effectiveness of the solution was not scientific evidence but observable results. In workshops, first-time participants weren't given a scientific account of how or why the formula worked, but focused instead on methods for cultivating the most effective microbes. DIYers often exchanged stories about their successes experimenting with different recipes. Traditional ingredients like soapberry were added to a formula meant for cleansing. Aloe vera plants were fermented to make a skin potion.

Participants attributed the popularity of eco-enzymes to their capacity to produce effects that could be seen and felt. They invoked scientific explanations only when pressed for an account of how the enzymes worked. At one workshop, Yun Tan suggested that the formula is slightly acidic, allowing it to dissolve fats such as grease and oil. Guiyang, on the other hand, contended that the solution was actually basic. Reluctant to argue and eager to stress its usefulness across a wide range of contexts, Guiyang referred to a biochemical formula inside the promotional pamphlet:

Eco-enzyme begins a biochemical reaction from starch and sugar that produces an acetic acid ($Ch2COOH$), which when combined with water, disintegrates into starch, fat, and protein producing Acetyl-CO-A (Acetyl coenzyme A) a molecule that participates in many biochemical reactions in protein, carbohydrate, and lipid metabolism.

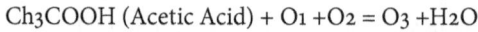

Ch3COOH (Acetic Acid) + O1 +O2 = O3 +H2O

The product O3 ozone, has the capacity to kill bacteria, and also to reduce the number of pollutants and toxins in the air. It can also increase the amount of oxygen in the air.

Eco-enzyme brewers appeal to scientific language to legitimate the formula. Yet, among a limited but growing number of scientific studies, there is a lack of consensus on the efficacy of waste enzymes (or eco-enzymes).[9] The lack of scientific consensus, however, has done little to dampen enthusiasm among practitioners. DIYers might refer new participants to the existence of scientific evidence, but in workshops, their discussion turns to an insistence on the efficacy of eco-enzymes based on observable results.

The biochemical formula, however, captures the scientific process that practitioners believe supports the efficiency of eco-enzymes: the ability of enzymes to catalyze chemical reaction at the smallest scale. Enzymes are proteins that act alone or in larger groups (complexes) to accelerate chemical reactions by lowering the activation energy, or the minimum energy required for a chemical reaction. Enzymes harbor a transformative capacity due to their catalytic ability to speed up biochemical reaction. In order to break down nutrients in the environment to aid cellular digestion, enzymes are secreted beyond the membranes of cells. In this process, the environment is absorbed into the cell itself, rendering indistinct the self-contained organism and its environment. In doing so, enzymes exemplify the concept of *sympoiesis,* the collective production of systems without defined spatial or temporal boundaries (Haraway 2016). Instead, individual organisms transform matter by taking in various agents in their environment.

At the heart of the metabolic process, enzymes facilitate the biochemical reactions that precipitate the transformation of matter. Elizabeth Povinelli (2016) argues that if signs of life are reduced to the smallest capacity for biochemical change, enzymes, as a catalyst of change, mediate the very process that separates the inert from the living. Catalysts ensure the continuity of cellular transformations, or the capacity to continue to transfer electrons. The formula is the biochemical representation of change and transformation between an organism and its environment. An enzyme catalyzes change by transcending the boundary of an organism, and then it incorporates outside nutrients as a part of itself.

By catalyzing the breakdown of organic waste, eco-enzymes produce visible effects of material transformation that precipitate further experimentation. As Povinelli notes of American fermentation activist Sandor Katz, his experiment in fermenting oil was political because it turned the material excess of "capitalist waste production" into an anti-consumption movement and "a set of new relations" that undergird them (Povinelli 2011). Eco-enzymes' felt effects on the bodies it was applied to were further evidence of the brew's capacity to transform bodies and ecologies. The effects of eco-enzymes were uncertain. Yet, it was precisely the uncertainty of these material changes that gathered a community of sympathetic users who viewed these material transformations as impetus for further collective experimentation.

During DIY classes, community activists willingly grew, ingested, and smeared bacterial enzymes from fermented organic waste on their bodies as a way to bring about a hoped-for fortification. The capacity of enzymes to catalyze change is experienced as a shared material affect, the "intensity [that] is embodied . . . at its interface with things" (Massumi 2002, 25). Just as enzymes transgress cellular boundaries to effect biochemical transformation of an exchange between an organism and the environment, the cultivation and use of eco-enzymes facilitate the transgression of a social boundary—the one that encourages people to be repelled by rotting organic matter and waste. Brewers reject a culture of a hygienic modernity where bacteria cultures are viewed as a threat. Instead, anti-waste activists engage in a probiotic act of environmental resuscitation by creating "conditions in which naturally occurring wild organisms thrive and proliferate" (Katz 2008, 3).

Bruno Latour made clear that modern regimes of sanitation and health emerged alongside the discovery, management, and governance of microbial life (Latour 1988). Modern sanitation and health practices that regularize life and biological processes exemplify what Michel Foucault (1997) calls biopolitics. Biopolitics, according to Heather Paxson, was accompanied by a "microbiopolitics," an impulse to govern and regularize life "predicated on the indirect control of human bodies through direct control over microbial bodies" (Paxson 2008, 38). Pasteurization and the Pasteurian regime in particular produced categories and a method for the anthropogenic management of microscopic biological agents "engaged in infection, inoculation, and digestion" (Paxson 2008, 17). A significant legacy of pasteurization is the production of a germophobic subject who has internalized a broader attitude toward microbes, generated through public health: the elimination of microbial life is perceived to be central to the practice of safeguarding bodies.

Esposito argues that Foucault's biopolitics is not only concerned with a negative biopolitics, or a power over life, expressed through efforts to discipline, normalize, and optimize bodies. Instead, Esposito identifies an affirmative biopolitics that contains the seeds of "a power of life" invested in the unknown potentials that stem from the proliferation of life (2008, 32). Esposito uses microbial interactions to demonstrate his political theory of immunity. In the eighteenth and nineteenth centuries, the advent of medical bacteriology and the discovery of vaccines shifted immunity from a natural to an acquired condition. With vaccination, immunity is brought about by the purposeful introduction of "an attenuated form of infection to protect against a more virulent form of the same type" (Esposito 2011, 7). Rather than expelling poisons and guarding the body against impurities, life is preserved and fortified by neutralizing and absorbing its contradiction. Throughout much of the twentieth century, the association of microbes with pathogens and disease meant that immunity was and is understood as a process of inoculating an enemy force that emanates from the outside (Martin 1994). Instead of purging microbes from a social community, an affirmative biopolitics means immunity is understood as an investment in the proliferation of microbial life.

In workshops at Garden Villa, the conversation revolved around the material effects of enzymes and when and how brewers could tell the solution was working. Yun Tan first introduced Jun to me as the brewer who resided outside of Garden Villa, and who famously began to dump eco-enzymes into the local waterway close to her village in hopes of combatting pollution. When I ask Jun why she resisted the urge to commercialize her eco-enzyme formula fermented from a wide range of herbs and fruits that she proclaims cures her daughter's stomachaches, she explains:

When you drink eco-enzymes there's a reaction period, because it is supposed to help your entire body adjust. It's [the eco-enzymes] trying to help you to restore your body's functions. But during this period, some people have high blood pressure, diabetes, they say that after a period of drinking eco-enzymes, they will feel dizzy, faint, have diarrhea, fever, coughs, but these are all signs that the eco-enzyme is chasing the illness out of your body; then it will restore it slowly. A lot of people don't understand these effects, or they try to control these situations. If you sell it, you might mean well, but end up causing harm. Even if you give a bottle of eco-enzyme to friends and they drink it for a few days, but end up feeling ill . . . people will feel like you don't have their best interests at heart. . . . you must, at the same time, be able to convince people to believe in eco-enzymes, not just as a product to sell.[10]

Jun's account suggests a turn toward private, individual self-cultivation for the preservation of health and environment. Judith Farquhar and Qicheng Zhang documented the *yangsheng* movement of the 1990s which revived the ancient practice of cultivating well-being through mountain walks, calisthenics, and the consumption of nutritious food (Farquhar and Zhang, 2012). The *yangsheng* movement provided a way to "escape without leaving" (22) via the cultivation of body and self within the parameters of what was permitted by the state. In Jun's account, the cultivation of eco-enzymes is distinct both from *yangsheng* and from Chinese traditional medicine (Zhan 2009), and she emphasizes the enzymes' dependence on a community of sympathetic brewers collectively invested in the unknowable outcome and effects of the practice. Members of this community must not only be willing to tolerate the uncertain terms and effects of eco-enzymes but acknowledge and prepare for a gradual process of adaptation that may cause illness.

The brewing of eco-enzymes can be understood in one sense as a form of more-than-human anti-toxic politics. Eco-enzyme brewing, as with anti-incineration protests, not only emerged from a citizen response to a top-down solution for waste management but can be read as a response to a pervasive condition of toxic exposure. In an era where bodies and ecologies are so thoroughly enveloped in chemicals and toxins, scholars have argued that it is no longer possible to contemplate a politics of purity that aims to purge substances of danger from the social body (Douglas 1991). Persistent and ever-present chemical entanglements undermine attempts to manage waste through containment and displacement. Instead, eco-enzymes mobilize the unknown potential of microbes to neutralize and reincorporate waste back into bodies and environments in an act of fortification. A return to "an ideal of uncontaminated body, has become unthinkable practically and politically" (Langwick 2018, 421). Yun Tan did not explain her cultivation of eco-enzymes using the same language, but her practices are in line with feminists' and post-humanist scholars' call for practices that make possible "partial and robust biological-cultural-political-technological recuperation and re-compositions" (Haraway 2015, 160). Microbial advocacy challenges the fortress mentality of guarding bodies from chemicals, germs, and other microorganisms. The material effects of microbes facilitate an experimental approach to determining what constitutes a social and political collective that exceeds the project of environmental governance.

As people cultivate microbial life to work with nature to ensure community and environmental health, they engage in instances of "microbial advocacy," the purposeful cultivation and deployment of microbes as a way to shape the relationship between bodies and environments by enacting ecological change at the smallest scale (see Ford 2019). Waste, once viewed as something to be ejected from communities, is transformed and neutralized through the logic of immunity for the purposes of strengthening community protection. Immunity highlights the process of a continuous exchange between the self and the surrounding environment. In immunity, the outside is absorbed into organisms as a critical strategy for the fortification of life (Esposito 2011, 165). An investment in microbes lays the groundwork for experimenting with novel collectives and recompositions that address an environment of pollution and waste.

A POLITICS OF SCALE: RECONSTITUTING ECOLOGICAL COLLECTIVES

The road to Jun's house follows the urban waterway. Urban water channels are a ubiquitous and visible part of the delta city. Long before this region became a center of China's industrial production, fishing was an important form of livelihood. As the region turned into the world's factory floor, these waterways changed visibly, polluted with pesticides and industrial effluent.

One Sunday morning, I met with Jun to walk the length of the riverway outside her village. Jun wanted to show me the results of years of
dumping eco-enzymes in the water. Jun was an active member of the local
eco-enzyme chat group in QQ[11] and one of the earliest members to join the
online eco-enzyme forum. Unlike the activists in Garden Villa, who were
mostly white-collar workers, Jun lived in a peri-urban village home that she
shared with her parents, husband, and two young children. Jun told me that
she came from a line of fishermen dating back generations. As a child, she
remembered walking barefoot down the same mud path along the riverway.
When Jun first started using eco-enzymes, it was primarily for washing
dishes and for household cleaning. When an online friend told her that in
Taiwan they also use eco-enzymes to clean waterways, Jun immediately
brought her leftover enzyme dregs and poured them in front of her door.
"At the time I didn't think of pouring it on the bottom of the river bed, and
ended up pouring it on the dirt. When I went to look the next day, I realized
that the mud was much cleaner, the dirt and black spots were gone. A few
days after, it was even clearer."

Jun has been pouring the enzyme into the river since 2006. "I didn't
know why before, but since I started making eco-enzyme, I realized that I
was raised by the water and I should also give back." Jun's understanding of
pollution comes from being connected to the river. "When I was little my
mom used to be able to catch fish that weighed over 10 catty (over 10 lbs.),
but now all the fish are the size of a palm; you can't even sell it for money.
We used to talk about how delicious the fish was, but now it tastes of gaso-
line. Once we catch all the fish, what will children eat?"

By deploying eco-enzymes as an agent of remediation, Jun is engaging
in a form of "ethical doing" an act geared toward care and obligation for
future generations (Puig de la Bellacasa 2011). Ethics here is not imagined
as a moral disposition but as mundane acts of monitoring and repairing
ecologies. The slow and methodical application of the formula to the waterway over time highlights how microbes constitute a material substrate,
not only for Jun to articulate a critique of the polluting effects of development. The act of pouring eco-enzymes into the river is also a way for
Jun to reconnect with older historical practices of dwelling with the river.
The question of whether or not eco-enzymes are taking effect remains to
be seen.

By acting with microbes, the significance of Jun's action is to demon-

FIGURE 5.3   The river delta and village by Jun's home, 2013. Photo by author.

strate a turn toward a co-laboring with nature that resists an understanding of environmental remediation as carried out through technoscience. Instead, microbes' uncertain and experimental effect enable an investigation into how humans and nonhumans can be recomposed to practice an ethic of daily care and to reconstitute a connection to local ecologies and histories in a contaminated landscape. In the eco-enzyme project, decomposing waste is an act of transformation as the substance that was once waste is welcomed back into bodies and environments as an agent of remediation. The cultivation of microbes represents a "probiotic turn" and an environmental mode of the biopolitical aimed at the transformation of the body and the local ecology (Lorimer 2017).

The significance of eco-enzyme brewing lies not in its efficacy in combatting pollution, but rather in what is produced out of the "doing," an energy and fervor that prompts brewers to gather (with each other and microbes) in acts of experimental speculation. On the afternoon of January 1, 2014, members of the eco-enzyme collective gathered at the Yingzhou ecological park in front of steps leading down to the riverway. DIYers from all over Guangzhou came with half bottles, buckets, and one-liter containers of solution. Ling had secured permission from the local police to transport eco-enzymes to the river. Participants planned to mark the New Year to collectively expand on Jun's individual efforts to purify the local waterway and, after passing around pamphlets, they proceeded to pour one hundred liters of eco-enzymes into the river.

As eco-enzyme brewers started to organize more publicly, critics began to challenge its proclaimed efficacy. Some in the popular media argued that the effects of the brew were at best exaggerated and at worst a form of magical thinking. Other anti-waste activists were similarly skeptical. They argued that eco-enzyme brewing focused too much on the transformative effects of the enzyme rather than on waste reduction itself. Like the state's agenda of building WTE incinerators, eco-enzyme brewers also rested their hopes for environmental resuscitation narrowly on a singular technology.

ADDICTION

One of my most vivid memories of Green Family comes from one of the first workshops I attended. We watched as Ling turned the cap on a plastic two-liter water bottle with a slight bulge that dissipated with a hiss as the air escaped. Assembled participants talked excitedly about the first time they opened the lid to release the built-up gas. A woman smiled as she recounted a fondness for her daily routine of listening to the familiar hiss as the air escaped whenever she squeezed the bottle to feel how much pressure had built up over the previous day. Her neighbor nodded in agreement and called the process "addictive" (*shangyin*).

Confronted with an ecological crisis, addiction has increasingly been evoked in characterizing social and ecological relations under capitalism. Contemporary societies are addicted to consumption, fossil fuels, and cheap nature (Patel and Moore 2017). The evocation of addiction is purposeful and describes the ways that agency, understood as the free capacity to act, is constrained by a set of material conditions. Addiction emerges from the interaction of people and things (Povinelli 2011, 124). To be addicted, however, is not passive habituation. Addiction describes a proclivity or a will to act, an impulse to pursue a path of action or an outcome that becomes difficult to rein in. A shift away from collective ecological crisis might depend on the cultivation of new addictions. The energy that emerges from acting with microbes generates a force for investing in new types of action.

Toward the end of my fieldwork in August 2013, I met Yun Tan one last time. I waited for her in front of the strip of restaurants, fruit markets, and convenience stores toward the front entrance of Garden Villa. Over the previous few months, the production of eco-enzyme had scaled up. The workshop participants found that they had quickly used up their own household kitchen scraps. Yun Tan turned to gathering additional scraps and fruit peels from the neighborhood juice stand.

It was a typical weekday afternoon. I watched the once quiet suburban complex grow increasingly crowded with a stream of commuters arriving in buses delivering them home from the center of the city. In the late August heat, they marched from the bus depot one by one. Yun Tan might have blended in were it not for the giant bags of fruit peels she was trying to balance, the weight of the plastic bags dragging her down as we wrapped up our round of organic waste collection from fruit stands and restaurants. She looked at the crowd and turned to me and laughed. She told me that she used to come home from work and surf the web to relax. Now, all of her free time has been committed to hauling waste from fruit stands, her hands often sore the next morning from chopping up vegetables.

Perhaps this is what Yun Tan is referring to when she used the word *addiction*. Her anti-waste activism had created not only a practice of care for waste, but in doing so, ensconced her in habits and conditions that she found increasingly difficult to extricate herself from. Yun Tan told me that what drove her was the idea that each bag of organic waste that she processed was kept out of landfills. Yun Tan's actions suggest that the solution to consumption requires not only that we wean ourselves from some addictions, but that we cultivate new ones.

With the rise of consumer society, a growing waste crisis, and pervasive toxicity, the Chinese state has chosen to invest in centralized solutions, typically technological infrastructure, to address the environmental crisis. Faced with the pace and extent of China's urban waste problem, eco-enzyme's uncertain microbial effects appeared miniscule at best. Yet, as waste activists point out, China's authoritarian approach to environmental governance favors quick-fix solutions at the expense of grassroots experiments and meaningful citizen participation. In this context—of severe environmental decline and authoritarian repression—the scale and energy of eco-enzyme brewing speaks to the will of citizens to redirect their desire to care for the environment toward everyday practice. Brewers invest in an expansion of the scope and form of environmental action, even if the real scale of their work is at the level of microbial transformation.

Eco-enzyme brewing provoked more than just individual actions or small-scale interventions but facilitated a collective experiment in reengagement and the reconstitution of material and labor infrastructures of waste management. The material effects of microbes, particularly their catalytic function, is central to the collective inquiry of how to devise community strategies to move waste politics beyond an opposition to top-down state policies. The cultivation and application of eco-enzymes pushes participants toward a more expansive experiment with the types of actions and collectives that might sustain Guangzhou's urban ecology.

By reconstituting human and nonhuman collectives in acts of cooperation and care for the environment, brewers enact an alternative mode of ecological relation to waste in a more-than-human anti-toxic politics. Brewers' investment in the cultivation of microbes demonstrates a desire among everyday citizens to not only reduce waste but to labor and invest in everyday acts of care and environmental repair. The consequence of their work, environmental transformation, is achieved and sustained not by brewers laboring alone but in close collaboration with the microbes that catalyze the visible effects of change. To take seriously, as the brewers do, the "magical quality" of microbial interactions is to assert the political potential of unknown effects.[12] Against a more muscular definition of what constitutes the political, brewers invest in the space of the unknown and the indeterminate effects of matter in an experimental inquiry. Through the recomposition of mundane everyday matter and practices, of infusing organic waste, sugar, and water with time and human care, brewers transform waste into an agent to fortify the capacity of bodies, homes, and the local ecology, and to forge more-than-human collectives in in a toxic environment.

EPILOGUE
POLITICS AT THE END
OF NATURE

AS I NEARED THE END of my long-term fieldwork in 2013, I interviewed an official from the National Resources Recycling Association, the national association of the recycling industry in China. When I asked him to talk about the future of waste management, he responded by describing three stages in the country's recent history of waste management. From 1990 until 2000, the export of waste from the West to China was the biggest force shaping waste management in China. Over the next twenty years, from the early 2000s to 2020, the country was focused on establishing a modern domestic waste management system. Finally, from 2020 onward, China would emerge as a leader in environmental technology, exporting sustainable waste management technologies and expertise to the world.

At the time, I dismissed his comment as just another ambitious state pronouncement, an established official discourse of planning and explicit goal setting (a common feature of China's approach to development). After wrapping up the fieldwork phase of my research on this book, I continued working on the topic as I completed my PhD, published articles, and began teaching. I have continued to reflect on the scope of transformation implicit in his reply, both in regard to China's pattern of consumption and the state's approach to waste. In the official's periodization, the country would reinvent its relationship to waste in the span of just twenty years. From 2000 to 2020, China would shift from being a dump for the West to a nation of sophisticated consumers and waste producers. Along the way, Chinese officials and engineers would come up with the technology and governance strategies to resolve their own waste crisis and then export the model to the world. Implicit in the official's description was the assumption that development in China would continue to be characterized both by investments in science and technology and by increasing rates of consumption and waste generation. Ten years on, in 2023, some of the official's predictions appear, on the surface, to have become reality. The state's strategy for urban waste, however, has repeatedly been circumscribed or undermined by unanticipated events and historical contingencies.

In 2017 the National Sword policy banned the import of foreign waste and recyclables. In response, waste producers in the West instead began to ship plastics and electronic waste to countries across Southeast Asia and West Africa for processing or simply sent it to landfills closer to home (Harrabin and Edgington 2019). The closure of Chinese ports to waste imports made abundantly clear that even as the world continued to generate millions of tons of plastic waste each day, the West lacked the will and the capacity to manage its own waste and continued to rely on developing countries to absorb and displace pollution. The toxic and contaminating effects of waste treatment and disposal are still displaced and continue to reproduce colonial relations of pollution and harm.

In the last decade, China has built a new generation of waste treatment facilities. In 2021 municipal officials proclaimed that Guangzhou had become the first city in China to abandon landfilling and that the city had the largest WTE incineration capacity in the nation (CCTV 2021). Guangzhou is now home to seven Circular Economy Industrial Parks, large-scale waste processing zones home to incinerators, waste-sorting facilities, and plants to treat organic waste. On the surface, the city seems to have successfully built a system of infrastructures and technologies in support of the vision of a circular mode of waste management. The operation of such facilities, however, continues to pose challenges. A July 2023 article in the *Nanfang Daily* chronicled repeated failures at the Phoenix Comprehensive Waste Processing Facility since it was built in November 2019 and reported that the facility had been all but abandoned by 2022 (*Nanfang Daily* 2023). At the same time, in China and across the globe, disposability, hastened by digital commerce and the popularity of food delivery apps, accelerated the generation of packaging and consumer waste. Public education programs have done little to curtail the persistent flood of waste created by a modern consumer lifestyle. The COVID-19 pandemic reasserted a regime of sanitation and the containment of waste. Whether municipalities will continue to invest in ecological approaches to waste management following the pandemic remains to be seen.

Since 2013, the Chinese state has deepened political control and reshaped the country's social and political landscape with the aid of a new generation of technologies. The Xi Jinping regime has established an increasingly restrictive political climate, cracking down on civil society organizations and online dissent and tightening control over cities. At the end of 2017 and in early 2018, the Beijing government waged a forty-day campaign to raze thousands of "illegal" structures, displacing many migrant workers. China has rolled out a digital tracking system combining geospatial data, personal financial transactions, and the monitoring of private communication. The response to COVID-19 in China made clear that spatial containment, digital tracking, and facial recognition first put in place in China's borderlands are now a prominent feature of urban life.[1] As the world emerged from the global lock-down, the roaring economic growth that China experienced in the first four decades following reform has slowed dramatically. China faces challenges on multiple fronts: shifting geopolitical alliances, the prospect of a new "cold war" with the US, rising unemployment (particularly among recent graduates), spiraling real estate debt and a housing market crash, and a succession of ecological crises (flooding, food insecurity, extreme heat, and drought).

At the same time, investments in science, technology, and infrastructure, once a critical strategy of domestic development, now constitute key aspects of the state's plans to become a global power and green leader. The three-trillion-dollar Belt and Road Initiative (BRI) uses the financing and construction of infrastructure to establish influence in Southeast Asia, Latin America, Africa, and Europe. China was projected to overtake the US as the number one source of research and development investment by 2022 (Ekrem 2020). At home, the state has continued to pursue the creation of ecological cities through investments in urban infrastructures, green spaces, the remediation of urban waterways, and by controlling population through de-densification (Zhao 2020).

In some ways, the controversies and actions taken by citizens described in this book index a moment of political opening that now appears distant.

Guangzhou's experiments with the circular economy nevertheless remain instructive especially as China doubles down on consumption-led urban growth and techno-scientific environmental governance. Citizen politics in Guangzhou did not reduce the production of waste nor did they overturn the state's techno-scientific authoritarian project. Guangzhou's experiments with waste, however, are a reminder that authoritarian ecological governance in China has not been exclusively a project of top-down control. Instead, the ecological project in China is both complicated by and developed in collaboration with diverse actors and alongside political contestations.[2] In Guangzhou, the realization of a modern ecological city was made possible only by a variety of labor practices and daily improvisations. Citizen actions proved capable of articulating an alternative vision for waste's continuous renewal and circulation, and to some extent of altering or reshaping the state's capacity to realize a techno-scientific approach to waste management.

Guangzhou's experiments with the circular economy speak both to how environmental governance has become an important part of what makes a city modern and to the reality that the creation of ecological cities often amplifies rural-urban inequality. Projects of ecological governance and urbanization prioritized an aesthetic of order, catered to the desires of the urban elite, and hastened the displacement of rural lives. The introduction of new infrastructures increasingly displaced rural people's access to land and restricted informal livelihood and labor practices. In Guangzhou, contestations over the transformation of waste point to how the pursuit of ecological projects are intricately tied to the valuation of land and labor, who has a claim to urban space and resources, and who can speak against the state.

In Guangzhou, techno-scientific green development provoked contestations and controversies around the public reception of science and technology. Citizens engaged science and technology to generate new discourses, knowledge practices, and novel alliances suited to an authoritarian context (Anderson 2002; Law and Lin 2017; Kreimer 2022). State-driven techno-scientific environmental governance shaped the distribution of labor and of the impact of techno-scientific innovation on the lives of the poor.[3] Under China's ecological regime, techno-science reconfigured and redistributed the labor of clean-up, maintenance, and ecological remediation.

The techno-scientific governance of waste in Guangzhou demands a consideration of how ecological projects are reshaping land, labor, and livelihood. A sensitivity to and understanding of how environmental projects and techno-science redistribute value and harm is critical to the formation of a more just and sustainable future.

The Guangzhou case is an instructive example of how we might understand experiments with the circular economy not only in China but globally, particularly as technological investments and innovations are increasingly presented as either the ideal mechanism or the only option for dealing with the ecological crises we face. As implemented in China, the circular economy preserved the aggressive growth and consumption that the state valued and forestalled the radical aims of waste movements focused on anti-consumption, degrowth, and the conservation of matter (Hickel 2020; Livingston 2019). Guangzhou's efforts to modernize its waste infrastructure undermined the circular economy's promise to deploy techno-fixes to circumvent the onset of ecological crisis in order to uphold the existing regime of production (Mah 2021). In Guangzhou, neither the promotion of technologies that promised to seamlessly turn waste into energy nor the claim that waste could be effortlessly recirculated back into channels of production slowed or shifted the proliferation of waste. Instead, technologies like WTE incineration displaced pollution, and the promotion of citywide recycling contributed to the illusion of citizen environmental participation while obscuring the political economy of labor.

Given the Chinese state's commitment to a techno-political mode of ecological governance, even at a time when the political climate in China has become increasingly restrictive, Guangzhou's waste politics are a useful way to imagine modes of collaboration and collective action formed alongside China's ecological project. Experiments with the circular economy facilitated new forms of political articulation, livelihood practices, and networks of collaboration. Waste's tendency to proliferate and to persist in a diverse array of forms—as toxic aerosols, scrap commodities, and as fertilizers and cleansers that circulate through the urban ecology—moved distinct communities to action in varied yet interconnected ways. As a matter of shared concern, waste facilitated debates that challenged the premise of China's regime of production and growth and its environmental management. The practices in this book suggest that more sustainable waste practices might emerge out of a deeper *dwelling with* waste, as a simultaneously toxic and potentially life-giving substance woven into every feature of the city and its ecology. Following in the footsteps of sanitation workers, informal collectors, and waste activists, the path toward more sustainable waste practices might lie in carefully attuning the set of relations generated by waste's transformation—a set of temporally emergent, dynamic, and flexible alliances.

Glossary

baihuaqifang, 百花齐放: "let one hundred flowers bloom"

chengguan, 城管: urban management

chengxiang tongchou, 城乡统筹: The Rural-Urban Coordination campaign

chengzhongcun, 城中村: "village in the city," urban village or city enclave

chuyu laji, 厨余垃圾: organic waste or kitchen waste

ci tang, 祠堂: ancestral hall

danwei, 单位: work unit

dayouji, 打游击: "guerrilla" collectors

dixiaohao, diwuran, dipaifang, **gaoxiaolü**; 低消耗，低污染，低排放，高效率: low energy consumption, low emission, low pollution, and high efficiency

"ditan jingji, zhihui chengshi," 低碳经济 智慧城市: "low-carbon economy, knowledge city"

du, 毒: toxicity

feipin, 废品: scrap commodities

fengbishi, 封闭式: enclosed system

fenjian zhongxin/ zhan, 分拣中心/ 站: sorting centers/ stations

gongzheng heli, 公正合理: fair and reasonable

gongxiaoshe, 供销社: Bureau of Supply and Marketing

guojia huanjing baohu ju, 国家环境保护局: State Environmental
   Protection Administration (SEPA)

Guangzhou shi chengshi guanli weiyuanhui (chengguanwei), 广州市城
   市管理委员会 (城管委): Urban Management Committee of Guangzhou
   Municipality (Municipal Urban Management Committee)

Guangzhou shi shirong huanjing weisheng ju, 广州市市容环境卫生局:
   Guangzhou Municipal Bureau for Environment and Hygiene

Guangdong sheng zaisheng ziyuan hangye xiehui, 广东省再生资源行业协
   会: Regenerative Resources Association (RRAG)

**Guangzhou shi chengshi feiqiwu chuli gongzhong zixun jiandu
   weiyuanhui,** 广州市城市废弃物处理公众咨询监督委员会: Guangzhou
   Public Consultation and Supervision Committee for Urban Waste
   Management

hexie shehui, 和谐社会: harmonious society

huanbaojiaosu, 环保酵素: eco-enzyme

huanjing weisheng, 环境卫生: environmental sanitation

huanjing, 环境: environment

huishouwangdian, 回收网点: recycling collection depots

hukou, 户口: household registration system

hunhe laji, 混合垃圾: mixed waste

"jianliang hua, ziyuan hua, wuhai hua," 减量化，资源化，无害化:
   "reduction, resourcification, detoxification"

"jianshe zhihui Guangzhou, ditan Guangzhou, xingfu Guangzhou," 建设
   智慧广州、低碳广州、幸福广州: "Build a smart Guangzhou, low-carbon
   Guangzhou, and a happy Guangzhou"

jiaojing, 交警: traffic police

jiedao banshi chu, 街道办事处: sub-district offices

"jiediqi", 接地气: "work from the ground up"

Jin, 斤: catty (unit of mass)

jisan jiaoyi shichang, 集散交易市场: exchange markets

jiti, 集体: collectives

jiti shengchan, 集体生产: collectivization

ke huishou laji, 可回收垃圾: recyclable waste

laji, 垃圾: garbage

"lajibuluodi," 垃圾不落地: "No waste touches the ground"

laji weicheng, 垃圾围城: waste besieged the city

laobaixing, 老百姓: commoner (everyday citizen)

laoban, 老板: boss

laoxiang, 老乡: migrants from the same region

louba, 楼巴: private bus service to gated complexes

qita laji, 其他垃圾: other waste

shangyin, 上瘾: addictive

shequ jianshe, 社区建设: community and neighborhood governance

shengtai chengshi, 生态城市: ecological city

shihuangzhe / shihuang dajun, 拾荒者/ 拾荒大军: waste pickers/ scavenging team

shoumailao, 收买佬: itinerant buyers

suzhi, 素质: (moral) quality

tamen weijian, 他们违建: building in violation of building codes

weisheng, 卫生: sanitation

"women bu zang, tamen cai zang," 我们不脏，他们才脏: "We're not dirty, they're dirty"

"women gen zhengfu gekongduihua," 我们跟政府隔空对话: "We engaged the government [in a dialogue] across space"

"women yiqian fa zhan de henhao," 我们以前发展的很好: "previous era of good development"

xiandaihua huayuanshi gongchang, 现代化花园式工厂: modern garden- style or an eco-industrial facility

xiaoqu, 小区: (local) community

xiaokang shehui, 小康社会: moderately prosperous society

xinfang / shangfang, 信访/上访: petitioning

xunhuan, ditan, lüse, 循环 低碳 绿色: circularity, low-carbon, greenness

xunhuan jingji, 循环经济: circular economy

yangsheng, 养生: self-cultivation

"yi ge shoumailao, ban ge xiaotou," "一个收买佬， 半个小偷": "Any full-time collector is always part thief"

youhai laji, 有害垃圾: toxic waste

Yue ban yue qiong, 越搬越穷: to loss one's wealth in the process of relocation

zangluancha, 脏乱差: dirt, chao, backwardness (deficiency)

"zhe ge ganjing bu liao," 这个 干净 不了: "There's no way that this can be clean"

zhengfu, 政府: government

Notes

Introduction

1. Phoenix is an alias.

2. Environmental justice movements host "toxic tours" for outsiders to witness and mobilize against the effects of contamination and pollution on local communities (Pezzullo 2009).

3. For a discussion of how states showcase technology and infrastructure see Nye (1994) and Schwenkel (2015).

4. See Guangzhou Municipal Statistics Bureau, Guangzhou Statistical Yearbook, 1986 to 2014.

5. See Pellow (2004) and Little (2014) for accounts of the global offshoring of waste. Minter (2013) and Schulz (2015) provide accounts of the effects of the offshoring of electronic waste to China.

6. See Assa and Doron (2018) and Chalfin (2023).

7. I use *ecological urbanism* to describe top-down imaginaries, programs, and projects for the realization of modern cities on behalf of the Chinese state. Urban political ecology focuses on the sociopolitical processes and contestations that have produced urban ecologies and landscapes.

8. Discard scholars have theorized waste as a symbolic form that facilitates structures of marginalization and that perpetuates capitalist relations of disposability and discard (Douglas 1991; Bauman 2004; Bataille 1991; Gidwani 2011).

9. My use of urban nature and environments encompasses both the production of ecological imaginaries and the physical process of transformation within cities (Gandy 2006; Rademacher and Sivaramakrishnan 2017). See also Angelo 2021; Günel 2019; and Rademacher 2011.

10. While not undertaken explicitly to address climate change, technopolitical interventions on waste in Chinese cities are aligned with efforts to engineer resil-

ience and sustainability using renewable energy and urban design in other contexts (Boyer 2019; Günel 2019; Howe 2019; Lennon 2017; Rademacher 2017).

11. In contrast to earlier scholarship examining ecological degradation caused by modernization projects and development undertaken by the Chinese state (Economy 2004; Mertha 2008; Shapiro 2001; Tilt 2010), recent studies explore how contemporary governance regimes in China center sustainability and ecology (Byrnes 2019; Harrell 2023; Li and Shapiro 2020; Rodenbiker 2023; Yeh 2022; Zee 2022).

12. Ethnographic studies of development frequently distinguish between planning and the realities of implementation (Collier 2011; Mosse 2005; Tsing 2005).

13. Science and technology studies and political ecology scholars have advocated for closer attention to matter and elements. See Papadopoulos, Puig de la Bellacasa, and Myers (2021).

14. Lefebvre (1996) and Harvey (2008) both use the concept of "the right to the city" to refer to collective efforts by citizens to forge social ties, relations to nature, technologies, and aesthetic values in cities outside of engineers, planners, and political elites. I use the word *claims* rather than *rights* as a rights-based approach to urban politics is more suited to Western liberal political contexts. The idea of "claims to the city" similarly encapsulates how waste served as a political vehicle for Chinese urban citizens to explore how to make demands or to engage an authoritarian state.

15. For a discussion on nonhumans and cities, see Barua (2023).

16. Scholars have studied Chinese investments in science and technology from biomedicine to computer hardware (Lindtner 2020; Ong and Chen 2010; Zhang 2023).

17. Since the rise of the anti-waste movement in the West, political movements have coalesced around the offshoring and displacement of waste, lobbying against waste policies, and on imagining radical anti-consumption movements (Pellow 2007; MacBride 2012; Little 2014; Barnard 2016; Giles 2021).

18. The household responsibility system meant that the village collective retained public ownership of land but farming became the responsibility of households.

19. Special economic zones are special manufacturing enclaves with tariff protection. In 1984 China established fourteen additional SEZs in its coastal cities.

20. For examples of the real estate–led mode of development elsewhere see Shatkin (2017), Rabie (2021), and Harms (2016).

21. Per capita income doubled between 1978 and 1990 and increased another 50 percent between 1990 and 1994 (Davis 2000).

22. The Guangzhou Municipal Plan presented a comprehensive and coordinated vision for Guangzhou's urban expansion, redevelopment, and transformation.

23. The names of all interlocutors are pseudonyms.

24. Policymakers in the Netherlands and Germany first used the principles of the circular economy to devise measures for waste prevention and reduction (Mol and Sonnenfeld 2000).

25. In 2002, the first circular economy programs were launched under the State Environmental Protection Administration as pilot programs in industrial parks (McDowall et al. 2017).

26. The circular economy was meant to resolve ecological degradation caused by rapid urbanization and industrialization over the previous thirty years of reform and especially during the era of the Eleventh Five-Year Plan (2006–2010). The CE envisioned environmental action at three scales of actions and interventions. At the micro level, the CE would reform production and targets emissions at the scale of industries or corporations. Next, interfirm production would be coordinated via green supply chain management practices and pollution controls in eco-industrial parks (EIPs) (Yuan et al. 2006). Finally, in "eco-cities" or "eco-provinces," large-scale land developments dedicated to the design of new housing and manufacturing would facilitate resource conservation and clean production (Caprotti 2014).

27. Guangzhou Economic and Trade Commission and Guangzhou Circular Economy and Cleaner Production Association 2013. Guangdong Province also issued its own circular economy law in 2013.

28. Guangzhou jingji maoyi weiyuanhui (Guangzhou Economic and Trade Commission) 2013, 149.

29. Guangzhou jingji maoyi weiyuanhui (Guangzhou Economic and Trade Commission) 2013, 150.

30. The Chinese state has used the centralized management of environmental resources to consolidate state power and control. Li and Shapiro characterize China's twenty-first century environmental governance as a mode of authoritarian environmentalism, a political process in which environmental projects are tools to extend state political control and for the shaping of economic, social, and political life (Li and Shapiro 2020). For a description of the state's deployment of science and technology for environmental management through the Imperialist, Nationalist, and Socialist Periods, see Shapiro (2001), Schmalzer (2016), Seow (2021), and Harrell (2022).

31. Industrial ecologists challenge the vision of the circular economy in biophysical terms. The injection of new materials and energy is necessary in every cycle to overcome the effects of dissipation, to address entropy, losses in quantity (physical material losses, by-products), and the quality (mixing, downgrading) of matter (Cullen 2017; Velis 2018).

32. Wang Jiuliang's photographs also use the concept of waste siege to describe Beijing's waste crisis. See discussion in Landsberger (2019).

33. Actor-network theory holds that science and technology are fields of human and nonhuman material agencies that evolve through networks. A "hybrid collectif" forms when agency and social effects derive not from human intention alone but alongside objects throughout the network (Latour 1987; Callon and Law 1997).

34. In studies of globalization in the 1990s and 2000s, circulation emerged as a key concept to describe forms of flows, spatial arrangements, and political connectivity (Castells 2000; Sassen 2001).

35. Cowen (2014) argues that supply chain capitalism requires an examination of the materiality of circulation in order to secure infrastructures and ensure continuous flows.

36. Durkheim (1995) wrote of how bodies gathered in space during rituals or social occasions produced "energy" and a sense of cohesion. Butler (2018) describes

an assembly as a political gathering or demonstration where bodies come together to voice demands.

37. Mary Douglas (1991) wrote that "where there is dirt, there is system" (44). Cassie Fennell suggested the term "systemic irritant" in feedback on an early draft.

38. Stern (2013) chronicles the rise of environmental courts in China. Fu (2017) characterizes authoritarian rule under the Hu Jintao administration (2003–2013) as "flexible repression" in which the Party or central state handed discretionary control to the local state to experiment and improvise (10–11).

39. By 1989, environmental sanitation (*huangjin weisheng*) combined municipal sanitation with the control of urban environmental pollution in areas ranging from noise control to the measurement and regulation of industrial pollution. Tengxun Web, August 10, 2013, "Environmental Industry: Twelfth Five-Year Plan: Waste Management Brings Historical Opportunities" [Huanbao hangye: 'shierwu' laji chuli yinglai lishi jiyu]. [In Chinese.] https://web.archive.org/web/20130907195908/ http://finance.qq.com/a/20130810/005300.htm.

40. For the Guangzhou Environmental Sanitation Comprehensive Plan I (2000–2010) and II (2010–2020), see Guangzhou shi jianshe weiyuanhui [Guangzhou Municipality Construction Commission] and Guangzhou shirong huanjing weishengju [Guangzhou Municipality Bureau of City Appearance, Environment and Sanitation] (1999), and Guangzhou shi chengshi guanli weiyuanhui [Urban Management Committee of Guangzhou Municipality] (2012).

41. Guangzhou aimed to actualize the goals set out in the Twelfth Five-Year Plan (2011–2015) to transition from landfill to incineration as the primary strategy of waste management. In the Twelfth Five-Year Plan, the state planned to invest around 78 billion RMB (12 billion USD) to build another 218 incinerators across China, up from only 104 in 2010.

42. Data from 2012 fieldnotes.

43. The newly formed Guangzhou Urban Management Committee of Guangzhou Municipality (Municipal Urban Management Committee [Guangzhou shi chengshi guanli weiyuanhui]) was responsible for the implementation of waste management planning including the siting and construction of WTE facilities.

44. Guangzhou shi renmin zhengfu [Guangzhou Municipal Government], 2011.

45. Guangzhou was a center of the Maritime Silk Road. As early as the Tang Dynasty (618–907 AD), Arab traders erected mosques, and the city exported ceramics and porcelain. In the Qing Empire, merchants set sail from the city to carry tea, textiles, and spices abroad. The Treaty of Nanjing (1842) opened Guangzhou as a treaty port. Occupation by the English and French led to the rise of anti-foreign and nationalist movements. Anti-Manchu sentiments eventually paved the way for the Guangzhou Uprising and the Chinese revolution. Guangzhou was the base for Sun-Yat Sen and the Nationalist Party (Kuomintang) in the Nationalist Period (under the official control of the Party from 1928 to 1937). After the Japanese occupation from 1938 to 1945, Communists gained control in 1949. As early as the 1960s, the Chinese Ministry of Foreign Trade experimented with export production in the region (Kelly 2021).

46. The 2012 map was the result of a 2005 redistricting that eliminated Dong-shan and Fangcun and merged them into Yuexiu and Liwan respectively and created the two new districts Nansha and Luogang (KK News 2019).

47. In 2014 Guangzhou's boundaries underwent another round of redistricting that left eight districts in the city center along with three additional suburban districts (*Nanfang Daily* 2014). Redistricting in 2013 and 2014 combined Luogang and Huangpu into an expanded Huangpu district. Chonghua and Zengcheng went from county to district designations. In December 2021, Guangzhou underwent another round of redistricting that yielded the current eleven-district map (Guang-zhou Municipality Web page 2023).

48. I use *infrastructural extension* in contrast to scholarship that highlights how slowly crumbling infrastructures or the sudden disconnection or termination of services such as housing or social services permit citizens to intervene and negotiate with the state (Chu 2014; Fennell 2015).

49. Carse argues that infrastructure highlights the relationship between "infra" or what lies beneath, below, or within structures and that which creates "relationships of depth and hierarchy" (2016, 27).

50. Urban political ecologists have elaborated on the metaphor of circulation particularly in relation to water infrastructures (Gandy 2014; Kaika 2005).

51. Almost all Cantonese interlocutors had excellent if not native command of both Mandarin and Cantonese. In Guangzhou, it is common to have exchanges that switch between Mandarin and Cantonese. More than half of my informants (from middle-class homeowner protesters to informal collectors and sanitation workers) did not speak Cantonese and preferred to communicate in Mandarin. I also conducted brief interviews in Mei Village in Hakka with the help of a research assistant.

52. The environmental justice literature in the US has been particularly interested in the entanglement of race and toxicity (Checker 2005; McGurty 2007; Pellow 2004; Shevory 2007).

Chapter 1

1. "Guerrillas" is also used for a range of informal urban service providers such as delivery drivers, food stall managers, and home repair workers (Guang 2005).

2. Materials redirected for reuse were commonly known as "scraps" (*feipin*) during the Maoist Era. State-run recycling campaigns in the post-reform period preferred to use the term "recyclables" (*huishou laji*).

3. Scholars have argued that waste and waste work have enabled migrants and the urban poor to devise different forms of life to resist the effects of neoliberal urbanization. In her study of informal waste pickers in Rio, Millar (2018) argues that the landfill offers a flexible alternative to the rigid demands of waged labor. Similarly, Doherty (2021) demonstrates that in contemporary Uganda, socially devalued and deemed symbolically polluting waste work enabled "the expression of competing regimes of value and urban belonging" (25).

4. The displacement of rural migrants occurring in China's megacities accompanies other ongoing processes of displacement. For instance, Smith (2021) and

Rodenbiker (2023) document how China's urban-rural coordination campaign and projects of ecological conservation hastened the movement of villagers off of peri-urban or agricultural land and away from agrarian livelihoods.

5. In her analysis of sanitation strikes and participatory waste movements in Senegal, Fredericks (2018) suggests urban waste management is not only a system of technological infrastructures but "vital infrastructures" of labor (Fredericks 2018, 14). In cities of the Global South, "vital infrastructures" such as waste work fill a gap in services delivery amid state disinvestment. At the same time, waste work reveals how neoliberal urban reform allocates precarity by assigning disposability. Informal waste work not only reflects neoliberal disinvestment, the state's withdrawal from public services, and a shift away from permanent work, but highlights how an association with discard renders bodies as disposable, polluted, and dirty and thus the target of improvement.

6. As Goldstein (2021) points out, in China waste was historically governed by two distinct branches of the municipal administration. The Municipal Sanitation Bureau provided services such as waste collection (*laji*), street cleaning, handling human waste, regulating public toilets (*weisheng bu*), and built end-of-life facilities such as landfills and WTE incinerators. In contrast, scrap commodities or recyclables were primarily managed by street peddlers prior to the establishment of the Mao-era recycling system.

7. Goldstein (2021) also argues that the management of the scrap sectors, however, was shaped by periods of state intervention in and retreat from the system. See also Liebman (2019).

8. Throughout the 1980s to the early 2000s, China's rising industrialization occurred at the same time as the process of deindustrialization that has unfolded in Western Nations. In the West, with the decline of social security and the disassociation of labor and social-reproduction, firms shifted production offshore and the growth of the service economy drove the casualization of labor (Weeks 2011; Boltanski, Chiapello, and Elliott 2018).

9. Informal collectors are alternatively known as scavengers, the scavenging army (*shihuang zhe, shihuang dajun*) or itinerant buyers (*shoumailao*).

10. Since the mid-2000s, the "Build a New Socialist Countryside" campaign has promoted the modernization and reform of villages.

11. A number of villages within cities are also undergoing a process of shrinkage and expansion alongside Guangzhou's annexation of neighboring counties. In 2007 Guangzhou had over 138 "village enclaves." In 2018, with the expansion of urban jurisdiction into Panyu, Luogang, and Huangpu, the number of villages within the city increased to 272 as the geographical boundaries of the city were broadened (see *Nanfang Daily* 2018, 9, 18).

12. Chapters 2 and 3 elaborate on the effects of urban reconstruction on the peri-urban edge.

13. In the US, gentrification is often predicated on a form of racial capitalism that relies on discourses of "blight" and naturalizes the need for improvement (Solomon 2019).

14. Writing on an informal waste market in the peripheries of Beijing from 2003 to 2013, Goldstein (2021) notes that continuity of residence and access to land was critical to the growth of the scrap trade and wealth (192).

15. Ecological corridors are a land and wildlife protection method used in conservation. Ecological corridors connect fragmented habitats and aid biodiversity. Urban ecological corridors are a technique of urban planning and design that describe protected natural habitats, green open spaces, or artificially created environments (Peng, Zhao, and Liu 2017).

16. Elyachar (2010) refers to the social infrastructure of channels that facilitate circulation and exchange as "phatic labor."

17. An ordinary three-wheel carts costs around 150 RMB; the modified version costs over 500 RMB in 2012–2013.

18. Tianhe is also being transformed into a mall city. Globalization has perpetuated the standardization of commerce and obliterated local street culture in service of a private public space (Dávila 2016).

19. Ling (2019) describes a similar dynamic with migrant workers who rely on scraps in peri-urban Shanghai.

Chapter 2

1. The start of the project was delayed for two years and Phase II of the Phoenix WTE facility began construction in 2012.

2. In the 1990s and 2000s, development strategy focused on foreign technological imports. Western technological hardware was considered higher quality than domestic technology. However, since then, China has prioritized investments in domestic research and development (Lazonick, Zhou, and Sun 2016; Economy 2018; Lindtner 2020). Veolia, as a foreign firm, conferred a level of legitimacy to China's claims of using state-of-the-art technology in waste management. At the same time, Veolia was increasing their own presence in China where rapid urbanization created a market for environmental technology (Ma 2004).

3. Villagers also recounted a similar transformation during interviews.

4. The concept of a modern garden-style or eco-industrial facility (*xiandaihui huayuanshi gongchang*) borrows from the language of industrial ecology. The idea of a "garden-style" facility references a style of building achieved through aesthetic features that connote the ecological.

5. Fieldnotes, 2012.

6. Village Township Enterprises meant that small and medium-scale workshops sprang up all over villages.

7. "Green grabbing" describes the process by which sustainability is used as justification for the dispossession and appropriation of land, forests, and other forms of nature from local communities for the purposes of facilitating capitalist commodification. Examples include parks, forests, reserves, or farms, especially in food security initiatives, ecotourism, biofuels, biodiversity conservation, and ecosystem services (Fairhead, Leach, and Scoones 2012).

8. Li (2014) advocates for a focus on the specificities of the conjuncture, the par-

ticular ways that a set of elements, processes, and events shape peoples' lives at a particular place and time as a way of tracing capitalism's effects.

9. The survey conducted by villagers reported that from 1993 to 2005, nine people died near the facility but between 2005 and 2009, after the facility was built, there were over forty-two registered deaths from cancer as a result of increased exposure to the emissions of the facility (Fieldnotes 2012).

10. Social surveys and popular epidemiology have long gathered accounts, personal narratives, and sociological data to link social conditions to the environment. Popular epidemiology has served as a powerful tool to reveal the uneven distribution of health and environmental problems and its spatial proximity to industries, toxic dump sites, and waste facilities (Brown 1992).

11. Elsewhere I elaborate on how states rely on organized tours to perform the efficacy of WTE incinerators and their capacity to dematerialize pollution for citizens (Zhang, 2024).

12. See Barlow (2023) for a discussion of a similar problem with burning wet waste in India.

Chapter 3

1. "Being invited to tea" is a euphemism for being taken in for questioning by public security officials.

2. An extension of the traditional political practice of petitioning, ordinary citizens bring their grievances and sit face to face with officials to present their case. Starting in 2009, the Guangzhou city management bureau, in charge of decisions on waste infrastructure, established a monthly reception of cases. Visits to petitioning days were dominated by anti-incineration cases.

3. See Map I.2 in the introduction to this book for Panyu and Huadu Districts.

4. Scholars have increasingly focused on the process of suburbanization as a key driver of urban expansion and development in Asia (Shen and Wu 2016; Wu and Keil 2020).

5. Writing on the toxic politics at Love Canal, Fowlkes and Miller (1987) note that parental conservativism, the unwillingness of parents to tolerate gratuitous risk in their children's environment, tended to elevate their anticipation of risk.

6. In the US, homeownership was historically not only a vehicle for securing a form of family-based autonomy, but an institution connected to concerns with quality of life (Fowlkes and Miller 1987).

7. See Yang and Calhoun (2007), Repnikova (2017), and Lei (2018) for a discussion of the rise of a green public sphere and media activism in China.

8. Fieldnote, June 6, 2012.

9. The anti-incineration movement in the US has successfully stopped and stalled the construction of new WTE incinerators. In 2015, Florida proposed building an WTE incinerator, the first in the US in over fifteen years. See Waste 360 (2022).

10. This is the current site of the Panyu facility.

11. As the experience of Mei villagers demonstrates, more often than not, vil-

lager appeals against harms incurred from industrial facilities are typically ignored or met with violence and repression (Lora-Wainwright 2017).

12. In projects of nation-building or in the contemporary era of globalized science, developing nations often perceive that the "lack" they experience can be remedied through the transfer of science and technology (Greenhalgh 2020).

13. Petitioning is an official channel of citizen appeal to the state in China where ordinary citizens are encouraged to bring their grievances to bypass local governments and appeal to higher level officials. Starting in 2009, the newly formed Guangzhou Municipal Urban Management Committee, in charge of implementing the construction of waste infrastructures, established monthly petitioning days.

14. Fieldnotes 2013.

15. This group was officially named the Guangzhou Public Consultation and Supervision Committee for Urban Waste Management (Guangzhou shi chengshi feiqiwu chuli gongzhong zixun jiandu weiyuanhui).

16. Elsewhere I describe the ways that rational resistance served as the primary strategy of the middle class to distinguish themselves from both villagers and the state (Zhang 2014).

Chapter 4

1. See also Checker (2020).

2. "Suggestions for Accelerating Marketization in the Public Utilities Industry" and "Regulation on Public Utilities Franchising" (Xu and Dou 2021).

3. Interview with an official from the Guangzhou All-China Federation of Trade Unions (ACFTU) (January 25, 2013).

4. In the case of veteran workers, the rise of collective action depended on a shared sense of identity and community cultivated by the old socialist work unit. In the case of a younger proletariat class, the emergence of a new sense of class-based identity emerged at the point of production and in shared living spaces such as dormitories and migrant communities. See also Chan and Ngai (2009).

5. In 2012 and 2013, municipal sanitation strikes in Guangzhou did not spill over to workers in the private waste sector. On the impact of *hukou* on rural migrants see Chan and Zhang (1999) and Peng (2011).

6. The concept of knowledge city (*zihui chengshi*) refers to the creation of the networked city—investments in digital infrastructure to create a seamless connectivity across financial institutions, commerce, transportation, and telecommunication. In 2012, the notion of a knowledge city remained abstract—visible only through subway cards that could also be used at convenience stores and refilled through a bank machine. By the summer of 2018, the contours of the knowledge city were apparent. Smartphones and Alipay had all but replaced cash, restaurant menus replaced with QR codes. By the summer of 2018, citizens could find someone to recycle their goods through local WeChat groups.

7. The slogan "Reduce Reuse Recycle" was coined on Earth Day in 1970 in the US and marks the beginning of associating the recuperation of scraps with sustainabil-

ity and environmental benefit. Shortly thereafter, the cultivation of citizen behavior to recuperate and sort waste would become synonymous with a nascent environmental consciousness. Like tree-planting, anti-littering, and other environmental campaigns, recycling campaigns aimed not only to alter the quality of the urban environment but they sought to reshape urban subjects by concretely connecting citizens to everyday environmental actions in order to forge subjects capable of caring for the environment (Agrawal 2005; MacBride 2012).

8. The other cities are Beijing, Shanghai, Nanjing, Hangzhou, Guilin, Shenzhen, and Xiamen.

9. The Green Community concept was put forth by the National Environmental Bureau in 2001 under the environmental education guidelines and then again in 2004 under the green community guidelines.

10. The recuperation of scraps as commodities constituted a waste commons for the urban poor where communities devised and implemented arrangements to recuperate resources in more or less shared and nonsubtractable ways (Gidwani 2013).

11. Waste pickers in Uruguay characterize landfills as a "mother," a reference to their historical function as a refuge for those excluded from formal work (O'Hare 2019).

12. Representatives from the local resident association (*juwei*) believed residents needed better incentives and suggested that Eco-Canton run a giveaway to convince them to turn up at events to promote recycling. The volunteers observed that residents barely looked at recycling pamphlets before tossing them. Building management, fearing complaints about uninvited solicitors, quickly rejected an alternative plan for volunteers to canvas door to door.

13. Taipei authorities also introduced an economic incentive to promote recycling and introduced legislation mandating that all waste be disposed of in special waste bags. Sorting waste and removing recyclables reduced the volume of discard and cut costs.

14. The experiment took place in early 2014, shortly after I completed my fieldwork.

15. The rudimentary equipment and tools of street cleaning—the wheat-bristled mops and three-wheel carts responsible for hauling waste—remained little changed since the republic and socialist era.

16. Fieldnotes, September 5, 2013.

Chapter 5

1. Eco-enzyme became popular across China after its initial introduction in Taiwan, Thailand, and Malaysia. By 2014 a Chinese eco-enzyme website had over 66,000 registered members; the website was still active as of 2021. See also Lou (2017).

2. Silvia Lindtner (2020) argues that China's economic rise hinges on its transformation into a prototype nation as both scientific institutions and everyday entrepreneurs adopted the spirit of the makers movement in which "the testing and

modeling of a technological alternative . . . was no longer reserved for elites, for scientists, designers, or engineers" (2) but was available to everyone.

3. See Latour (2010), Haraway (2016), and Tsing et al. (2017).

4. Over seven million digesters were built in the countryside primarily to treat animal manure and other agricultural byproducts such as grain husks and stocks. See Li (1984).

5. Municipal governments proposed building biogas digesters next to existing waste management facilities such as WTE incinerators.

6. The black soldier fly project exemplifies the reconfiguration of nature and nonhuman life in service of the capitalist drive to standardize life. See also Blanchette (2020) and Besky and Blanchette (2019).

7. The phrase "let a hundred flowers bloom" (*baihuaqifang*) refers to a Maoist Era campaign that encouraged citizens to openly express their own opinions to the Communist Party. Colloquially, the phrase is used to describe moments of experimentation.

8. Fieldnotes 2013.

9. According to these studies, an eco-enzyme catalyzes the digestion of large organic compounds and can be effective in diluting ammonia nitrogen and phosphorus. There are a limited number of scientific publications that study the effects of eco-enzymes in controlled environments such as gray water treatment plants, but scientific verification of eco-enzymes as a biotechnology is growing. See Nazim and Meera (2013) and Tang and Tong (2011). No scientific study addresses the broad range of effects proclaimed by cultivators.

10. Fieldnotes 2013.

11. QQ is a popular instant chat app in China similar to MSN Messenger.

12. I follow J. K. Gibson-Graham's proposal (2008) to amplify the heterogeneous effects of counterhegemonic practices in scholarly work as a method for imagining alternative economies and political futures.

Epilogue

1. Digital surveillance is a prominent feature of state control in Xinjiang (Byler 2022).

2. Such reminders are particularly important at a moment when there is an increasing tendency to reify the totalizing nature of the authoritarian state and as an increasingly restrictive political climate limits foreign journalists and researchers. At the same time, the eruption of protests across China's major cities that effectively overturned the state's zero-COVID policy in 2022 is evidence of how temporarily emergent collectives in China harbor the power to overturn state policy.

3. For an elaboration of how techno-science entrenches existing class, race, and social inequalities in design and computing, see Amrute (2016) and Irani (2019).

Bibliography

Aga, Aniket. 2021. *Genetically Modified Democracy: Transgenic Crops in Contemporary India*. New Haven and London: Yale University Press.

Agard-Jones, Vanessa. 2013. "Bodies in the System." *Small Axe: A Caribbean Journal of Criticism* 17 (3): 182–92.

Agrawal, Arun. 2005. *Environmentality: Technologies of Government and the Making of Subjects*. Durham, NC, and London: Duke University Press.

Ahmann, Chloe. 2020. "Atmospheric Coalitions: Shifting the Middle in Late Industrial Baltimore." *Engaging Science, Technology and Society* 6: 462–85.

Alaimo, Stacy. 2010. *Bodily Natures: Science, Environment, and the Material Self*. Bloomington: Indiana University Press.

Amrute, Sareeta. 2016. *Encoding Race, Encoding Class: Indian IT Workers in Berlin*. Durham, NC: Duke University Press.

Anagnost, Ana. 2004. "The Corporeal Politics of Quality (Suzhi)." *Public Culture* 16 (2): 189–208.

Anand, Nikhil. 2017. *Hydraulic City: Water and the Infrastructures of Citizenship in Mumbai*. Durham, NC, and London: Duke University Press.

Anderson, Warwick. 2002. "Introduction: Postcolonial Technoscience." Special Issue: Postcolonial Technoscience. *Social Studies of Science* 32 (5/6): 643–658.

Andreas, Joel. 2009. *Rise of the Red Engineers: The Cultural Revolution and the Origins of China*. Stanford, CA: Stanford University Press.

Angelo, Hillary. 2021. *How Green Became Good: Urbanized Nature and the Making of Cities and Citizens*. Chicago: University of Chicago Press.

Auyero, Javier, and Débora Alejandra Swistun. 2009. *Flammable: Environmental Suffering in an Argentine Shantytown*. Oxford and New York: Oxford University Press.

Balayannis, Angeliki. 2020. "Toxic Sights: The Spectacle of Hazardous Waste Removal." *Environment and Planning D: Society and Space* 38 (4): 772–90.

Ballestero, Andrea. 2015. "The Ethics of a Formula: Calculating a Financial-Humanitarian Price for Water." *American Ethnologist* 42 (2): 262–78.

Barlow, Matt. 2023. "Burning Wet Waste: Environmental Particularlity, Material Specificity, and the Universality of Infrastructure." *Asia Pacific Journal of Anthropology* 24 (2): 134–52.

Barnard, Alex V. 2016. *Freegans: Diving into the Wealth of Food Waste in America.* Minneapolis: University of Minnesota Press.

Barua, Mann. 2023. *Lively Cities: Reconfiguring Urban Ecology.* Minneapolis: University of Minnesota Press.

Bataille, George. 1991. *The Accursed Share: An Essay on General Economy.* Translated by Robert Hurley. New York: Zone Books.

Bauman, Zygmunt. 2004. *Wasted Lives: Modernity and Its Outcasts.* Polity.

Bayat, Asef. 2000. "From 'Dangerous Classes' to 'Quiet Rebels': Politics of the Subaltern in the Global South." *International Sociology* 15 (3): 533–57.

Bear, Laura. 2015. *Navigating Austerity: Currents of Debt along a South Asian River.* Stanford, CA: Stanford University Press.

Benanav, Aaron. 2019. "The Origins of Informality: The ILO at the Limit of the Concept of Unemployment." *Journal of Global History* 14 (1): 107–25.

Benezra, Amber. 2023. *Gut Anthro: An Experiment in Thinking with Microbes.* Minneapolis: University of Minnesota Press.

Benezra, Amber, Joseph DeStefano, and Jeffrey I. Gordon. 2012. "Anthropology of Microbes." *Proceedings of the National Academy of Sciences of the United States of America* 109 (17): 6378.

Besky, Sarah, and Alex Blanchette. 2019. *How Nature Works: Rethinking Labor on a Troubled Planet.* Santa Fe: School for Advanced Research Press; Albuquerque: University of New Mexico Press.

Bize, Amiel. 2020. "The Right to the Remainder: Gleaning in the Fuel Economies of East Africa's Northern Corridor." *Cultural Anthropology* 35 (3): 462–86.

Blanchette, Alex. 2020. *Porkopolis: American Animality, Standardized Life, and the Factory Farm.* Durham, NC: Duke University Press.

Boland, Alana, and Jiangang Zhu. 2012. "Public Participation in China's Green Communities: Mobilizing Memories and Structuring Incentives." *Geoforum* 43 (1): 147–57.

Boltanski, Luc, and Ève Chiapello. 2018. *The New Spirit of Capitalism.* Translated by Gregory Elliott. London and New York: Verso.

Bondes, Maria, and Thomas Johnson. 2017. "Beyond Localized Environmental Contention: Horizontal and Vertical Diffusion in a Chinese Anti-Incinerator Campaign." *Journal of Contemporary China* 26 (104): 504–20.

Bosworth, Kai. 2022. *Pipeline Populism: Grassroots Environmentalism in the Twenty-First Century.* Minneapolis: University of Minnesota Press.

Boyer, Dominic. 2019. *Energopolitics: Wind and Power in the Anthropocene.* Durham and London: Duke University Press.

Bray, David. 2005. *Social Space and Governance in Urban China: The Danwei System from Origins to Reform*. Stanford, CA: Stanford University Press.

Brown, Phil. 1992. "Popular Epidemiology and Toxic Waste Contamination: Lay and Professional Ways of Knowing." *Journal of Health and Social Behavior* 33 (3): 267–81.

Butler, Judith. 2018. *Notes toward a Performative Theory of Assembly*. Cambridge, MA: Harvard University Press.

Butt, Waqas. 2023. *Life beyond Waste: Work and Infrastructure in Urban Pakistan*. Stanford, CA: Stanford University Press.

Byler, Darren. 2022. *Terror Capitalism: Uyghur Dispossession and Masculinity in a Chinese City*. Durham, NC: Duke University Press.

Byrnes, Corey. 2019. *Fixing Landscape: A Techno-Poetic History of China's Three Gorges*. New York: Columbia University Press.

Caldeira, Teresa Pires do Rio. 2000. *City of Walls: Crime, Segregation, and Citizenship in São Paulo*. Berkeley: University of California Press.

Callison, Candis. 2014. *How Climate Change Comes to Matter: The Communal Life of Facts*. Durham and London: Duke University Press.

Callon, Michel, and John Law. 1997. "Agency and the Hybrid Collectif." In *Mathematics, Science, and Postclassical Theory*, 95–117. Durham, NC: Duke University Press.

Calvillo, Nerea. 2018. "Political Airs: From Monitoring to Attuned Sensing Air Pollution." *Social Studies of Science* 48 (3): 372–88.

Calvino, Italo. 1997. *Invisible Cities*. London: Vintage.

Caprotti, Federico. 2014. "Critical Research on Eco-Cities? A Walk through the Sino-Singapore Tianjin Eco-City, China." *Cities* 36 (February): 10–17.

Carse, Ashley. 2014. *Beyond the Big Ditch*. Cambridge and London: MIT Press.

———. 2016. "Keyword: Infrastructure: How a Humble French Engineering Term Shaped the Modern World." In *Infrastructure and Social Complexity*, edited by Penelope Harvey, Casper Bruun Jensen, and Atsuro Morita, 45–57. Abingdon, Oxon, and New York: Routledge.

Castellini, Valentina. 2019. "Environmentalism Put to Work: Ideologies of Green Recruitment in Toronto." *Geoforum* 104 (August): 63–70.

Castells, Manuel. 2000. *The Rise of the Network Society*. Malden, MA: Wiley-Blackwell.

CCTV. 2021. "Guangzhou shixian yuansheng shenghuo laji lingtianmai, zhuli Dagangqu lüse ditan fazhan" [Guangzhou achieves zero-landfilling of municipal waste, helps Dagang district's green, low-carbon development]. [In Chinese.] September 23, 2021. http://m.news.cctv.com/2021/09/24/ARTIyKweE48VpFQ17z uIdkH9210924.shtml.

Chalfin, Brenda. 2023. *Waste Works: Vital Politics in Urban Ghana*. Durham, NC: Duke University Press.

Chan, Chris King-Chi, and Pun Ngai. 2009. "The Making of a New Working Class? A Study of Collective Actions of Migrant Workers in South China." *China Quarterly* (198), 287–303.

Chan, Kam Wing. 2007. "Misconceptions and Complexities in the Study of China's

Cities: Definitions, Statistics, and Implications. Eurasian Geography and Economics." *Eurasian Geography and Economics* 48: 382–412.

Chan, Kam Wing, and Li Zhang. 1999. "The Hukou System and Rural-Urban Migration in China: Processes and Changes." *China Quarterly* 160: 818–55.

Checker, Melissa. 2005. *Polluted Promises: Environmental Racism and the Search for Justice in a Southern Town.* New York: New York University Press.

———. 2020. *The Sustainability Myth: Environmental Gentrification and the Politics of Justice.* New York: New York University Press.

Chen, Angela. 2018. "China Generates More Waste Than Any Other Country. How Does It Deal with It?" World Economic Forum. 2018. https://www.weforum.org/agenda/2018/12/no-chopsticks-with-my-takeaway-how-china-is-tackling-food-waste-with-digital-innovation/.

Chen, Fu. 1981. *Chen Fu Agricultural Book* 陈旉农书. Beijing: Nongye Chubanshe 农业出版.

Chen, Jia-Ching. 2013. "Sustainable Territories: Rural Dispossession, Land Enclosures and the Construction of Environmental Resources in China." *Human Geography* 6 (1): 102–25.

Chen, Xi. 2012. *Social Protest and Contentious Authoritarianism in China.* Cambridge: Cambridge University Press.

Chi, C. 2008. "Ban Renmin Manyi de Dahuanwei" [Providing satisfactory sanitation services.] *Chengshi Guanli Yu Keji* [Urban management and technology.] [In Chinese.] 1: 70–74.

Choy, Timothy. 2011. *Ecologies of Comparison: An Ethnography of Endangerment in Hong Kong.* Durham, NC: Duke University Press.

Choy, Timothy, and Jerry Zee. 2015. "Condition—Suspension." *Cultural Anthropology* 30 (2): 210–23.

Chu, Julie Y. 2014. "When Infrastructures Attack: The Workings of Disrepair in China." *American Ethnologist* 41 (2): 351–67.

Chu, Nellie, Ralph A. Litzinger, Mengqi Wang, and Qian Zhu. 2022. "Guest Editors' Introduction: The Urban In-Between." *Positions: East Asia Cultures Critique* 30 (3): 411–27.

Chuang, Julia. 2020. *Beneath the China Boom: Labor, Citizenship, and the Making of a Rural Land Market.* Oakland: University of California Press.

Cody, Francis. 2011. "Publics and Politics." *Annual Review of Anthropology* 40 (September): 37–52.

Collier, Stephen. 2011. *Post-Soviet Social: Neoliberalism, Social Modernity, Biopolitics.* Princeton, NJ: Princeton University Press.

Corson, Catherine, and Kenneth Iain MacDonald. 2012. "Enclosing the Global Commons: The Convention on Biological Diversity and Green Grabbing." *Journal of Peasant Studies* 39 (2): 263–83.

Cowen, Deborah. 2014. *The Deadly Life of Logistics: Mapping Violence in Global Trade.* Minneapolis: University of Minnesota Press.

Cullen, Jonathan M. 2017. "Circular Economy: Theoretical Benchmark or Perpetual Motion Machine?" *Journal of Industrial Ecology* 21 (3): 483–86.

Davies, Thom. 2022. "Slow Violence and Toxic Geographies: 'Out of Sight' to Whom?" *Environment and Planning C: Politics and Space* 40 (2): 409–27.

Dávila, Arlene. 2016. *El Mall: The Spatial and Class Politics of Shopping Malls in Latin America*. Oakland: University of California Press.

Davis, Deborah. 2000. *The Consumer Revolution in Urban China*. Berkeley: University of California Press.

Davis, Heather. 2022. *Plastic Matter*. Durham, NC: Duke University Press.

Davis Jackson, Deborah. 2011. "Scents of Place: The Dysplacement of a First Nations Community in Canada." *American Anthropologist* 113 (4): 608–18.

Degani, Michael. 2022. *The City Electric: Infrastructure and Ingenuity in Postsocialist Tanzania*. Durham, NC: Duke University Press.

Dewey, John. 2016. *The Public and Its Problems: An Essay in Political Inquiry*. Athens, OH: Swallow Press.

Doherty, Jacob. 2021. *Waste Worlds: Inhabiting Kampala's Infrastructures of Disposability*. Oakland: University of California Press.

Doron, Assa, and Robin Jeffrey. 2018. *Waste of a Nation: Garbage and Growth in India*. Cambridge, MA: Harvard University Press.

Douglas, Mary. 1991. *Purity and Danger*. London and New York: Routledge.

Duara, Prasenjit. 1991. "Knowledge and Power in the Discourse of Modernity: The Campaigns Against Popular Religion in Early Twentieth-Century China." *Journal of Asian Studies* 50 (1): 67–83.

Durkheim, Émile. 1995. *The Elementary Forms of Religious Life*. Translated by Karen E. Fields. New York: The Free Press.

Economy, Elizabeth C. 2004. *The River Runs Black: The Environmental Challenge to China's Future*. Ithaca, NY: Cornell University Press.

———. 2018. *The Third Revolution: Xi Jinping and the New Chinese State*. New York: Oxford University Press.

Ekrem, Janni. 2020. "China's Historic Rise in Science and Technology Stir Criticism." Science Business, April 6, 2020. https://sciencebusiness.net/international -news/chinas-historic-rise-science-and-tech-stirs-criticism.

Elyachar, Julia. 2010. "Phatic Labor, Infrastructure, and the Question of Empowerment in Cairo." *American Ethnologist* 37 (3): 452–64.

Esposito, Roberto. 2008. *Bíos: Biopolitics and Philosophy*. Translated by Timothy C. Campbell. Minneapolis: University of Minnesota Press.

Esposito, Roberto. 2011. *Immunitas: The Protection and Negation of Life*. Translated by Zakiya Hanafi. Cambridge, Malden, MA: Polity Press.

Ezrahi, Yaron. 2012. *Imagined Democracies: Necessary Political Fictions*. New York: Cambridge University Press.

Fairhead, James, Melissa Leach, and Ian Scoones. 2012. "Green Grabbing: A New Appropriation of Nature?" *Journal of Peasant Studies* 39 (2): 237–61.

Farquhar, Judith, and Qicheng Zhang. 2012. *Ten Thousand Things: Nurturing Life in Contemporary Beijing*. New York: Zone Books.

Fennell, Catherine. 2015. *Last Project Standing: Civics and Sympathy in Post-Welfare Chicago*. Minneapolis: University of Minnesota Press.

Ferguson, James. 1994. *The Anti-Politics Machine: "Development," Depoliticization, and Bureaucratic Power in Lesotho*. Minneapolis and London: University of Minnesota Press.

Fitzpatrick, Sheila. 2005. *Tear Off the Masks: Identity and Imposture in Twentieth-Century Russia*. Princeton, NJ: Princeton University Press.

Ford, Andrea. 2019. "Introduction: Embodied Ecologies." Cultural Anthropology Fieldsights. https://culanth.org/fieldsights/introduction-embodied-ecologies.

Forment, Carlos A. 2018. "Trashing Violence/Recycling Civility: Buenos Aires' Scavengers and Everyday Forms of Democracy in the Wake of Neoliberalism." *Anthropological Theory* 18 (2–3): 409–31.

Fortun, Kim. 2001. *Advocacy after Bhopal: Environmentalism, Disaster, New Global Orders*. Chicago: University of Chicago Press.

———. 2014. "From Latour to Late Industrialism." *HAU: Journal of Ethnographic Theory* 4 (1): 309–29.

Foucault, Michel. 1997. "Society Must Be Defended." In *Lectures at the Collège de France, 1975–76*. Edited by Mauro Bertani and Alessandro Fontana. Translated by David Macey. New York: Picador.

Fournier, Lauren. 2020. "Fermenting Feminism as Methodology and Metaphor: Approaching Transnational Feminist Practices through Microbial Transformation." *Environmental Humanities* 12 (1): 88–112.

Fowlkes, Martha R., and Patricia Y. Miller. 1987. "Chemicals and Community at Love Canal." In *The Social and Cultural Construction of Risk*. Vol. 3, *Technology, Risk and Society*, edited by B. B. Johnson and V. T. Covello, 55–78. New York: Springer.

Fredericks, Rosalind. 2018. *Garbage Citizenship: Vital Infrastructures of Labor in Dakar, Senegal*. Durham, NC, and London: Duke University Press.

———. 2021. "Anthropocenic Discards: Embodied Infrastructures and Uncanny Exposures at Dakar's Dump." *Antipode* (December 2021).

Friedman, Eli. 2022. *The Urbanization of People: The Politics of Development, Labor Markets, and Schooling in the Chinese City*. New York: Columbia University Press.

Frosch, R. A., and N. E. Gallopoulos. 1989. "Strategies for Manufacturing." *Scientific American* 261 (3): 144–52.

Fu, Diane. 2017. *Mobilizing without the Masses: Control and Contention in China*. Cambridge: Cambridge University Press.

Gamble, Sidney. 1921. *Peking: A Social Survey*. New York: George H. Doran Company.

Gandy, Matthew. 2006. "Urban Nature and the Ecological Imaginary." In *In the Nature of Cities: Urban Political Ecology and the Politics of Urban Metabolism*, edited by Nikolas C. Heynen, Maria Kaika, and Erik Swyngedouw, 62–72. London: New York: Routledge.

———. 2014. *The Fabric of Space: Water, Modernity, and the Urban Imagination*. Cambridge and London: MIT Press.

Gaubatz, Piper. 1999. "China's Urban Transformation: Patterns and Processes of Morphological Change in Beijing, Shanghai and Guangzhou." *Urban Studies* 36 (9): 1495–1521.

Ghertner, D. Asher. 2015. *Rule by Aesthetics: World-Class City Making in Delhi*. New York: Oxford University Press.

Gibson-Graham, J. K. 2008. "Diverse Economies: Performative Practices for Other Worlds." *Progress in Human Geography* 32 (5): 613.

Gidwani, Vinay. 2013. "Value Struggles: Waste Work and Urban Ecology in Delhi." In *Ecologies of Urbanism in India: Metropolitan Civility and Sustainability*, edited by Anne M. Rademacher and K. Sivaramakrishnan, 169–200. Hong Kong: Hong Kong University Press.

Gidwani, Vinay, and Amita Baviskar. 2011. "Urban Commons." *Economic and Political Weekly* 46 (50): 42–43.

Gidwani, Vinay, and Anant Maringanti. 2016. "The Waste-Value Dialectic: Lumpen Urbanization in Contemporary India." *Comparative Studies of South Asia, Africa and the Middle East* 36 (1): 112–33.

Gidwani, Vinay, and Rajyashree N. Reddy. 2011. "The Afterlives of 'Waste': Notes from India for a Minor History of Capitalist Surplus." *Antipode* 43 (5): 1625–58.

Giles, David Boarder. 2021. *A Mass Conspiracy to Feed People: Food Not Bombs and the World-Class Waste of Global Cities*. Durham, NC: Duke University Press.

Gille, Zsuzsa. 2007. *From the Cult of Waste to the Trash Heap of History: The Politics of Waste in Socialist and Postsocialist Hungary*. Bloomington and Indianapolis: Indiana University Press.

———. 2010. "Actor Networks, Modes of Production, and Waste Regimes: Reassembling the Macro-Social." *Environment and Planning A* 42 (5): 1049–64.

Gillespie, Tom. 2016. "Accumulation by Urban Dispossession: Struggles over Urban Space in Accra, Ghana." *Transactions of the Institute of British Geographers* 41 (1): 66–77.

Goh, Kian. 2021. *Form and Flow: The Spatial Politics of Urban Resilience and Climate Justice*. Cambridge, MA: MIT Press.

Goldstein, Jesse. 2018. *Planetary Improvement: Cleantech Entrepreneurship and the Contradictions of Green Capitalism*. Cambridge, MA: MIT Press.

Goldstein, Joshua. 2021. *Remains of the Everyday: A Century of Recycling in Beijing*. Oakland: University of California Press.

Graeber, David. 2001. *Toward an Anthropological Theory of Value: The False Coin of Our Own Dreams*. New York: Palgrave.

Greenhalgh, Susan. 2020. "Introduction: Governing through Science: The Anthropology of Science and Technology in Contemporary China." In *Can Science and Technology Save China?*, edited by Susan Greenhalgh and Zhang Li, 1–24. Ithaca, NY, and London: Cornell University Press.

Gregson, Nicky, A. Metcalfe, and L. Crewe. 2007. "Moving Things Along: The Conduits and Practices of Divestment in Consumption." *Transactions of the Institute of British Geographers* 32 (2): 187–200.

Guang, Lei. 2005. "Guerilla Workfare: Migrant Renovators, State Power, and Informal Work in Urban China." *Politics & Society* 33 (3): 481–506.

Guangzhou jingji maoyi weiyuanhui [Guangzhou Economic and Trade Commission] and Guangzhou shi xunhuan jingji he qingjie shengchan xiehui [Guangzhou Circular Economy and Cleaner Production Association]. 2013. "Guangzhou shi xunhuan jingji fazhan guihua 2012–2020" [Guangzhou circular economy development plan]. In *Guangzhou shi xunhuan jingji duben* [Guangzhou circular economy reader]. [In Chinese.], 145–227.

Guangzhou Municipal Statistics Bureau (GSB). 1986-2014. Guangzhou zongji nianjian. Guangzhou Statistical Yearbook. 1986-2014. China Statistics Press, Beijing [In Chinese].

Guangzhou Municipality Webpage. 2023. "Governing Districts" [xingzhenquyu]. [In Chinese.] February 8, 2023. https://www.gz.gov.cn/zlgz/gzgk/xzqy/index.html.

Guangzhou shi chengshi guanli weiyuanhui [Urban Management Committee of Guangzhou Municipality]. 2012. "Guangzhou shi huanjing weisheng zongti guihua 2010–2020." [Guangzhou environmental sanitation comprehensive plan 2010–2020]. [In Chinese].

Guangzhou shi jianshe weiyuanhui [Guangzhou Municipality Construction Commission] and Guangzhou shirong huanjing weishengju [Guangzhou Municipality Bureau of City Appearance, Environment and Sanitation]. 1999. "Guangzhou shi huanjing weisheng zongti guihua" [Guangzhou environmental sanitation comprehensive plan]. [In Chinese]. Zhongguo huanjing kexue chubanshe.

Guangzhou shi renmin zhengfu [Guangzhou Municipal Government]. 2011. "Guangzhou shi chengshi shenghuo laji fenlei guangli zanxing guiding [Guangzhou municipal waste sorting provisional regulations]. In *Guangzhou Shi Xunhuan Jingji Duben* [Guangzhou circular economy reader]. [In Chinese]: 233–39.

Guangzhou shi renmin zhengfu [Guangzhou Municipal Government]. 2012. "Guangzhou shi zongti guihua 2011–2020 [Guangzhou municipal plan 2011–2020].

Guangzhou zaisheng ziyuan hangye xiehui [Guangzhou Resources Industry Association]. 2006. "Zaisheng ziyuan huishou liyong yewu zhishi" [Renewable resource recycling and reuse practical knowledge]. [In Chinese.]

Günel, Gökçe. 2019. *Spaceship in the Desert: Energy, Climate Change, and Urban Design in Abu Dhabi*. Durham, NC: Duke University Press.

Haraway, Donna. 2015. "Anthropocene, Capitalocene, Plantationocene, Chthulucene: Making Kin." *Environmental Humanities* 6 (1): 159–65.

Haraway, Donna J. 2016. *Staying with the Trouble: Making Kin in the Chthulucene*. Durham, NC, and London: Duke University Press.

Harms, Erik. 2016. *Luxury and Rubble: Civility and Dispossession in the New Saigon*. Oakland: University of California Press.

Harrabin, Roger, and Tom Edgington. 2019. "Recycling: Where Is the Plastic Waste Mountain?" BBC Reality Check, January 1, 2019. https://www.bbc.com/news/science-environment-46566795.

Harrell, Stevan. 2022. "Prometheus Brings Water: Development and Fix-Fixing in China." *Made in China Journal* 7 (2): 108–15.

———. 2023. *An Ecological History of Modern China*. Seattle: University of Washington Press.

Hart, Keith. 1973. "Informal Income Opportunities and Urban Employment in Ghana." *Journal of Modern African Studies* 11 (01): 61–89.

Harvey, David. 1997. *Justice, Nature and the Geography of Difference*. Cambridge, MA: Wiley-Blackwell.

———. 2005. *A Brief History of Neoliberalism*. Oxford and New York: Oxford University Press.

———. 2008. "The Right to the City." *New Left Review* 53, September to October: 1–16.

Hathaway, Michael J. 2013. *Environmental Winds: Making the Global in Southwest China*. Berkeley: University of California Press.

He, Baogang, and Mark E. Warren. 2011. "Authoritarian Deliberation: The Deliberative Turn in Chinese Political Development." *Perspectives on Politics* 9 (2): 269–89.

Hébert, Karen. 2016. "Chronicle of a Disaster Foretold: Scientific Risk Assessment, Public Participation, and the Politics of Imperilment in Bristol Bay, Alaska." *Journal of the Royal Anthropological Institute* 22 (S1): 108–26.

Hess, David. 2016. *Undone Science: Social Movements, Mobilized Publics and Industrial Transitions*. Cambridge, MA: MIT Press.

Hickel, Jason. 2020. *Less Is More: How Degrowth Will Save the World*. London: Penguin Random House.

Howe, Cymene. 2019. *Ecologics: Wind and Power in the Anthropocene*. Durham and London: Duke University Press.

Hsing, You-Tien. 2010. *The Great Urban Transformation: Politics of Land and Property in China*. Oxford and New York: Oxford University Press.

Hsu, Shu-Hsiang. 2006. "NIMBY Opposition and Solid Waste Incinerator Siting in Democratizing Taiwan." *Social Science Journal* 43(3): 453–59.

Huang, Gengzhi, Desheng Xue, and Zhigang Li. 2014. "From Revanchism to Ambivalence: The Changing Politics of Street Vending in Guangzhou." *Antipode* 46 (1): 170–89.

Huang, Shaohong. 2013. "'Datianshan Project Halted for Adjustments." [In Chinese.] *Nanfang Daily* October 28, 2013. http://gz.fzg360.com/news/201310/466265_1.html.

Huang, Yanzhong. 2020. *Toxic Politics: China's Environmental Health Crisis and Its Challenge to the Chinese State*. Cambridge: Cambridge University Press.

Irani, Lilly. 2019. *Chasing Innovation: Making Entrepreneurial Citizens in Modern India*. Princeton and Oxford: Princeton University Press.

Irwin, Alan. 1995. *Citizen Science: A Study of People, Expertise, and Sustainable Development*. London and New York: Routledge.

Jasanoff, Sheila, ed. 2004. *States of Knowledge: The Co-Production of Science and the Social Order*. New York: Routledge.

Jasarevic, Larisa. 2015. "The Thing in a Jar: Mushrooms and Ontological Speculations in Post-Yugoslavia." *Cultural Anthropology* 30 (1). 36–64.

Kaika, Maria. 2005. *City of Flows: Modernity, Nature, and the City*. New York: Routledge.

Katz, Sandor Ellix. 2008. *Wild Fermentation: The Flavor, Nutrition, and Craft of Live-Culture Foods*. Chelsea Green Publishing.

Kelly, Jason M. 2021. *Market Maoists: The Communist Origins of China's Capitalist Ascent*. Cambridge and London: Harvard University Press.

Kimura, Aya Hirata. 2016. *Radiation Brain Moms and Citizen Scientists*. Durham, NC: Duke University Press.

King, F. H. 1927. *Farmers of Forty Centuries: Organic Farming in China, Korea, and Japan*. New York: Harcourt, Brace & Company.

Kipnis, Andrew. 2007. "Neoliberalism Reified: Suzhi Discourse and Tropes of Neoliberalism in the People's Republic of China." *Journal of the Royal Anthropological Institute* 13 (2): 383–400.

Kirksey Eben, and Sophie Chao. 2022. "Introduction: Who Benefits from Multispecies Justice?" In *The Promise of Multispecies Justice*, edited by Sophie Chao, Karin Bolender, and Eben Kirksey. Durham and London: Duke University Press.

KK News. 2019. "Guangzhou xingzhenqu guigaigeshi, jin 30 niande jiuci datiaozhen" [Guangzhou political district reform history: Nine reforms over the last thirty years (1985–2014)]. [In Chinese.] January 14, 2019. https://kknews.cc/news/4nbnja3.html.

Kreimer, Pablo. 2022. "Constructivist Paradoxes Part 1: Critical Thoughts about Provincializing, Globalizing, and Localizing STS from a Non-Hegemonic Perspective." *Engaging Science, Technology, and Society* 8 (2): 159–75.

Krupar, Shiloh. 2013. *Hot Spotter's Report: Military Fables of Toxic Waste*. Minneapolis: University of Minnesota Press.

Lam, Tong. 2011. *A Passion for Facts: Social Surveys and the Construction of the Chinese Nation-State, 1900–1949*. Berkeley: University of California Press.

Lamoreaux, Janelle. 2019. "'Swimming in Poison': Reimagining Endocrine Disruption through China's Environmental Hormones." *Cross Current: East Asian History and Culture Review* (e-journal) 8 (1): 195–223. https://muse.jhu.edu/article/727335.

Landsberger, Stefan. 2019. *Beijing Garbage: A City Besieged by Waste*. Amsterdam: Amsterdam University Press.

Langwick, Stacey Ann. 2018. "A Politics of Habitability: Plants, Healing, and Sovereignty in a Toxic World." *Cultural Anthropology* 33 (3): 415–43.

Lardy, Nicholas. 2016. "China: Toward a Consumption-Driven Growth Path." In *Seeking Changes: The Economic Development in Contemporary China*, edited by Yanhui Zhou, 85–111. Central Compilation and Translation Bureau, China.

Larkin, Brian. 2008. *Signal and Noise: Media, Infrastructure, and Urban Culture in Nigeria*. Durham, NC: Duke University Press.

Latour, Bruno. 1987. *Science in Action*. Cambridge, MA: Harvard University Press.

———. 1988. *The Pasteurization of France*. Translated by Alan Sheridan and John Law. Cambridge and London: Harvard University Press.

———. 2005. *Reassembling the Social: An Introduction to Actor-Network-Theory*. Oxford; New York: Oxford University Press.

———. 2010. "An Attempt at a 'Compositionist Manifesto.'" *New Literary History* 41 (3): 471–90.

Law, John, and Wen-yuan Lin. 2017. "Provincializing STS: Postcoloniality, Symmetry, and Method." *East Asian Science, Technology and Society: An International Journal* 11 (2): 211–27.

Lawhon, Mary, David Nilsson, Jonathan Silver, Henrik Ernstson, and Shuaib Lwasa. 2017. "Thinking through Heterogeneous Infrastructure Configurations." *Urban Studies* 55 (4): 720–32.

Lazonick, William, Yu Zhou, and Yifei Sun. 2016. "Introduction: China's Transformation to an Innovation Nation." In *China as an Innovation Nation*, edited by Yu Zhou, William Lazonick, and Yifei Sun, 1–32. Oxford and New York: Oxford University Press.

Lee, Ching Kwan. 2007. *Against the Law: Labor Protests in China's Rustbelt and Sunbelt*. Berkeley and Los Angeles: University of California Press.

Lefebvre, Henri. 1996. "The Right to the City." In *Writings on Cities*, edited by Eleanore Kofman and Elizabeth Lebas. Cambridge, MA: Wiley-Blackwell.

Lei, Ya-Wen. 2018. *The Contentious Public Sphere: Law, Media, and Authoritarian Rule in China*. Princeton, NJ: Princeton University Press.

Lennon, Myles. 2017. "Decolonizing Energy: Black Lives Matter and Technoscientific Expertise amid Solar Transitions." *Energy Research & Social Science* 30: 18–27.

Li, Jiawen. 2012. "Likeng Laji Fenshao Chang 850 C Gao Wendu Shaoburong Suliaodai" [Likeng WTE incineration plant can't burn plastic at 850 degrees celsius?]. [In Chinese.] *Xinhua News*, 2012. Accessed September 23, 2016. http://epaper .xkb.com.cn/view/808649.

Li, Nianguo. 1984. "Biogas in China." *Trends in Biotechnology* 2 (3): 77–79.

Li, Tania Murray. 2014. *Land's End: Capitalist Relations on an Indigenous Frontier*. Durham, NC, and London: Duke University Press.

Li, Yifei, and Judith Shapiro. 2020. *China Goes Green: Coercive Environmentalism for a Troubled Planet*. Cambridge and Medford: Polity Press.

Li, Zhigang, Yanyan Chen, and Rong Wu. 2020. "The Assemblage and Making of Suburbs in Post-reform China: The Case of Guangzhou." *Urban Geography* 41 (7) 990–1009.

Liboiron, Max. 2021. *Pollution Is Colonialism*. Durham, NC: Duke University Press.

Liboiron, Max, and Josh Lepawsky. 2022. *Discard Studies: Wasting, Systems, and Power*. Cambridge and London: MIT Press.

Liebman, Adam. 2019. "Reconfiguring Chinese Natures: Frugality and Waste Reutilization in Mao Era Urban China." *Critical Asian Studies* 51 (4): 537–57.

Lin, George C. S. 2016. "Reproducing Spaces of Chinese Urbanisation: New City-Based and Land-Centred Urban Transformation." *Urban Studies* 44 (9): 1827–55.

Lin, George C. S., and Shih-Yang Kao. 2019. "Contesting Eco-Urbanism from Below: The Construction of 'Zero-Waste Neighborhoods' in Chinese Cities." *International Journal of Urban and Regional Research* 44 (1): 72–89.

Lindtner, Silvia. 2020. *Prototype Nation: China and the Contested Promise of Innovation*. Princeton, NJ, and Oxford: Princeton University Press.

Ling, Minhua. 2019. *The Inconvenient Generation: Migrant Youth Coming of Age on Shanghai's Edge*. Stanford, CA: Stanford University Press.

Little, Peter C. 2014. *Toxic Town: IBM, Pollution, and Industrial Risks.* New York: New York University Press.

Livingston, Julie. 2019. *Self-Devouring Growth: A Planetary Parable as Told from Southern Africa.* Durham, NC, and London: Duke University Press.

Lora-Wainwright, Anna. 2017. *Resigned Activism: Living with Pollution in Rural China.* Cambridge, MA: MIT Press.

Lora-Wainwright, Anna, Yiyun Zhang, Yunmei Wu, and Benjamin Van Rooij. 2012. "Learning to Live with Pollution: The Making of Environmental Subjects in a Chinese Industrialized Village." *China Journal* 68 (1): 106–24.

Lorimer, Jamie. 2017. "Probiotic Environmentalities: Rewilding with Wolves and Worms." *Theory, Culture & Society* 34 (4): 27–48.

———. 2020. *The Probiotic Planet: Using Life to Manage Life.* Minneapolis and London: University of Minnesota Press.

Lou, Loretta Ieng Tak. 2017. "The Material Culture of Green Living in Hong Kong." *Anthropology Now* 9 (1): 70–79.

Luthra, Aman, and William Monteith. 2021. "Of Market Vendors and Waste Collectors: Labour, Informality, and Aesthetics in the Era of World-Class City Making." *Antipode* 55 (4): 1–21.

Lyons, Kristina. 2016. "Decomposition as Life Politics: Soils, Selva, and Small Farmers under the Gun of the U.S.–Colombia War on Drugs." *Cultural Anthropology* 31 (1): 56–81.

Ma, Zhiping. 2004. "Veolia Environment to Increase China Presence." Chinadaily .com.cn, May 21, 2004. http://www.chinadaily.com.cn/english/doc/2004-05/21/content_332582.htm.

MacBride, Samantha. 2012. *Recycling Reconsidered: The Present Failure and Future Promise of Environmental Action in the United States.* Cambridge, MA: MIT Press.

Mackenzie, Adrian. 2013. "From Validating to Verifying: Public Appeals in Synthetic Biology." *Science as Culture* 22 (4): 476–96.

Mah, Alice. 2021. "Future-Proofing Capitalism: The Paradox of the Circular Economy for Plastics." *Global Environmental Politics* 21 (2): 121–42.

Mao, Tse-Tung. 1965. *Selected Works Of Mao Tse-Tung,* Vol. III. Beijing: Foreign Languages Press.

Marres, Noortje. 2012. *Material Participation: Technology, the Environment and Everyday Publics.* New York: Palgrave Macmillan.

Martin, Emily. 1994. *Flexible Bodies: Tracking Immunity in American Culture from the Days of Polio to the Age of AIDS.* Boston: Beacon Press Books.

Marx, Karl.1976. *Capital, Volume I.* Translated by Ben Fowkes. London: Penguin Books.

Marx, Karl. 1987. *Capital, Volume II.* London: Lawrence and Wishart.

Massumi, Brian. 2002. *Parables for the Virtual: Movement, Affect, Sensation.* Durham, NC: Duke University Press.

Mathews, Andrew S., and Jessica Barnes. 2016. "Prognosis: Visions of Environmental Futures." *Journal of the Royal Anthropological Institute* 22 (S1): 9–26.

May, Shannon Kathleen. 2011. "Practices of Ecological Citizenship: Global Dreams for a Chinese Village." University of California, Berkeley.

McDowall, Will, Yong Geng, Beijia Huang, Eva Barteková, Raimund Bleischwitz, Serdar Türkeli, René Kemp, and Teresa Doménech. 2017. "Circular Economy Policies in China and Europe." *Journal of Industrial Ecology* 21 (3): 651–61.

McFarlane, Colin. 2021. *Fragments of the City: Making and Remaking Urban Worlds.* Oakland: University of California Press.

McGurty, Eileen. 2007. *Transforming Environmentalism: Warren County, PCBs, and the Origins of Environmental Justice.* New Brunswick, NJ, and London: Rutgers University Press.

McKee, Emily. 2015. "Trash Talk: Interpreting Morality and Disorder in Negev/ Naqab Landscapes." *Current Anthropology* 56 (5): 733–52.

Merrifield, Andy. 2014. *The New Urban Question.* New York: Pluto Press.

Mertha, Andrew C. 2008. *China's Water Warriors: Citizen Action and Policy Change.* Ithaca and London: Cornell University Press.

Michaud, Kristy, Juliet E. Carlisle, and Eric R.A.N. Smith. 2008. "Nimbyism vs. Environmentalism in Attitudes toward Energy Development." *Environmental Politics* 17 (1): 20–39.

Millar, Kathleen M. 2018. *Reclaiming the Discarded: Life and Labor on Rio's Garbage Dump.* Durham, NC: Duke University Press.

Minter, Adam. 2013. *Junkyard Planet: Travels in the Billion-Dollar Trash Trade.* New York: Bloomsbury Publishing.

Mol, Arthur P. J., and David Allan Sonnenfeld. 2000. *Ecological Modernisation around the World: Perspectives and Critical Debates.* London and Portland, OR: Frank Cass.

Moore, Jason W. 2015. *Capitalism in the Web of Life: Ecology and the Accumulation of Capital.* London and New York: Verso.

Moore, Sarah A. 2012. "Garbage Matters: Concepts in New Geographies of Waste." *Progress in Human Geography* 36 (6): 780–99.

Morimoto, Ryo. 2023. *Nuclear Ghost: Atomic Livelihoods in Fukushima's Gray Zone.* Oakland: University of California Press.

Mosse, David. 2005. *Cultivating Development: An Ethnography of Aid Policy and Practice.* London and New York: Pluto Press.

Murphy, Michelle. 2006. *Sick Building Syndrome and the Problem of Uncertainty: Environmental Politics, Technoscience, and Women Workers.* Durham, NC: Duke University Press.

———. 2017. "Alterlife and Decolonial Chemical Relations." *Cultural Anthropology* 32 (4): 494–503.

Nanfang Daily. 2014. "Guangzhou Shi Xingzhenqu Gushi Zhenfang Gongbu, Shiqu Ershi Bian Shiyiqu" [Guangzhou planning plan publicized, ten district, two counties converted to eleven districts]. [In Chinese.] *Nanfang Daily*, February 19, 2014.

Nanfang Daily. 2018. "Guangzhou 272 Chengzhongcun, naru, 'sanjiu' gaizao lidu jinnian hanjian" [Guangzhou's 272 village enclaves included in the "three olds"

scope of reform rarely seen]. [In Chinese.] Accessed July 20, 2023. http://gz
.house.163.com/18/0918/08/DRVK9CKP008786F3.html.

Nanfang Daily, 2023. Zhang Diyang, Dong Tianjian, Wan Wenlong. "Guangzhou
Likeng quanguo zuida chuyu lajichuli xiangmu tingba, yiying jishu louhou
shouzhi" [Guangzhou Likeng nation's largest kitchen waste treatment project
halted due to suspected technological problems.] [In Chinese.] July 5, 2023.
https://ujoy.net/topics/9401358.

Naustdalslid, Jon. 2014. "Circular Economy in China—the Environmental Dimension of the Harmonious Society." *International Journal of Sustainable Development & World Ecology* 21 (4): 303–13.

Nazim, Fazna, and V. Meera. 2013. "Treatment of Synthetic Greywater Using 5%
and 10% Garbage Enzyme Solution." *Bonfring International Journal of Industrial Engineering and Management Science* 3 (4): 111–17.

Nguyen, Victoria. 2020. "Breathless in Beijing: Aerial Attunements and China's
New Respiratory Publics." *Engaging Science, Technology, and Society* 6 (November): 439–61.

Nixon, Rob. 2011. *Slow Violence and the Environmentalism of the Poor.* Cambridge,
MA: Harvard University Press.

Nye, David E. 1994. *American Technological Sublime.* Cambridge and London: MIT
Press.

O'Brien, Kevin. 2003. "Neither Transgressive nor Contained: Boundary-Spanning
Contention in China." *Mobilization: An International Quarterly* 8 (1): 51–64.

O' Hare, Patrick. 2019. "'The Landfill Has Always Borne Fruit': Precarity, Formali-
sation and Dispossession among Uruguay's Waste Pickers." *Dialectical Anthropology* 43 (1): 31–44.

Ong, Aihwa, and Nancy N. Chen, eds. 2010. *Asian Biotech: Ethics and Communities
of Fate.* Durham NC: Duke University Press.

Oreskes, Naomi, and Erik M. Conway. 2010. *Merchants of Doubt: How a Handful of
Scientists Obscured the Truth of Issues from Tobacco Smoke to Global Warming.*
New York and London: Bloomsbury Press.

Ottinger, Gwen. 2013. *Refining Expertise: How Responsible Engineers Subvert Environmental Justice Challenges.* New York: New York University Press.

———. 2010. "Buckets of Resistance: Standards and the Effectiveness of Citizen
Science." *Science, Technology, & Human Values* 35 (2): 244–70.

Papadopoulos, Dimitris, María Puig de la Bellacasa, and Natasha Myers, eds. 2021.
Reacting Elements: Chemistry, Ecology, Practice. Durham, NC: Duke University
Press.

Parreñas, Juno Salazar. 2018. *Decolonizing Extinction: The Work of Care in Orang-
utan Rehabilitation.* Durham, NC: Duke University Press.

Patel, Raj, and Jason W. Moore. 2017. *A History of the World in Seven Cheap Things:
A Guide to Capitalism, Nature and the Future of the Planet.* Oakland: University
of California Press.

Paxson, Heather. 2008. "Post-Pasteurian Cultures: The Microbiopolitics of Raw-
Milk Cheese in the United States." *Cultural Anthropology* 23 (1): 15–47.

Paxson, Heather, and Stefan Helmreich. 2014. "The Perils and Promises of Microbial Abundance: Novel Natures and Model Ecosystems, from Artisanal Cheese
to Alien Seas." *Social Studies of Science* 44 (2): 165–93.

Pellow, David N. 2004. *Garbage Wars: The Struggle for Environmental Justice in
Chicago*. Cambridge and London: MIT Press.

Pellow, David Naguib. 2007. *Resisting Global Toxics: Transnational Movements for
Environmental Justice*. Cambridge, MA: MIT Press.

Peng, Jian, Huijuan Zhao, and Yanxu Liu. 2017. "Urban Ecological Corridors Construction: A Review." *Acta Ecologica Sinica* 37 (1): 23–30.

Peng, Thomas. 2011. "The Impact of Citizenship on Labour Process: State, Capital
and Labour Control in South China." *Work, Employment & Society* 25 (4): 726–
41.

Perry, Elizabeth J. 2011. "From Mass Campaigns to Managed Campaigns: 'Con-
structing a New Socialist Countryside.'" In *Mao's Invisible Hand: The Political
Foundations of Adaptive Governance in China*, edited by Sebastian Heilmann
and Elizabeth J. Perry, 30–61. Boston: Brill.

Petryna, Adriana. 2002. *Life Exposed: Biological Citizens after Chernobyl*. Princeton, NJ: Princeton University Press.

Pezzullo, Phaedra Carmen. 2009. *Toxic Tourism: Rhetorics of Pollution, Travel, and
Environmental Justice*. Tuscaloosa: University of Alabama Press.

Polleri, Maxime. 2019. "Conflictual Collaboration: Citizen Science and the Governance of Radioactive Contamination after the Fukushima Nuclear Disaster."
American Ethnologist 46 (2): 214–26.

Povinelli, Elizabeth A. 2011. *Economies of Abandonment: Social Belonging and Endurance in Late Liberalism*. Durham, NC: Duke University Press.

———. 2016. *Geontologies: A Requiem to Late Liberalism*. Durham, NC, and London:
Duke University Press.

Prakash, Gyan. 1999. *Another Reason: Science and the Imagination of Modern India*.
Princeton, NJ: Princeton University Press.

Puig de la Bellacasa, Maria. 2011. "Matters of Care in Technoscience: Assembling
Neglected Things." *Social Studies of Science* 41 (1): 85–106.

Rabie, Kareem. 2021. *Palestine Is Throwing a Party and the Whole World Is Invited:
Capital and State Building in the West Bank*. Durham, NC: Duke University
Press.

Rademacher, Anne. 2011. *Reigning the River: Urban Ecologies and Political Transformation in Kathmandu*. Durham and London: Duke University Press.

———. 2017. *Building Green: Environmental Architects and the Struggle for Sustainability in Mumbai*. Oakland: University of California Press.

Rademacher, Anne, and K. Sivaramakrishnan. 2017. *Places of Nature in Ecologies of
Urbanism*. Hong Kong: Hong Kong University Press.

Ren, Xuefei. 2011. *Building Globalization: Transnational Architecture Production in
Urban China*. Chicago: University of Chicago Press.

Renmin Web. 2013."Guangzhou shizhang Chengjianhua chengnuo: Jinnianqi tigao
huanweigong shouru" [Guangzhou's Mayor Chengjianhua promises to increase

sanitation workers' wages this year.] [In Chinese.] *People*, February 28, 2013. http://finance.people.com.cn/n/2013/0228/c357591-20633447-2.html.

Reno, Joshua. 2016. *Waste Away: Working and Living with a North American Landfill*. Oakland: University of California Press.

———. 2020. *Military Waste: The Unexpected Consequences of Permanent War Readiness*. Oakland: University of California Press.

Repnikova, Maria. 2017. *Media Politics in China: Improvising Power under Authoritarianism*. Cambridge: Cambridge University Press.

Resnick, Elana. 2021. "The Limits of Resilience: Managing Waste in the Racialized Anthropocene." *American Anthropologist* 123 (2): 222–36.

Rodenbiker, Jesse. 2023. *Ecological States: Politics of Science and Nature in Urbanizing China*. Ithaca, NY, and London: Cornell University Press.

Rogaski, Ruth. 2004. *Hygienic Modernity: Meaning of Health and Disease in Treaty-Port China*. Berkeley and Los Angeles: University of California Press.

Rooij, Benjamin van. 2010. "The People vs. Pollution: Understanding Citizen Action against Pollution in China." *Journal of Contemporary China* 19 (63): 55–77.

Rowe, Gene, and Lynn J. Frewer. 2000. "Public Participation Methods: A Framework for Evaluation." *Science, Technology & Human Value* 25 (1): 3–29.

Roy, Ananya, and Aihwa Ong. 2011. *Worlding Cities: Asian Experiments and the Art of Being Global*. Chichester, West Sussex, Malden, MA: Wiley-Blackwell.

Sanyal, Kalyan, and Rajesh Bhattacharyya. 2009. "Beyond the Factory: Globalisation, Informalisation of Production and the New Locations of Labour." *Economic and Political Weekly* 44 (22): 35–44.

Sassen, Saskia. 2001. *The Global City: New York, London, Tokyo*. Princeton, NJ: Princeton University Press.

Schmalzer, Sigrid. 2016. *Red Revolution, Green Revolution: Scientific Farming in Socialist China*. Chicago and London: University of Chicago Press.

Schnitzler, Antina von. 2017. *Democracy's Infrastructure: Techno-Politics and Protest after Apartheid*. Princeton, NJ: Princeton University Press.

Schulz, Yvan. 2015. "Towards a New Waste Regime?: Critical Reflections on China's Shifting Market for High-Tech Discard." *China Perspectives* 3 (September): 43–50.

Schwenkel, Christina. 2015. "Spectacular Infrastructure and Its Breakdown in Socialist Vietnam." *American Ethnologist* 42 (3): 520–34.

Seow, Victor. 2021. *Carbon Technocracy: Energy Regimes in Modern East Asia*. Chicago and London: University of Chicago Press.

Shapiro, Judith. 2001. *Mao's War against Nature: Politics and the Environment in Revolutionary China*. Leiden: Cambridge University Press.

Shapiro, Nicholas. 2015. "Attuning to the Chemosphere: Domestic Formaldehyde, Bodily Reasoning, and the Chemical Sublime." *Cultural Anthropology* 30 (3): 368–93.

Shatkin, Gavin. 2017. *Cities for Profit: The Real Estate Turn in Asia's Urban Politics*. Ithaca, NY: Cornell University Press.

Shen, Jie, and Fulong Wu. 2016. "The Suburb as a Space of Capital Accumulation: The Development of New Towns in Shanghai, China." *Antipode* 49 (3): 761–80.

Shevory, Thomas C. 2007. *Toxic Burn: The Grassroots Struggle against the WTI Incinerator.* Minneapolis and Bristol: University of Minnesota Press.

Shin, Hyun Bang. 2014. "Contesting Speculative Urbanisation and Strategising Discontents." *City: Analysis of Urban Trends, Theory, Action* 18 (4/5): 509–16.

Siu, Helen F. 2007. "Grounding Displacement: Uncivil Urban Spaces in Postreform South China." *American Ethnologist* 34 (2): 329–50.

Smith, Neil. 2005. *The New Urban Frontier: Gentrification and the Revanchist City.* London: Routledge.

———. 2008. *Uneven Development: Nature, Capital, and the Production of Space.* 3rd ed. Athens: University of Georgia Press.

Smith, Nick R. 2021. *The End of the Village: Planning the Urbanization of Rural China.* Minneapolis, London: University of Minnesota Press.

Solinger, Dorothy J. 2012. "The New Urban Underclass and Its Consciousness: Is It a Class?" *Journal of Contemporary China* 21 (78): 1011–28.

Solomon, Marisa. 2019. "'The Ghetto Is a Gold Mine': The Racialized Temporality of Betterment." *International Labor and Working-Class History* 95 (March): 76–94.

Stallybrass, Peter. 1990. "Marx and Heterogeneity: Thinking the Lumpenproletariat." *Representations* 31, Special Issue: The Margins of Identity in Nineteenth-Century England (Summer 1990): 69–95.

Stamatopoulou-Robbins, Sophia. 2020. *Waste Siege: The Life of Infrastructure in Palestine.* Stanford, CA: Stanford University Press.

Star, Susan Leigh. 1999. "The Ethnography of Infrastructure." *American Behavioral Scientist* 43 (3): 377.

Stengers, Isabelle. 2005. "Deleuze and Guattari's Last Enigmatic Message." *Angelaki—Journal of the Theoretical Humanities* 10 (2): 151–67.

Stern, Rachel E. 2013. *Environmental Litigation in China: A Study in Political Ambivalence.* Cambridge and London: Cambridge University Press.

Stoetzer, Bettina. 2022. *Ruderal City: Ecologies of Migration, Race, and Urban Nature in Berlin.* Durham, NC: Duke University Press.

Swanson, Heather Anne. 2018. "Landscapes, by Comparison: Practices of Enacting Salmon in Hokkaido, Japan." In *The World Multiple: The Quotidian Politics of Knowing and Generating,* edited by Omura, Keiichi, Grant Jun Otsuki, Shiho Satsuka, and Atsuro Morita, 105–22. Abingdon, Oxon, New York: Routledge.

Swider, Sarah. 2015. "Chengguan and Struggles over the Right to the City." *Critical Sociology* 41 (5): 701–16.

Swyngedouw, Erik. 2006. "Circulations and Metabolisms: (Hybrid) Natures and (Cyborg) Cities." *Science as Culture* 15 (2): 105–21.

Sze, Julie. 2007. *Noxious New York: The Racial Politics of Urban Health and Environmental Justice.* Cambridge, MA: MIT Press.

———. 2015. *Fantasy Islands: Chinese Dreams and Ecological Fears in an Age of Climate Crisis.* Oakland: University of California Press.

Táíwò, Olúfẹ́mi, O. 2022. *Reconsidering Reparations: Worldmaking in the Case of Climate Crisis.* New York: Oxford University Press.

Tang, Fu E., and Chung W. Tong. 2011. "A Study of the Garbage Enzyme's Effects in

Domestic Wastewater." *World Academy of Science, Engineering and Technology* 60: 1143–48.

Tarr, Joel. 1996. *The Search for the Ultimate Sink: Urban Pollution in Historical Perspective*. Akron, OH: University of Akron Press.

Tengxun Web. 2013. "Huanbao hangye: 'shierwu' laji chuli yinglai lishi jiyu" [Environmental industry, twelfth five-year plan: Waste management brings historical opportunities.] [In Chinese.] August 10, 2013. https://web.archive.org/web/20130907195908/http://finance.qq.com/a/20130810/005300.htm.

Tilt, Bryan. 2010. *The Struggle for Sustainability in Rural China: Environmental Values and Civil Society*. New York: Columbia University Press.

Tironi, Manuel. 2018. "Hypo-Interventions: Intimate Activism in Toxic Environments." *Social Studies of Science* 48 (3): 438–55.

Tsing, Anna Lowenhaupt. 2005. *Friction: An Ethnography of Global Connection*. Princeton and Oxford: Princeton University Press.

———. 2015. *The Mushroom at the End of the World: On the Possibility of Life in Capitalist Ruins*. Princeton, NJ, and Oxford: Princeton University Press.

Tsing, Anna Lowenhaupt, Heather Swanson, Elaine Gan, and Nils Bubandt. 2017. "Introduction: Haunted Landscapes of the Anthropocene." In *Arts of Living on a Damaged Planet: Ghosts of the Anthropocene*, 1–14. Minneapolis: University of Minnesota Press.

Vaughn, Sarah E. 2022. *Engineering Vulnerability: In Pursuit of Climate Adaptation*. Durham, NC: Duke University Press.

Velis, Costas. 2018. "No Circular Economy If Current Systemic Failures Are Not Addressed." *Waste Management and Research* 36 (9): 757–59.

Vogel, Sarah A. 2013. *Is It Safe?: BPA and the Struggle to Define the Safety of Chemicals*. Berkeley: University of California Press.

Wang, Jing. 2011. "Yige Yu Lajichang Gongsheng 20 Nian de Cunluo Likengkangzhengshi" [A village that's lived with a waste plant for over 20 years, Likeng's resistance history.] [In Chinese.]) Caixin, November 6, 2011. http://finance.sina.com.cn/roll/20111106/225510762893.shtml.

Waste 360. 2022. "The State of Waste-to-Energy in the U.S." https://www.waste360.com/waste-energy/state-waste-energy-us.

Weeks, Kathi. 2011. *The Problem with Work: Feminism, Marxism, Antiwork Politics, and Postwork Imaginaries*. Durham, NC: Duke University Press.

Weston, Kath. 2017. *Animate Planet: Making Visceral Sense of Living in a High-Tech, Ecologically Damaged World*. Durham, NC, and London: Duke University Press.

Wong, Natalie W. M. 2015. "Advocacy Coalitions and Policy Change in China: A Case Study of Anti-Incinerator Protest in Guangzhou." *Voluntas* 27, 2037–54.

———. 2016. "Environmental Protests and NIMBY Activism: Local Politics and Waste Management in Beijing and Guangzhou." *China Information* 30 (2): 143–64.

World Bank. 2005. "Waste Management in China: Issues and Recommendations May 2005." Working Paper No. 9. https://globalrec.org/wp-content/uploads/2014/03/China-Waste-Management-2005.pdf.

Wu, Fulong, and Roger Keil. 2020. "Changing the Geographies of Sub/Urban Theory: Asian Perspectives." *Urban Geography* 41 (7): 947–53.

Wu, Fulong, and Anthony Gar-On Yeh. 2007. "Urban Spatial Structure in a Transitional Economy." *Journal of the American Planning Association*, 65 (4): 377–94.

Wu, Fulong, and Jingxing Zhang. 2007. "Planning the Competitive City-Region: The Emergence of Strategic Development Plan in China." *Urban Affairs Review* 42 (5): 714–40.

Wu, Ka-Ming, and Jieying Zhang. 2019. "Living with Waste: Becoming 'Free' as Waste Pickers in Chinese Cities." *China Perspectives* 2019 (2): 67–74.

Wu, Yanyan, Shuyuan Li, and Shixiao Yu. 2016. "Monitoring Urban Expansion and Its Effects on Land Use and Land Cover Changes in Guangzhou City, China." *Environmental Monitoring and Assessment* 188 (54): 1–15.

Wylie, Sara Ann. 2018. *Fractivism: Corporate Bodies and Chemical Bonds*. Durham and London: Duke University Press.

Wynne, Brian. 1991. "Knowledges in Context." *Science, Technology, & Human Values* 16 (1): 111–21.

———. 2007. "Public Participation in Science and Technology: Performing and Obscuring a Political-Conceptual Category Mistake." *Technology and Society: An International Journal* 1: 99–110.

Xu, Jiang, and Anthony G. O. Yeh. 2003. "Guangzhou: City Profile." *Cities* 20 (5): 361–74.

Xu, Jiang, and Anthony G. O. Yeh. 2005. "City Repositioning and Competitiveness Building in Regional Development: New Development Strategies in Guangzhou, China." *International Journal of Urban and Regional Research* 29 (2): 283–308.

Xu, Yi, and Xuewei Dou. 2021. "From Empowerment to Encapsulation: Sanitation Workers' Struggles and Sources of Power in South China." *Labor History* 62(4): 413–33.

Yan, Hairong. 2003. "Neoliberal Governmentality and Neohumanism: Organizing Suzhi/Value Flow through Labor Recruitment Networks." *Cultural Anthropology* 18 (4): 493–523.

Yan, Yunxiang. 2009. *The Individualization of Chinese Society*. Oxford and New York: Berg 2009.

Yang, Guobin, and C. Calhoun. 2007. "Media, Civil Society, and the Rise of a Green Public Sphere in China." *China Information* 21 (2): 211–36.

Yates, Michelle. 2011. "The Human-as-Waste, The Labor Theory of Value and Disposability in Contemporary Capitalism." *Antipode* 43 (5): 1679–95.

Yeh, Emily. 2013. *Taming Tibet: Landscape Transformation and the Gift of Chinese Development*. Ithaca and London: Cornell University Press.

———. 2022. "Sky River: Promethean Dreams of Optimising the Atmosphere." *Made in China Journal* 7 (2): 96–101.

Yuan, Zengwei, J. Bi, and Y. Moriguichi. 2006. "The Circular Economy: A New Development Strategy in China." *Journal of Industrial Ecology* 10 (1 2): 4–8.

Zee, Jerry C. 2022. *Continent in Dust: Experiments in a Chinese Weather System.* Oakland: University of California Press.

Zhan, Mei. 2009. *Other-Worldly: Making Chinese Medicine through Transnational Frames.* Durham, NC: Duke University Press.

Zhang, Amy. 2014. "Rational Resistance: Homeowner Contention against Waste Incineration in Guangzhou." *China Perspectives* 2014 (2): 46–52.

———. 2020a. "The Black Soldier Fly: An Indigenous Innovation for Waste Management in Guangzhou." In *Can Science and Technology Save China?* edited by Susan Greenhalgh and Li Zhang, 163–83. Ithaca, NY: Cornell University Press.

———. 2020b. "Circularity and Enclosures: Metabolizing Waste with the Black Soldier Fly." *Cultural Anthropology* 35 (1): 74–103.

———. 2024. "Spectacular Technology, Invisible Harms: Waste Tours and Witnessing Green Techno-Science in China." *Science Technology and Human Values.*

Zhang, Hao, and Eli Friedman. 2019. "Informality and Working Conditions in China's Sanitation Sector." *China Quarterly* 238: 375–95.

Zhang, Lei, Arthur P. J. Mol, and David A. Sonnenfeld. 2007. "The Interpretation of Ecological Modernisation in China." *Environmental Politics* 16 (4): 659–68.

Zhang, Li. 2010. *In Search of Paradise: Middle-Class Living in a Chinese Metropolis.* Ithaca, NY: Cornell University Press.

Zhang, Lin. 2023. *The Labor of Reinvention: Entrepreneurship in the New Chinese Digital Economy.* New York: Columbia University Press.

Zhao, Yimin. 2020. "Folding Beijing in Houchangcun Road, or, the Topology of Power Density." *Urban Geography* 41 (10): 1247–59.

Zhu, Annah Lake. 2022. *Rosewood: Endangered Species Conservation and the Rise of Global China.* Cambridge, MA: Harvard University Press.

Index

Note: page numbers in *italics* refer to illustrations; those followed by "n" indicated endnotes.

The authorized representative in the EU for product safety and compliance is:
Mare Nostrum Group
B.V Doelen 72
4831 GR Breda
The Netherlands

www.ingramcontent.com/pod-product-compliance
Lightning Source LLC
Chambersburg PA
CBHW030824270326
41928CB00007B/886